DRAMA + THEORY

MANCHESTER
UNIVERSITY PRESS

DRAMA + THEORY

Critical approaches to modern British drama

Peter Buse

MANCHESTER UNIVERSITY PRESS
Manchester and New York

distributed exclusively in the USA by Palgrave

Published by Manchester University Press
Oxford Road, Manchester M13 9NR, UK
and Room 400, 175 Fifth Avenue, New York, NY 10010, USA
http://www. manchesteruniversitypress.co.uk

Distributed exclusively in the USA by
Palgrave, 175 Fifth Avenue, New York,
NY 10010, USA

Distributed exclusively in Canada by
UBC Press, University of British Columbia, 2029 West Mall,
Vancouver, BCV, Canada V6T 1Z2

British Library Cataloguing-in-Publication Data
A catalogue record for this book is available from the British Library

Library of Congress Cataloging-in-Publication Data applied for

ISBN   0 7190 5721 3 *hardback*
       0 7190 5722 1 *paperback*

First published 2001

10 09 08 07 06 05 04 03 02 01   10 9 8 7 6 5 4 3 2 1

Typeset by Special Edition Pre-press Services, London
Printed in Great Britain by Bell & Bain Ltd, Glasgow

To my parents

Contents

Illustrations

Look Back in Anger, Royal Court Theatre, 1956; photographer: Houston Rogers; reproduced by permission of the Victoria and Albert Picture Library (page 12).

The Homecoming, Royal Shakespeare Company, 1965; photographer: Zoe Dominic; reproduced by permission of the photographer (page 40).

What the Butler Saw, National Theatre, 1995; photographer: Catherine Ashmore; reproduced by permission of the photographer (page 82).

Top Girls, Royal Court Theatre, 1982; photographer: Catherine Ashmore; reproduced by permission of the photographer (page 118).

Pravda, National Theatre, 1986; photographer: Catherine Ashmore; reproduced by permission of the photographer (page 147).

Acknowledgements

I was able to write this book in large part because of a semester's leave granted to me by the Department of English at the University of Salford. The European Studies Research Institute at Salford has given me all the support I have asked for, and the University's Embryonic Research Fund allowed me to attend the School of Criticism and Theory at Cornell University in the summer of 1999. I must also thank my students at the University of Salford, who heard most of it, went along with some of it and kept me sharp.

I am grateful to Alistair Stead of the University of Leeds, who first taught me modern British drama and let me mix it up with theory; and to Jo-Ann Wallace and Jonathan Hart of the University of Alberta, who introduced me to critical theory. I could not have written this book without the stimulating years I spent at the Centre for Critical and Cultural Theory in Cardiff, and I am especially indebted to Catherine Belsey for her teaching, rigour and clarity.

Angus Easson, Mags Martin, Sue Powell and Stella Walker provided me with an enviable working environment in Salford. Paul Callick, Avril Horner and Scott McCracken commented helpfully on the project in its early stages. Antony Easthope talked to me about Lacan, Fred Botting helped me think about jokes, Melissa Jacques and Deborah Staines introduced me to trauma theory, and Sarah E. Evans gave me her reading of Sarah Kane. Thanks to Simon O'Sullivan for advice on Lyotard and for long productive walking conversations. Thanks, as well, to Matthew Frost of Manchester University Press, who encouraged the project and pushed it forward at the right times.

For their friendship and insight, I would like to thank Sara Ahmed, Carson Bergstrom, Ellie Byrne, Rainer Emig, Angela Keane, Michaela Lea, Martin McQuillan, Angelica Michaelis, Rajeet Pannu, Antony Rowland, Simon Spooner and Andy Stott. My greatest debt is to Núria Triana-Toribio.

Introduction

+

Drama *plus* theory. It is an unusual sort of arithmetic. This book proceeds on the assumption that critical and cultural theory can productively add to our understanding of modern British plays. Caryl Churchill plus Walter Benjamin, Tom Stoppard plus Jean-François Lyotard, Joe Orton plus Michel Foucault, Timberlake Wertenbaker plus Edward Said: such additions are more than the sums of their parts; they are exciting and illuminating combinations. In other words, I take for granted that challenging and provocative plays can only benefit from an encounter with the sharpest of critical thinking. Times are changing, but there are still many who feel quite the opposite: that theory can only subtract from drama, diminishing it somehow. This feeling may come from a sense that theory is too often set up in a position of mastery with regard to the dramatic text – a map applied to a play but unaffected by it. It is always a danger, but it is one I hope that I avoid in *Drama + theory*. Not only can theory add to drama, but drama can add to theory, inflecting it in ways previously unanticipated. Rather than seeking the failings in any individual theory – and undoubtedly there are some – this book asks in what ways the texts of theory can gain from the theoretical insights that drama itself has to offer. The ambition of *Drama + theory* is therefore largely positive, as marked by the '+' sign of the title.

Which drama, then, and what theories? There are now so many theoretical movements that fall under the general designation of 'theory' that this text, like any other, must narrow down its field of reference. Psychoanalysis, Marxism, postmodernism, structuralism, post-colonialism, queer theory and trauma theory are all represented here, but the core of the book lies with the ideas which emerged from France in the late 1960s and early 1970s. Accordingly, *Drama + theory* leans heavily towards post-structuralism in its overall theoretical perspective, and chapters are dedicated to texts by Jacques

Lacan, Michel Foucault, Jean-François Lyotard, Louis Althusser and Jean Baudrillard. The two earlier thinkers who make an appearance – Sigmund Freud and Walter Benjamin – in many ways presaged the insights of post-structuralism. Of the two later thinkers, Shoshana Felman has been one of the most successful American proponents of Lacanian psychoanalysis, while Edward Said is a lone dissenting voice, suspicious of post-structuralism, but nevertheless conversant with its terms and points of reference. Theory is plural in this book, then, and presents nine different positions; but at the same time the reader will find recurrent themes and common assumptions from chapter to chapter.

The drama, meanwhile, takes in nine plays performed on the British stage since 1956. And as the title indicates, *Drama + theory* examines drama rather than theatre or performance. That is to say, it tends to concentrate, in its theoretical readings, on printed plays rather than staged productions. By doing this, it goes slightly against the grain of recent times, which have tended to privilege questions of *mise-en-scène* and performance. Over the past two or three decades theatre studies and performance studies have taken great strides in addressing those areas of the theatrical event which were neglected when the main object of study was the playtext. Yet a great many students still study theatre primarily as drama, reading printed plays rather than analysing performance. It is with such readers in mind that I focus on the conceptual content of plays over and above problems of production, acting, audience reception, theatrical venue, stage design or theatrical history. Having said that, I am loath to draw a rigid line between theatre and drama, so I address specifically theatrical questions where relevant, and I ask what special challenges the facts of performance pose for theory.

Drama + theory follows a straightforward pattern: each chapter brings together a single play and a single theoretical text and places them in direct dialogue with each other. The spirit of this book is therefore one of testing: it asks, What if Jacques Lacan were paired off with John Osborne, Louis Althusser with Trevor Griffiths, Shoshana Felman with Sarah Kane? So, to the 'plus' of the title, can be added the 'with' of each chapter sub-title. Each playwright is linked *with* a particular theorist, under the assumption that the play and the theoretical text will work in tandem. In the first instance I am looking for what light the theory might shed on the play, but at the same time I am examining the relation of reciprocity and exchange that the 'with' implies; and the play often gives new insight on the theoretical text and even tests its limits.

It would be possible to test in this manner many different theories on a single play, and I do want to emphasize at all times that theory opens up new possibilities in reading. All books on drama work from certain theoretical assumptions, even if they are not always identified. *Drama + theory* seeks to make explicit the theoretical approach being adopted at every stage. This may imply that the choice of pairings is wholly arbitrary, that any theory can be read alongside any play. However, in most cases, the play itself has suggested a particular theory and has proven receptive to some theoretical insights more than others. Indeed, some of the links should seem almost immediately appropriate. For instance, Harold Pinter's *The Homecoming*, with the doubts it casts over the domestic setting, has clear affinities with Sigmund Freud's 'The "Uncanny"', an essay which probes the darker nooks of the *heimlich* (homely); *Pravda*, a joint effort of David Hare and Howard Brenton, places under the spotlight the mass media, which has always been a central concern of Jean Baudrillard, in *Simulacra and Simulation* as well as elsewhere; and Timberlake Wertenbaker's re-examination of colonial Australia chimes well with Edward Said's interests in *Culture and Imperialism*. The same goes to a greater or lesser extent for most chapters. If one of them were to raise an eyebrow, it would most likely be the first, where *Look Back in Anger* meets Jacques Lacan's 'The signification of the phallus'. This pairing is perhaps a trifle playful, or even perverse, but as it turns out, *Look Back in Anger* has just as many interesting things to say about desire as Lacan has. In fact, it is the surprise of the combination which can yield a new perspective on a familiar play.

Resistances to theory

Drama + theory enters a field that is still coming to terms with the seismic impact of theory. This book does not trouble itself overly with the validity or feasibility of its project. It is, however, worth noting some of the worries that have been registered in the past about the compatibility of theory and drama. It has been remarked more than once that the encounter with theory was slow to get started in the case of drama and theatre studies. For instance, as late as 1992, long after the theory wars had been fought in English literature departments, Adrian Page opened the edited collection, *The Death of the Playwright?: Modern British Drama and Literary Theory*, with the words, 'Despite the proliferation of literary theory in recent years, little attention has been paid to modern drama.'[1] That book began to redress the balance, if at times it still subscribed to what we might call the 'subtractive' school on theory and drama. Page, for one, feels that theory might still take away from drama rather than add to it and seeks to temper the post-structuralist announcement of the 'Death of the Author' by asking how 'the playwright can be resurrected as a wielder of meaning without suppressing the creative responses to his or her written text'.[2] Meanwhile, Mark Fortier, in *Theory/Theatre: An Introduction* (1997), claims that '[in] theatre studies especially, theory has not had … open-armed acceptance … Theory has often seemed too contemplative an activity to be more help than hindrance in such a practical pursuit as theatre.'[3] Fortier is probably right about the emphasis on the 'hands-on' within the theatrical community, but it is worth noting that there can be no practice without a theory, however submerged it is.

There is, however, more than knee-jerk reaction in the resistance to theory in some quarters of theatre studies. Fortier puts his finger on the problem when he points out that the theory of the late 1960s onwards was heavily marked by its linguistic orientation. 'Most of the theory under discussion', he writes, 'stresses the importance of language as the basis, even the fate of human activity.'[4] Saussurean linguistics, Lacanian psychoanalysis and Derridean deconstruction all give priority to language or writing, and all have helped to transform the study of the literary text. However, the linguistic turn in literary studies coincided with theatre studies paying more attention to precisely the *non*-linguistic aspects of theatre – the elements of drama and theatre that make it other than literature. For better or worse, the emphasis on language in theory was seen in many drama or theatre departments as unproductive: to give special status to language could only mean a narrow focus on the dramatic text at the expense of the performed event. The danger was that drama and theatre would only be subsumed again as mere genres of literature.

The sub-title of Page's book (*Modern British Drama and Literary Theory*) could only confirm such suspicions, since it implies that *literary* theory could be mapped wholesale on to drama with no consideration for the differences between literature and drama. In this

4

vision, theory, with its linguistic bias, rumbles roughshod over a medium in which language is only one element among many. There is some justification for such doubts, and the direct application of literary theory to dramatic texts is clearly wrongheaded. However, there is also a certain amount of misunderstanding at work: most theory is not first and foremost literary theory. Of the theoretical texts treated in *Drama + theory*, none could be said to be exclusively literary in their orientation, and most do not address literature at all. They are better described as critical and/or cultural theories, which make interventions in wider questions of subjectivity, sexuality, historiography, race, postmodernity and trauma. They are above all theories of culture and society, and since drama is very much a part of culture and society, they are of direct relevance to drama and theatre. It is obviously wrong to treat plays as if they were novels, but it would also be a mistake to quarantine drama and theatre within their own formal specificity and thereby ignore their participation in wider philosophical and cultural issues.

Recent years have seen the emergence of some excellent, theoretically informed work on modern British drama which takes something like the perspective just outlined. In his tremendous reconstruction of the cultural moment of the British New Wave (*British Realist Theatre: The New Wave in its Context*), Stephen Lacey deliberately states his debts to the theories of culture and ideology developed by the Birmingham Centre for Contemporary Cultural Studies. And although he does not explicitly acknowledge it, he also draws on discourse theory and post-structuralist notions of intertextuality.[5] Following a slightly different trajectory, Dan Rebellato's brilliant critique of the founding myths of modern British drama (*1956 and All That: The Making of Modern British Drama*) carefully weaves together the methods of Michel Foucault and Jacques Derrida in its re-telling of the Osborne era.[6] There are, then, signs that fruitful engagements between theory and modern British drama are now being undertaken, and that this book is not entering a void.

Texts, not -isms

Drama + theory does not assume any prior knowledge of the theories dealt with, and each chapter gives an accessible and in-depth exposition of the theorist's ideas. Knowledge of the plays is not absolutely indispensable, but the reader will profit more from a familiarity with them. What is slightly unusual about the method employed here is that it does not take an '-isms' approach to theory. Many books that attempt to apply theory in one way or another are organized around schools of thought, or '-isms'. I favour instead a sustained engagement with a single text. There are several reasons for this. The '-isms' approach risks flattening out differences and complexities, reducing a set of often disparate thinkers or texts to a single conglomerate position. Rather than carry out a generic 'psychoanalytic' reading of a play, I choose to concentrate on single issues within psychoanalysis – the Uncanny and desire – in separate chapters and by way of individual psychoanalysts (Freud and Lacan) and individual texts. This also allows the reader to consult what are often quite short texts in order to engage more fully with the ideas raised. I also insist on addressing specific texts because I firmly believe that theory is not just a set of abstract concepts 'out there' but something which is written and which therefore must be read. We cannot simply go straight to the theoretical content of any essay or book without at the same time thinking about the textual form that it takes. Accordingly, each chapter carries out a critical reading of the theoretical text at hand. This is not to say that the full range of '-isms' is not represented in *Drama + theory*, as has already been noted.

One '-ism' that is not directly represented here is feminism. Chapters 1, 2, 4, 6 and 9 address questions of gender or sexuality in one way or another, but no single chapter offers an explicitly feminist approach. This omission is made because of the huge wealth of feminist dramatic criticism that is already available. When many other recent theories had only been sporadically tested on drama, feminist dramatic criticism had been flourishing for some time. Along with semiotics, it has had much more of an impact on the study of drama and theatre than any other theoretical position.[7] Rather than duplicate work that has already been done, I can point the reader to the excellent writings of Elaine Aston, Sue-Ellen Case, Elin Diamond, Jill Dolan and Michelene Wandor, to mention just a few.[8]

I should also make clear what *Drama + theory* does not set out to achieve. It makes no claims for historical coverage in terms either of the changing material contexts of the plays or of the developments in time of dramatic form. Such matters are of course addressed where appropriate, and the chapter on *Top Girls* and Walter

Benjamin reflects at length on the making of history, but *Drama +
theory* does not provide a new narrative about post-war British
drama. There are plenty such works available, and those of Lacey
and Rebellato constitute two of the most provocative challenges to
the more familiar accounts. In such accounts, though, no more than
one or two pages can usually be dedicated to a single play. The same
fate all too often awaits theoretical texts or issues mentioned or
raised in passing but never explored in detail. In contrast, this book
pays close attention to a limited number of mainly well-known plays
from the post-war period. But rather than claiming to offer comprehensive accounts of the plays, it sets out to show the possibilities
theory provides for different reading strategies. Such an approach
may well complement the methods of the historical survey, but it
also seeks to displace the potential totalizing effects of this dominant
methodology through a set of disjunctive encounters between
theory and drama.

Finally, something needs to be said about the choice of plays.
It was impossible to include all the playwrights I would have liked
to, but I hope the book is fairly representative of post-war drama.
One notable absence is Samuel Beckett, but then the prodigious
output of the Beckett critical industry has seen to it that *Waiting for
Godot, Endgame, Happy Days* and other works have been seen
through every theoretical prism imaginable, and I have no wish to
tread repetitively in the paths of numberless Beckettians.[9] The plays
that I have chosen should, for the most part, be familiar to the
student of British drama. They are plays that are frequently taught –
certainly plays that I have taught and been taught in the past. This
book should be useful, then, not because it introduces unfamiliar
plays but because it gives new perspectives on familiar ones. Every
decade from the 1950s to the 1990s is represented, and the chronology of the plays determines the order of the chapters, although I
encourage you to read them in any order you see fit. Leaving aside
the Jewish, Czech, Welsh and American backgrounds of Pinter,
Stoppard, Griffiths and Wertenbaker, the plays have all emerged
from an English theatrical context – a function of my lack of expertise on Scottish, Welsh and Northern Irish theatre rather than an
oversight. Within that English context, though, there is a wide range
of venues of production. Four of the plays were first performed at
the Royal Court (*Look Back in Anger, Top Girls, Our Country's Good*
and *Blasted*), two in the commercial theatre (*The Homecoming* and

What the Butler Saw), one in a provincial theatre (*Comedians*), one at the National Theatre (*Pravda*), and one at the Edinburgh Fringe (*Rosencrantz and Guildenstern are Dead*). The weight of distribution therefore falls on the side of subsidized theatre, but this is the case in almost every university course on modern drama.

Inevitably, there were pairings of playwrights and theorists I contemplated but which the book could not accommodate, or which I thought better of. Some were serious: John Arden's *Serjeant Musgrave's Dance* with Mikhail Bakhtin's *Rabelais and his World*, or a Mark Ravenhill play with Georges Bataille's *The Accursed Share*, for instance. Others were more light-hearted: Pierre Bourdieu's *Distinction* with any one of Alan Ayckbourn's probing meditations on middle-class values; Roland Barthes' *A Lover's Discourse* with Terence Rattigan's *The Deep Blue Sea*; Arnold Wesker's *Roots* with Deleuze and Guattari's musings on the rhizome. These, or similar examples, are paths that the reader may wish to pursue. One theorist whose absence may seem surprising is Jacques Derrida. His thinking has affinities with many of the theorists in *Drama + theory*, but I am not convinced that deconstruction, with its intense emphasis on textuality, has immediate application to drama and theatre.[10] Nevertheless, for the reader who desires such an encounter, I might suggest that any number of Derrida's texts could be productively read alongside Noël Coward's *Blithe Spirit*.

Notes

1 Adrian Page, ed. *The Death of the Playwright?: Modern British Drama and Literary Theory* (Basingstoke: Macmillan, 1992), p. 1.
2 Page, *Death of Playwright*, p. 3.
3 Mark Fortier, *Theory/Theatre: An Introduction* (London and New York: Routledge, 1997), pp. 2–3.
4 Fortier, *Theory/Theatre*, p. 3.
5 Stephen Lacey, *British Realist Theatre: The New Wave in its Context* (London and New York: Routledge, 1995).
6 Dan Rebellato, *1956 and All That: The Making of Modern British Drama* (London and New York: Routledge, 1999)
7 Semiotics does not even make a guest appearance here, but the interested reader can turn to any number of books: Anne Ubersfeld, *Lire le théâtre* (Paris: Éditions Sociales, 1977); Keir Elam, *The Semiotics of Theatre and Drama* (London and New York: Methuen, 1980); Patrice Pavis, *Languages of the Stage*, trans. Susan Melrose (New York: Performing Arts Journal

Publications, 1982); Martin Esslin, *The Field of Drama: How the Signs of Drama Create Meaning on Stage and Screen* (London: Methuen Drama, 1987); Susan Melrose, *A Semiotics of the Dramatic Text* (Basingstoke: Macmillan, 1994)

8 See, for instance, Elaine Aston, *An Introduction to Feminism and Theatre* (London and New York: Routledge, 1995); Sue-Ellen Case, *Feminism and Theatre* (London and New York: Routledge, 1988); Elin Diamond, *Unmaking Mimesis: Essays on Feminism and Theatre* (London and New York: Routledge, 1997); and Jill Dolan, *The Feminist Spectator as Critic* (Ann Arbor: UMI Research Press, 1988); Michelene Wandor, *Carry On, Understudies: Theatre and Sexual Politics*, 2nd edn (London: Routledge and Kegan Paul, 1986) and *Orlando's Children: Sexuality and the Family in Post-War British Plays* (London: Methuen, 1986).

9 And yet, even within a saturated field, Peter Boxall reflects on 'the relative paucity of theoretical approaches to Beckett'. *Samuel Beckett: Waiting for Godot/Endgame: A Reader's Guide to Essential Criticism* (Cambridge: Icon Books, 2000), p. 5. 'Relative' is probably the key word, though, considering the vast quantities of ink spilt over Beckett.

10 Derrida concedes as much in his most sustained engagement with theatrical questions, the two essays on Antonin Artaud in *Writing and Difference*, trans Alan Bass (London: Routledge, 1978), 'La parole soufflée'; and 'The Theater of Cruelty and the Closure of Representation'. In both these pieces he resists to the end making direct comment on Artaud's theatrical practice, choosing instead to meditate on his texts on theatre.

1

What does Jimmy Porter want? – Osborne with Lacan

Something missing

Time has not been kind to *Look Back in Anger*. Although the date of its first production, 8 May 1956, has been retroactively fixed as the inauguration of a revolution in British drama, the play itself is now routinely seen as unequal to the status conferred on it. Formally and theatrically, it is rather timid in its experimentation; its politics are not nearly as radical as they at first seemed; and its hero, Jimmy Porter, is, after all, not much more than a misogynist lamenting the decline of British imperial hegemony. If *Look Back in Anger* is worth examining at all these days, the critical consensus seems to be, it is primarily as a sort of sociological document. It may not be highly significant as a piece of theatre, so this thinking goes, but its first production was still a crucial event in the social history of modern Britain. In other words, the play has come to be understood as relevant more for the effects it generated than for anything inherent in its contents. Alan Sinfield has convincingly argued that the young audience the play attracted constituted an emerging class fraction in the era of 'Affluence', and more recently, Stephen Lacey has offered an impressive and comprehensive reconstruction of the play's social contexts and intertexts.[1] In the light of such re-evaluations of *Look Back in Anger*, it may seem a little frivolous, if not perverse, to set aside temporarily the evident sociological significance of the play and propose a reading of it as an exemplary instance of the vicissitudes of the desiring subject.

What if Jimmy's oft-quoted line 'There aren't any good, brave causes left', a statement which has been read as a clarion-call to a disillusioned generation, is fundamentally a ruse, tricking us into believing that Jimmy Porter is a thwarted revolutionary or failed radical politician?[2] What if he is just looking for love in all the wrong places? So voluble is Jimmy in his opinions about the lamentable state of contemporary politics that we can lose sight of the

10

other fundamental dissatisfaction which animates him – that is, his inability or unwillingness to form reciprocal and happy relations with his wife Alison or her temporary substitute in Act Three, Helena. These two poles of dissatisfaction may not be unrelated, and they form the basic question of *Look Back in Anger*, which the play by no means answers unequivocally and which is, what exactly is it that Jimmy Porter wants? Desire in this play is problematic and troubled. Jimmy is not short of desires; indeed he announces them on a regular basis. Unfortunately, they do not seem to stay still; they shift and move, and sometimes even change into their opposite. And although the play centres on Jimmy, we might equally ask the question of the marginal characters.

Desire is hardly the most ironclad of theoretical terms. Fortunately, modern theory has its very own Doctor of Desire in the shape of the psychoanalyst Jacques Lacan, the thinker at the forefront of the French 'return to Freud'. Lacan would scoff at the thought of discovering the truth of Jimmy's desire, the answer to the question 'what does Jimmy want?' With the help of one of Lacan's texts, I propose instead to trace the contours of desire in *Look Back in Anger* without claiming to discover its 'truth'. In Lacan's hands, desire becomes strange and unfamiliar, because he rejects the normal truisms about the way it works. We might divide these truisms into two categories – the commonsensical and the metaphysical versions of desire. In the commonsense model, desire has objects and can be satisfied with the attainment of these objects. Clearly, this model finds its application in sexual desire, but it perhaps features most prominently in the relation of the consumer to commodities. Commodity culture constantly elicits the desire of consumers by offering them products – objects – which can be attained through a simple relation of exchange. Theoretically, desire is gratified through the possession of the new car, shirt, fast-food meal, can of pop. The shortcomings of this commonsense model are clear to many even without the aid of Jacques Lacan. The metaphysical model in Western culture finds its most common expression in what romantic fiction calls True Love. This is a desire which transcends the crass materiality of sexual intercourse and finds its resolution on a higher plane. It may be satisfied rather more rarely than the one posited by the commonsense model, but an impressive output of films, fiction and songs reassures us that this object of desire is also attainable.[3]

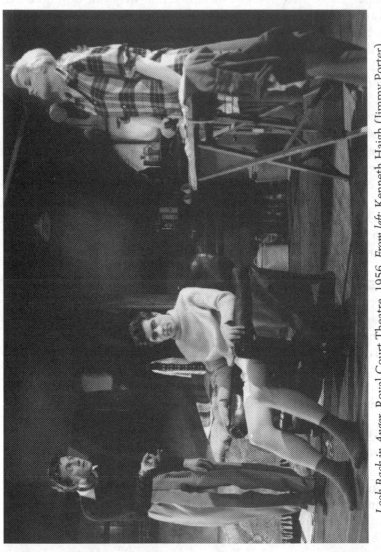

Look Back in Anger, Royal Court Theatre, 1956. *From left*: Kenneth Haigh (Jimmy Porter), Alan Bates (Cliff) and Mary Ure (Alison)

In both cases gratification is promised as a possible outcome for the person who desires.

In the face of such relatively comforting accounts of desire, Jacques Lacan consistently emphasizes its 'paradoxical, deviant, erratic, eccentric, even scandalous character'.[4] The quotation comes from Lacan's notorious essay 'The signification of the phallus' (1958), and although it is difficult to choose a single text from an oeuvre at every turn dedicated to analysing the mobile forces of desire, this one, by the very virtue of its notoriety, makes it an appropriate mate for Look Back in Anger. In this short but extremely dense essay Lacan spells out the fate of human subjectivity: to be constituted by a basic lack, or 'want-to-be', which generates an infinite chain of desires, none of which can be adequately fulfilled, but which propel the subject forward regardless. In 'The signification of the phallus' desire is no prelude to gratification, and in this sense, Look Back in Anger can be said to share Lacan's suspicion of both the commonsensical and metaphysical accounts of desire. More controversially, Lacan claims in this essay that desire is organized around a privileged signifier, the phallus, even though earlier in the same essay he suggests that desire is no respecter of anatomical distinctions between the sexes. In the reading that follows, the 'eccentric, even scandalous' nature of desire in Look Back in Anger will be the main focus, but the possible relevance of the so-called 'phallic signifier' will also be scrutinized.

How thin is desire?

In a famous photograph from the first production of Look Back in Anger, Mary Ure (Alison) is seen ironing Cliff's trousers, while Cliff (Alan Bates) sits trouserless in an armchair, looking sullen, and Kenneth Haigh (Jimmy) stands in mid-harangue (facing page). When I show this photograph to my students and ask them to identify Jimmy, four times out of five they choose the heavy-set Alan Bates over a rather scrawny Kenneth Haigh. They do this even though, for someone who has read the play, Alan Bates' lack of trousers immediately indicates that he is playing Cliff. Is it perhaps the stormy look on Alan Bates' face that makes us assume that he is the tormented anti-hero? Or could it be that Jimmy figures so large as the spokesman for a generation that we could not possibly imagine him as this wan, meagre fellow? Or do we guess that if either actor were to be the unassertive Welshman, it must be the skinny one? It may simply be that Alan Bates' subsequent fame and Kenneth Haigh's relative anonymity deceive us. I ask my students to do this exercise because I made the same error myself when I first glanced at the picture. This visual parapraxis, or slip of the eye, can be excused when we think that the rather more sturdy and heroic frame of Richard Burton took over the part of Jimmy in the more widely-seen film version of *Look Back in Anger*, but it nevertheless alerts us to a crucial dimension of the original play on stage: the physical slightness, the hungry demeanour of the actor playing Jimmy. The opening character descriptions are very clear about this, telling us that Jimmy is 'a tall, thin young man' and Cliff is 'dark, big-boned'.[5]

The obvious way to interpret Jimmy's skinniness is to say that it discourages an audience from seeing in him the features of the traditional masculine hero, and, further, that his slender stature is consistent with the play's wider thematics of a crisis in masculinity. However, we might equally say that what he clearly needs is a really good feeding. In fact, the state of Jimmy's appetite is a subject of conversation early in the play:

JIMMY: (Picks up a weekly.) I'm getting hungry.
ALISON: Oh no, not already!
CLIFF: He's a bloody pig.
JIMMY: I'm not a pig. I just like food – that's all.
[...]
CLIFF: Don't see any use in your eating at all. You never get any fatter.
JIMMY: People like me don't get fat. I've tried to tell you before. We just burn everything up. Now shut up while I read. You can make me some more tea.[6]

Appetite is not the same thing as desire, because appetite is something that can be gratified. In the case of Jimmy, though, there appears to be some unaccounted-for remainder. If he never gets any fatter *and* he eats exorbitantly, one is bound to ask, where does the surplus go? His own explanation is that he 'burns' it all up. Lacan has a deceptively simple formula in 'The signification of the phallus' for the measure of desire. He says, 'desire is neither the appetite for satisfaction, nor the demand for love, but the difference that results from the subtraction of the first from the second, the phenomenon

14

of their splitting'.[7] We need to be wary of the facility of such an equation, but we may loosely translate it as follows: Jimmy's appetite marks his *need* for sustenance, yet he seems to be making a *demand* for food in excess of this need. The residue left over – that part which goes who knows where and which he 'burns up' – may be said to be the marker left by desire of 'their splitting'. Therefore, the stage image of Jimmy's skinniness is crucial, since it is the embodiment of his exorbitant, desiring subjectivity. Jimmy's is the physiognomy of desire.

It could be argued that the entire opening scene of the play – the basic expository material of *Look Back in Anger* – is devoted to establishing the eccentric and fickle nature of Jimmy's desires. In short order we see and hear the following demands: he wants the 'posh paper' Cliff is reading, he wants food, he wants more tea, he wants Cliff's matches, then the paper again and more tea again, and he wants to listen to a Vaughan Williams concert on the radio. Most of these demands are gratified in one way or another, but being satisfied in one demand does not prevent Jimmy from making further ones. No wonder Alison later says of him 'you're like a child', a charge repeated in Act Two, scene one.[8] And this is precisely the Lacanian lesson about desire: it is perverse and restless, it pursues its objects only temporarily, and is certainly not satisfied when it reaches them, because it is in fact seeking something else. As Slavoj Žižek – one of the most brilliant contemporary interpreters of Lacan in recent years – succinctly puts it: 'desire is by definition caught in a certain dialectic, it can always turn into its opposite or slide from one object to another, it never aims at what appears to be its object, but always "wants something more"'.[9] Indeed, enclosed within this series of petulant demands for minor objects by Jimmy, is an altogether more extravagant one. In one of many invocations of religion by a supposed atheist, he cries out 'Oh heavens, how I long for a little ordinary human enthusiasm. Just enthusiasm – that's all. I want to hear a warm, thrilling voice cry out Hallelujah!'[10] This desire is of a rather different order from others articulated by Jimmy. Catherine Belsey writes that desire 'has no settled place to be. And moreover, at the level of the unconscious its objects are no more than a succession of substitutes for an imagined originary presence ... a completeness which is desire's final, unattainable object.'[11] Jimmy's longing for 'human

15

enthusiasm' is just such a longing: it goes beyond simple objects within grasping range and makes a request to what Lacan might call the 'big Other'.

A Lacanian anatomy of desire

A more explicit rendering of Lacanian precepts and vocabulary is in order. Terms like 'Other' (big O), 'other' (small o), 'signifier', 'symbolic order', the 'sexual relation' and 'lack' appear again and again within Lacan's texts, and 'The signification of the phallus' makes full use of their range of meanings. That essay could helpfully be broken down into three parts.

In the first part, Lacan distances himself from a dominant school of psychoanalytic thought around Freud's 'castration complex' and attempts to discredit the prominence given to the phallus within that framework. Traditionally, the little boy possesses a penis and therefore fears its loss, whereas the little girl never had one and therefore regrets its absence and envies the little boy. But Lacan rejects this basic sexual distinction, claiming that clinical facts 'reveal a relation of the subject to the phallus that is established without regard to the anatomical difference of the sexes'.[12] This is surprising, since the term 'phallus' would seem inevitably to refer, at least symbolically, to a physical organ, the penis, only found on male bodies. But it is precisely this logic of reference, of symbolization, which Lacan seeks to undermine. He resists the desire to ascribe a final signified to the phallus. Instead, he asserts, part way into the second section of the essay, that 'the phallus is a signifier'. To reach this conclusion he proceeds by a series of negations: 'the phallus is not a phantasy ... Nor is it as such an object ... It is even less the organ, penis or clitoris, that it symbolizes.'[13] It is effectively an element in a linguistic system, part of a chain of signifiers, which make sense only in relation to one another and not to a final signified. If there is a 'phallus' it is no more possessed by men than it is by women.

This fine-tuning of the meaning of the phallus by Lacan may appear arcane and obscure, but he has achieved two crucial theoretical points. First, he has dismissed peremptorily any account of human (sexual) identity based on biology. At the same time, though, he has retained the notion of loss or lack which originally energized debates around the castration complex and penis envy.

In the second part of the essay then, Lacan spells out a theory of human subjectivity based on lack or absence, but without taking recourse to the ground of biology. Instead of biology, Lacan sees the fundamental determinant of human subjectivity as language. Human beings are signifying animals; they are 'subjects' of language. Lacan calls language the 'symbolic order', and humans become human through entry into language, or the 'symbolic order'. As a result of this entry into a symbolic order, the subject is split: 'it is not only man who speaks, but that in man and through man *it* speaks [*ça parle*], that his nature is woven by effects in which is to be found the structure of language'.[14] Here is the source of lack, or the genesis of an inaugural loss: the speaking subject is not whole, because he or she is divided up within language. If to be human is to speak, and to speak is to speak a language which is not your own – which has come before you and exists without you – then to be human is to be radically split. Of course, to speak of 'being human' only clouds the issue, because it is precisely the humanist conception of a stable and centred identity that Lacan seeks to undermine. This is why he prefers 'the speaking subject' to the term 'human'.

Here is where desire comes in. If 'the speaking subject' is fundamentally split, what it wants above all is to be whole. In this quest he or she turns to the Other as the only thing likely to provide that plenitude. The Other is, alternatively, the symbolic order, or God – in any case, an authority or a place which is apparently complete and self-consistent in a way that the speaking subject is not. The Other is by definition inaccessible, but this does not stop the subject from making demands of it:

Demand constitutes the Other as already possessing the 'privilege' of satisfying needs, that is to say, the power of depriving them of that alone by which they are satisfied. This privilege of the Other thus outlines the radical form of the gift of that which the Other does not have, namely, its love.[15]

The demand for a lost presence is made in the form of a demand for Love. But the Other does not have this love to give. The subject then finds an endless procession of substitutes which act as stand-ins for the Other. These go by the shorthand *objet petit a* (object little a). These equally cannot satisfy the subject, because they are only *signifiers* of her or his desire: 'man cannot aim at being

17

whole ... while ever the play of displacement and condensation to which he is doomed in the exercise of his functions marks his relation as a subject to the signifier'.[16]

In the final section of the essay, Lacan returns to the phallus and explains how desire is organized around it, or rather, around its necessary absence, but an explanation of this function of the phallus must wait till later.

Love not marriage

In the course of *Look Back in Anger* Jimmy at once makes passionate arguments for love and dismisses it with scathing derision. Far from being a hopeless contradiction this is, in Lacanian terms, entirely consistent. Any demand for love made to a person is inevitably unconditional and absolute, because it is a demand addressed to the Other via its poor substitute, an other. The other, of course, is unable to fulfil the intense demands made upon her or him, and therefore risks the scorn and hatred of the one making the demand. Malcolm Bowie puts it like this: 'the paradox and the perversity to be found in any recourse to persons is that the other to whom the appeal is addressed is never in a position to answer it uncondition-ally'.[17] At times, Jimmy accepts with mature resignation this fate, this condition of receiving only inadequate substitutes for his desire. His well-known hunger for food provides him with a metaphor for women when he deflates Cliff's claims that things were different when Alison was around: 'Today's meal is always different from yesterday's and the last woman isn't the same as the one before. If you can't accept that, you're going to be pretty unhappy, my boy.'[18] This gastronomic account of women as infinitely substitutable is of course realized physically on stage when the beginning of Act Three mimics the beginning of Act One, with papers spread about, the two men reading in their armchairs and Helena standing at the ironing-board in the place of Alison.

However, we cannot accept too readily this adequation of Alison and Helena, nor should we accept Jimmy's resigned stance at face value. If the one acts as substitute for the other, it must be clear that Jimmy feels satisfied with neither. It is worth looking closely at what he considers their failings in love, because it transpires that Helena appears to give what Alison does not and vice versa. Here is the vituperative charge laid at Alison's feet by Jimmy:

> Do you know I have never known the great pleasure of lovemaking
> when I didn't desire it myself. Oh, it's not that she doesn't have her
> own kind of passion. She has the passion of a python. She just
> devours me whole every time.[19]

The complaint here is a version of the pop lyric which goes 'I want
you to want me.' Desire is not only desire for the other, but a desire
that the other should desire you. Or as Lacan puts it, 'It is not
enough to be subjects of need, or objects of love, but that they must
stand for the cause of desire.'[20] If this is the problem with Alison –
her lack of demand – then Helena at least appears to fulfil this
requirement, because Jimmy tells us that 'Right from that first
night, you have always put out your hand to me first. As if you
expected nothing, or worse than nothing, and didn't care.'[21] Here
he finds in Helena what was lacking in Alison, and yet we know very
well at the end of the play that it is still Alison whom he really
loves. Here is desire in all its perversity – it is not really interested in
getting what it wants, but is instead obsessed by the lack or loss
which propels it: 'by obtaining the object, we lose the fascinating
dimension of loss as that which captivates our desire'.[22]

The sexism of *Look Back in Anger* lies not so much in the
rantings of Jimmy against women as in the play's assumption
that while he is the desiring subject par excellence, the women's
desire is finite and quantifiable, and, indeed, a little embarrassing.
In Helena's melodramatic 'I've always wanted you – always!' we
have the sort of unconditional declaration unlikely to escape
Jimmy's lips.[23] Helena's exclamation directly echoes Alison's
earlier 'I've never really wanted anyone else.'[24] They differ from
Jimmy in being able to speak or name their desire. Jimmy, on the
other hand, keeps the thing he desires just out of reach, beyond
articulation: 'all because of something I want from that girl down-
stairs, something I know in my heart she is incapable of giving',
he says of Helena, without ever telling us exactly what that 'something' is.[25] In fact, Jimmy is particularly scornful of any direct
articulation of romantic sentiment, and the play prompts us to
think that women are more prone to such exclamations. The most
notable instance is the letter Alison leaves for Jimmy when she
leaves. After reading it out loud, Jimmy mocks it openly in front of

Helena, who is, of course, an actress:

> Oh, how could she be so bloody wet! Deep loving need! That makes
> me puke! [...] Deep, loving need! I never thought she was capable of
> being as phoney as that! What is that – a line from one of those plays
> you've been in?[26]

When desire is actually spoken, or in this case written, it sounds like
a cliché or a quotation. It does not originate from the person as an
authentic feeling but simply repeats well-worn phrases already in
circulation, like 'a line from one of those plays'. The mistake Jimmy
makes is to assume that he somehow has access to authentic expressions of love and desire.

What *Look Back in Anger* reveals here, while trying to distance
itself from the supposedly saccharine romantic plays which have
preceded it, is that desire is a discourse. There is no expression of
love which is not citational, which is not spoken from the place of
the Other.[27] That is to say, only the symbolic order can provide the
means for the subject to express her or his agonized split relationship to the symbolic order. The (failed) ruse of the play is to point
to the women's expressions of love as 'phoney' and thereby establish
Jimmy's passion as 'true'. However, he too is subject to the signifier
of romantic discourse, as the eminently conventional 'something I
want from that girl' proves, as does the melodramatic curtain scene
of Act Two:

> *She slaps his face savagely. An expression of horror and disbelief floods
> his face. But it drains away, and all that is left is pain. His hand goes up
> to his head, and a muffled cry of despair escapes him. Helena tears his
> hand away, and kisses him passionately, drawing him down beside her.*[28]

The play in fact endlessly finds ways to speak Jimmy's desire without
him having to speak it himself. Possibly the most obvious instance is
Cliff's action as proxy for Jimmy in a declaration of love for Alison:
'After all, he does love you. You don't need me to tell you that.'[29]
Perhaps not, but the audience needs to know, and functions as the
real interlocutor for a scene which might have been overheard in the
corridors of my high school during any average lunch hour. More
tellingly, Cliff plays the intermediary after Jimmy's recklessness leads
to Alison's burn from the iron, which just goes to prove the Lacanian
maxim 'I love you, but there is in you something more than you,
objet petit a, which is why I mutilate you.'[30]

20

There is no phallus

Lovers need to believe their relationship is unique, unparalleled; and yet the language of love is anything but unique. Lovers must have recourse to a vocabulary which ante-dates them by centuries, if it is not simply drawn from the latest Hollywood melodrama. *Look Back in Anger* presents us with a common strategy for avoiding this painful paradox of love – a retreat from language. When Alison and Jimmy reach a crisis, when it looks as if things cannot be resolved positively, they resort to their game of 'Bears and Squirrels'. We are led to understand that this is a familiar routine worked out well in advance of the time of the play, and involves Jimmy assuming the character of a 'jolly super bear' and Alison a 'beautiful, great-eyed squirrel'.[31] The audience is faced with the spectacle of the actors miming the actions of their respective animals: '*She jumps up and down excitedly, making little "paw gestures"*'.[32] This is nothing less than an attempt to exit the symbolic order for a while and find satisfaction at an imaginary level. As with any retreat from language, it can only fend off the pressures of the symbolic temporarily, as when Jimmy asks Alison to explain her 'dance':

JIMMY: What the hell's that?
ALISON: That's a dance squirrels do when they're happy.

They embrace again.

JIMMY: What makes you think you're happy?[33]

Clearly, it is a game which animates Alison rather more than it does Jimmy. Jimmy, as we know, is the talker, the speaking subject, who has a much greater investment in the symbolic order.

In Lacan's scheme, the symbolic order, the Other, gives the illusion that it can guarantee the ultimate meaning and consistency of the subject's experience. The subject has to presuppose another place, an ideal order which can issue such a guarantee. We could say that the phallus occupies that place, just so long as we realize that the phallus does not exist, or rather, that it can only function by being veiled, hidden, withheld. Desire is organized around a basic absence, the vacancy which is the veiled phallic signifier. This is what Lacan is getting at when he writes

The fact that the phallus is a signifier means that it is in the place of the Other that the subject has access to it. But since this signifier is only veiled, as ratio of the Other's desire, it is this desire of the Other

21

as such that the subject must recognize, that is to say, the other in so far as he is himself divided by the signifying *Spaltung*.[34]

Jimmy has a peculiar relation to the phallus as such. On the one hand, he is constantly pointing to the lack in the Other – that is to say, the fact that even the Other does not really possess the phallus, has no central point of consistency. On the other hand, he yearns for just such a central organizing principle, a way of organizing his desire. Just as the play sets up a dialectic between a false romantic discourse and Jimmy's authentic one, so it allows him to find fault with the lack in the Other, while at the same time setting up another place where the phallus continues to operate, veiled and unattainable.

In *Look Back in Anger*, the bad Other (to set up a crude designation) can be seen as the target of Jimmy's verbal attacks in Act One. The main representative of this degraded symbolic order is the Bishop of Bromley, whom Jimmy associates with Alison's father, Colonel Redfern. The Bishop has written in to one of the 'posh papers' with some magisterial comments about the H-bomb and the class system.

> JIMMY: (*to Alison*). You don't suppose your father could have written it, do you?
> ALISON: Written what?
> JIMMY: What I just read out of course.
> ALISON: Why should my father have written it?
> JIMMY: Sounds rather like Daddy, don't you think?
> ALISON: Does it?
> JIMMY: Is the Bishop of Bromley his *nom de plume*, do you think?[35]

Jimmy mocks the Bishop's language for much the same reason as he attacks the language of romance – it simply repeats certain well-worn phrases and clichés, and what is worse, from a position of symbolic authority. It cannot be stressed enough that it is *symbolic* authority the Bishop possesses. After all, the play makes very clear that the hold of religion in the contemporary world is weak at best. Much of the play is set on Sundays, and although going to church is certainly not an option for Jimmy, he nevertheless laments the lack opened up by this latterly sacred day.[36] The first words of the play are, of course, 'Why do I do this every Sunday?'[37] And what are the Sunday newspapers, if not organized religion's secular surrogate, churning out doctrines that Jimmy correctly identifies as shot through with middle-class ideology? Jimmy's problem is that he doubts the consistency of the Other, the symbolic position from which the newspapers speak.

The Bishop of Bromley and Daddy supposedly occupy the place of the possessor of the phallus, the wielder of authority, but in Jimmy's eyes they are merely laughable. Slavoj Žižek explains that this is the inevitable fate of the individual granted the power of the 'Name of the Father': 'the "real father" is a miserable individual obliged to sustain the burden of the Name of the Father, never fully adequate to his symbolic mandate'.[38] The stage directions in *Look Back in Anger* make the same point, if somewhat more delicately, when Colonel Redfern makes his brief appearance to fetch Alison away from the one-room flat. 'Brought up to command respect, he is often slightly withdrawn and uneasy now that he finds himself in a world where his authority has lately become less and less unquestionable.'[39] Certainly, on stage, the Colonel fits Žižek's picture of a faintly miserable individual, slightly querulous in his attitude to Alison and confused at the state of the world. And yet, in spite of this, the Colonel stills stands in for Jimmy's desire. In fact, the Colonel's own desire is not that different from Jimmy's, because it is effectively a desire marked by nostalgia for a prior moment of plenitude, forever lost.

The retroactive phallus

If what the split subject yearns for above all else is to be whole, then the most striking image of such a plenitude in *Look Back in Anger* can be found in the Colonel's elegiac account of imperial India between 1914 and 1947:

> I had the Maharajah's army to command – that was my world, and I loved it, all of it. At the time, it looked like going on forever. When I think of it now, it seems like a dream. If only it could have gone on forever. Those long, cool evenings up in the hills, everything purple and golden. Your mother and I were so happy then. It seemed as though we had everything we could want.[40]

Here is desire's final resting-place, where all demands are satisfied, and time is left over to command armies. The political reading of this Arcadia is obvious: plenitude for the few is only at the expense of privation for the many. This reading is in no way invalidated if we add that such nostalgic reminiscence, like all nostalgia, is for a state in the past which never existed in the first place. Nostalgia is simply

the projection of dissatisfactions with the present on to a past retroactively filled with meaning. Freud had a term for such retrospective
assignment of meaning – he called it *Nachträglichkeit* (deferred
action), and Lacan uses the term *après coup* (after the event).
Although Jimmy at times seems ready to debunk the Colonel's
regret for the past, he too relies on a retroactive understanding of
India as a place of plenitude:

> I think I can understand how her Daddy must have felt when he
> came back from India, after all those years away. The old Edwardian
> brigade do make their brief little world look pretty tempting [...]
> Still, even I regret it somehow, phoney or not.[41]

The phallus is now irretrievably lost, but at least we can console
ourselves with the thought that it once was possessed.

In an infinitely subtle reading of 'The signification of the phallus'
Jane Gallop seizes on the double occurrence of the word 'nostalgia'
in Lacan's text. She implies that Lacan marks a shift away from a
standard Freudian reading of castration as either 'a threat or a depri-
vation. Man is threatened with loss, woman is deprived.'[42] With the
term 'nostalgia', the subject's 'loss' is seen no longer as the result of
a definite event but as a retroactive effect. The important thing here
is not that the subject is devising intricate lies about her or his past
but that nostalgia is an ingenious method for keeping the phallus,
that which promises plenitude, at an inaccessible distance. As Lacan
tells us, this is the best, indeed the only, way for the phallic signifier
to function, since it works only as an absence that is veiled with the
illusion of presence.

To understand what, in *Look Back in Anger*, occupies the place
(or non-place) of the phallus in addition to India, we must look for
what or who is absent in the play. We could identify a chain of signifiers for Jimmy which are each substitutable for the next and read
like this: India–Madeline–Hugh–Webster. Jimmy finds no satisfaction in those around him or in his various temporary desires, but the
play tells a rather different story about certain off-stage characters
who exist only in the largely fictional world. Take, for instance,
Webster, Alison's jazz-loving friend who visits the flat occasionally,
but not in any of the scenes the audience witnesses.

JIMMY: [...] I like him. He's got bite, edge, drive—
ALISON: Enthusiasm.

JIMMY: You've got it. When he comes here, I begin to feel exhila-
rated. He doesn't like me, but he gives me something,
which is more than I get from most people. Not since—
ALISON: Yes, we know. Not since you were living with Madeline.[43]

Here again, we have 'enthusiasm' and that enigmatic 'something',
that unnameable kernel of satisfaction poor Alison cannot provide.
But which, evidently, Madeline could: 'JIMMY: Her curiosity about
things, and about people was staggering [...] With her, it was simply
the delight of being awake, and watching.'[44] Madeline, like India, is
located in the past and is a kind of retroactive nostalgia-effect. Hugh
Tanner, son of Mrs Tanner, who dies halfway though the play, also
occupies such a privileged past-tense position. In a long passage of
exposition in Act Two, Alison explains to Helena how Hugh was
Jimmy's comrade-in-arms in a war waged against her upper-class
friends. Although Hugh eventually abandoned Jimmy, we are led to
believe that while he was around, Jimmy had access to that pure
quicksilver, 'enthusiasm'.

India, Webster, Madeline, Hugh – for all of these, their privileged
position in the desiring network of the play lies in their absence.
If Webster, trombone in hand, actually made an appearance on stage,
he could no longer live up to the elevated status given to him by
Jimmy. Just as the 'real father' cannot possibly meet the symbolic
mandate of the Name of the Father, so no character realized on
stage and asked to fill the Other's shoes, as it were, could possibly
continue to stand for the phallic signifier. As Žižek puts it,

> Although any object can function as the object-cause of desire – inso-
> far as the power of fascination it exerts is not its immediate property
> but results from the place it occupies in the structure – we must, by
> structural necessity, fall prey to the illusion that the power of fasci-
> nation belongs to the object as such.[45]

Look Back in Anger finds the best way of avoiding the shattering of
this illusion – it keeps the objects of desire at a distance. Therefore
we do not see that it is the position they occupy and not the objects
themselves that exert the power of fascination. It is worth noting
that this position, whether it is the position of the phallus or not,
is not specifically gendered and can sustain both Madeline and
Webster, as well as all of imperial India and Edwardian England.
What is important is that this position is maintained through a
retroactive fixing of meaning.

The history of *Look Back in Anger* itself provides another excellent instance of the retroactive structure of meaning. The play occupies a privileged position in a narrative of twentieth-century British drama. It is usually given a power of inauguration in a dramatic set of changes on the English stage and is cited as an origin for them. Of course, this power was not inherent in the play from its first moment of production – the power and privileged position were ascribed to it later. More recently, as has already been noted, the play's importance has been called into question and it has come to be seen as less worthy of its special status. Apart from any qualities in the play itself, this set of doubts comes about because no 'real' play can live up to the mandate of such a symbolic position. Even if *Look Back in Anger* has now been dislodged from its 'false' position, the position itself, the empty place of the phallus, more often than not retains its value in critical circles.

The sweet-stall of surplus enjoyment

Although she is for the most part consigned to a position of inadequacy in relation to Jimmy's desire, Alison is granted a fine Lacanian insight about her husband's lack:

> HELENA: You think the world's treated you pretty badly, don't you?
> ALISON: [...] Oh, don't try and take his suffering away from him – he'd be lost without it.[46]

The implication is that Jimmy actually enjoys the various thwartings of his desire. In Lacanian terminology, this perverse pleasure gained from displeasure is called 'surplus enjoyment', or *jouissance*. If we remember that Lacan describes desire as a sort of residue or remainder, the result of a splitting of need and demand, it is this leftover that is the source of secret enjoyment. In a moment of rare verbal hesitation in Act One, Jimmy, head leant against Alison, utters an obscure and enigmatic statement: 'I think ... I must have a lot of— old stock... / Nobody wants it...'[47] He simply breaks off mid-sentence, and we get no explanation of what he is referring to. If we take 'old stock' literally, we can only assume that he refers to his sweet-stall, and that somewhere he has a surplus of candy tucked away that no one cares for. So few references are made to Jimmy's profession in the course of the play that we can easily forget that this sourpuss on Sundays is a dispenser of sweetness all week long.

There is something in him more than him that he distributes off-stage. The standard interpretation of Jimmy's profession would be to see it as ironic – he is a bitter man who sells candy. The irony is further compounded when we realize that in spite of all his apparent early socialist ideals, he has been forced to resort to the position of small entrepreneur. Certainly, the play seems to confirm Jimmy's aversion to all things sweet, as is seen in his notorious comparison of his wife to a chocolate meringue. Within the general economy of *Look Back in Anger*, to be sweet is to be the opposite of everything the play values – passion, enthusiasm, edge, drive. What could be more frivolous and insubstantial than sweets, so obviously surplus to requirements, generating desires which are gratified with the most fleeting of sugar rushes before giving way to more desire? And yet, there is Jimmy at the centre, with all his old stock, as the figure who promises to meet the fruitless desires of his customers – like the Other's very own candyman. We can almost imagine him there at his stall, secretly gorging himself on bon-bons, chocolates, custard cremes, toffee, licorice, even chocolate meringues ...

Notes

1 Alan Sinfield, 'The theatre and its audiences', in Alan Sinfield, ed., *Society and Literature 1945–1970* (London: Methuen, 1983), pp. 173–97, esp. 173–8. Stephen Lacey, *British Realist Theatre: The New Wave in its Context 1956–1965* (London and New York: Routledge, 1995), pp. 17–31. See also David Cairns and Shaun Richards, 'No good brave causes? The alienated intellectual and the end of empire', *Literature and History* 14 (1988), 194–206. Typical of the move towards discussion of context alone, Cairns and Richards outline in impressive detail the political circumstances of the Left in Britain leading up to Osborne's play, but they hardly spare any space for discussing the play itself. In contrast, Dan Rebellato pays close attention to both text and context in his tremendous polemic against the special canonical status of *Look Back in Anger* in his *1956 and All That: The Making of Modern British Drama* (London and New York: Routledge, 1999).
2 John Osborne, *Look Back in Anger* (London: Faber and Faber, 1960 [1957]), p. 84.
3 On the metaphysics of 'True Love', see Catherine Belsey, 'Reading love stories', Chapter 2 of *Desire: Love Stories in Western Culture* (Oxford: Blackwell, 1994).
4 Jacques Lacan, 'The signification of the phallus', *Écrits: A Selection*, trans. Alan Sheridan (New York and London: W. W. Norton and Co., 1977

[1966]), pp. 281–91. This quotation, p. 286. All subsequent references are to this translation, although it has also been translated by Jacqueline Rose as 'The meaning of the phallus' in Juliet Mitchell and Jacqueline Rose, eds, *Feminine Sexuality: Jacques Lacan and the école freudienne* (New York: Norton, 1982), pp. 74–85.

5 Osborne, *Look Back*, pp. 9, 10.

6 Osborne, *Look Back*, p. 12.

7 Lacan, 'Signification of the phallus,' p. 287.

8 Osborne, *Look Back*, pp. 24, 43.

9 Slavoj Žižek, *Looking Awry: An Introduction to Jacques Lacan through Popular Culture* (London and Cambridge, MA: The MIT Press, 1991), p. 134.

10 Osborne, *Look Back*, p. 15.

11 Belsey, *Desire*, p. 5.

12 Lacan, 'Signification of the phallus', p. 282.

13 Lacan, 'Signification of the phallus', p. 285.

14 Lacan, 'Signification of the phallus', p. 284.

15 Lacan, 'Signification of the phallus', p. 286.

16 Lacan, 'Signification of the phallus', p. 287.

17 Malcolm Bowie, *Lacan* (London: Fontana, 1991), p. 136.

18 Osborne, *Look Back*, p. 83.

19 Osborne, *Look Back*, p. 37.

20 Lacan, 'Signification of the phallus', p. 287.

21 Osborne, *Look Back*, p. 86.

22 Žižek, *Looking Awry*, p. 86.

23 Osborne, *Look Back*, p. 86.

24 Osborne, *Look Back*, p. 47.

25 Osborne, *Look Back*, p. 84.

26 Osborne, *Look Back*, p. 73.

27 Catherine Belsey claims that 'What is specific to postmodern writing is that it foregrounds the citationality of desire, affirms it, puts it on display. And in doing so both speaks desire and defers it' *Desire*, p. 82. In this sense, *Look Back in Anger* is still firmly on the other side of post-modernity.

28 Osborne, *Look Back*, p. 74.

29 Osborne, *Look Back*, p. 29.

30 Žižek, *Looking Awry*, p. 169.

31 Osborne, *Look Back*, p. 34.

32 Osborne, *Look Back*, p. 34.

33 Osborne, *Look Back*, p. 34.

34 Lacan, 'Signification of the phallus', p. 288.

35 Osborne, *Look Back*, p. 14.

36 Remarking on the biblical rhetoric pervading Jimmy's speech, David Simmonds interprets the gap opened up by the empty Sunday as symptomatic of a wider social and political malaise. 'As "spokesman of a generation", one that was spiritually floundering in the wake of two world wars, the holocaust and the nuclear bomb, Jimmy can only resist the absence he senses in society

through the discourse of lost authority. The significance of the play opening on a Sunday now becomes more apparent ... with the occasional chiming of the church bells throughout the play constantly reminding of an absent structure to the now empty and unchanging Sunday ritual.' Unpublished essay, 1998.

37 Osborne, *Look Back*, p. 10.
38 Slavoj Žižek, *Enjoy Your Symptom: Jacques Lacan in Hollywood and Out* (London and New York: Routledge, 1992), p. 6.
39 Osborne, *Look Back*, p. 63.
40 Osborne, *Look Back*, p. 68.
41 Osborne, *Look Back*, p. 17.
42 Jane Gallop, *Reading Lacan* (Ithaca and London: Cornell University Press, 1985), p. 146.
43 Osborne, *Look Back*, p. 18.
44 Osborne, *Look Back*, p. 19.
45 Žižek, *Looking Awry*, p. 33.
46 Osborne, *Look Back*, p. 54.
47 Osborne, *Look Back*, p. 33.

2

Home front – Pinter with Freud

An undecidable case

Near the start of *The Homecoming*, there is a puzzling exchange between Lenny and his uncle Sam, who has just returned from work. Sam, a chauffeur, tells of the rapport he built up that day with an American client:

> SAM: For instance, I told this man today I was in the second world war. Not the first. I told him I was too young for the first. But I told him I fought in the second.
>
> *Pause*
>
> So did he, it turned out.
>
> *LENNY stands, goes to the mirror and straightens his tie.*
>
> LENNY: He was probably a colonel, or something, in the American Air Force.
>
> SAM: Yes.
>
> LENNY: Probably a navigator, or something like that, in a Flying Fortress. Now he's most likely a high executive in a world-wide group of aeronautical engineers.
>
> SAM: Yes.
>
> LENNY: Yes, I know the kind of man you're talking about.
>
> *LENNY goes out, turning to his right.*[1]

As far as we can gather, Lenny was not in the car with Sam, and yet his 'guesses' about the identity of the American client are unerringly accurate. At least we assume they are accurate, because Sam answers simply and bluntly in the affirmative to both of Lenny's speculative statements. Whereas the net Lenny casts in his first guess – 'a colonel … in the American Air Force' – is wide enough, the detail of the second and the language it is couched in – 'a high executive in a worldwide group of aeronautical engineers' – are striking and peculiar. Lenny then exits abruptly, and there is no further elaboration on the sources of his intimate knowledge of the passenger in Sam's car. On the evidence available an audience might be forced to conclude that it had just witnessed a case of telepathic communication between uncle and nephew. Certainly, as the play progresses, we find this family is capable of doing more than a few surprising things.

The doubts raised by this passage of dialogue do not stop with the unconfirmed intimations of telepathy. In each case, the 'Yes' uttered by Sam, although apparently final and unequivocal, is open to at least two interpretations. It may be 'Yes', that Lenny has correctly described the military career and current occupation of the American client; but it may also simply be a sign of agreement with the 'probably [...] or something [...]' and the 'Probably [...] something like that [...] most likely' portion of Lenny's guesses. In other words, Sam may merely be agreeing with what Lenny claims is most 'probably' the case. To muddy murky waters even further, just before his exit Lenny talks of the American as a 'kind of man', a type, which seems in direct contradiction with the highly detailed and individualized picture he built up in his previous line. In other words, he makes it sound as if there are hundreds of retired American Air Force colonels who were navigators in Flying Fortresses and are now high executives in worldwide groups of aeronautical engineers.

We might try to resolve the mystery in miniature of this exchange by appealing to information divulged later in the play: we discover that Lenny is a pimp, that in the past Sam was a driver involved in prostitution and that Lenny envisages a clientele of wealthy Americans for his brother Teddy's wife Ruth. From this set of facts we might conclude that Sam is already engaged in such activities under Lenny's auspices and that Lenny displays his inside information as part of an ongoing conflict with his father, Max, who is witness to the entire exchange. Prior to Sam's arrival, Max and Lenny had been bickering, and Lenny's show of omniscience and his decisive exit may be read as a final thrust at his father. However, this explanation is no more than speculative detective work, since nothing in the play either confirms or disproves it. We must content ourselves with saying that the passage hovers between different possibilities, none of which takes precedence over the others: it is an instance of undecidability.

The enigma of the American Air Force colonel is only one of many such instances of undecidability in *The Homecoming*. Indeed it could be argued that the play generates its singular effect through a steady accumulation of similarly puzzling moments. The many critics and analysts of the play have registered their sense of this effect through a fascinating cluster of adjectives. Taken in chronological order in what is by no means a comprehensive survey, Philip Hope-Wallace calls it 'baffling', 'enigmatic', and 'veiled';[2] R. F. Storch, 'terribly familiar' and 'terrifying';[3] Bert O. States comes up with 'peculiar', 'uncanny', 'gothic', 'lurking', 'inexplicable' and 'mysterious';[4] Martin Esslin, 'strangely casual', 'mysterious' and 'apparently inexplicable';[5] Katherine Worth, 'oblique and haunting', 'alarming', 'uncanny', 'uneasy' and 'peculiar';[6] Simon Trussler musters 'uneasy';[7] and M.W. Rowe produces 'uneasy', 'brooding', 'murky', 'half-understood', and 'lurking'.[8] A number of the words – 'uneasy', 'peculiar', 'mysterious' – are used by several of these critics, and as a set they link up into a distinctive chain of associations. What these critics perceive in *The Homecoming* may be vague and ill-defined, but they seem to reach a discomfited consensus about that perception.

From this varied collection I would like to pick out Storch's paradoxical formulation, 'terribly familiar' and the use in passing of 'uncanny' by both States and Worth. The 'uncanny', in the sense in which it is used by Sigmund Freud in his essay of 1919, can in fact serve as an umbrella term to account for this grouping of adjectives brought to bear on Pinter's play. Storch in particular stands out because the first (although by no means the only) definition Freud gives of the uncanny is 'that class of the frightening which leads back to what is known of old and long familiar'.[9] The familiar is generally thought to be comforting, and in the unusual circumstances where it is terrifying, 'uncanny' is one way of describing what is happening. The main difference between Freud and this assortment of critics is that he seeks to define rigorously the uncanny, whereas they do not go beyond a sort of 'adjectival criticism', simply registering the uncanny impression the play has on them. For instance, neither States nor Worth attempt to explain what they mean when they call parts of the play 'uncanny'. Unfortunately, it is not so easy to separate the theoretical Freud from the more subjective critics, because Freud himself admits that the uncanny is dependent on the person who experiences it. He calls it a 'state of feeling' and therefore implies that the uncanny is necessarily subjective.[10] If this is the case, then the critics just cited provide more than enough empirical 'sense data' to embark on an account of the uncanniness of *The Homecoming*. What is needed first is a more thorough-going theoretical exploration of the term 'uncanny'.

The uncanny

Freud's essay 'The "Uncanny"' was published shortly after the first world war, but its critical insights have achieved prominence much more recently. Starting in 1970, when Jacques Derrida wrote three suggestive footnotes about it in 'The Double Session', post-structuralist theory in particular has been taken with the problem of the uncanny. Hélène Cixous, Samuel Weber, Sarah Kofman and Neil Hertz have all struggled extensively with Freud's piece, and rather than seeking to extract a final definition of the uncanny from Freud, they all remark on how difficult Freud himself finds it to pin the term down. Freud takes several stabs at producing a conclusive answer, but it is his ultimate hesitation that has animated his readers in more recent years.[11]

It all starts out well enough for Freud, who says that he wants to account for an area of aesthetics which has hitherto been neglected. Whereas aesthetics tends to concentrate on the beautiful and attractive, he wants to explore what brings forth the less positive emotions of distress, repulsion and fear. The German word he chooses for his subject is *unheimlich*, which translates literally as 'unhomely'. His essay unfolds in three sections. In the first, he engages in a lengthy linguistic exercise, noting the different words for *unheimlich* in various languages as well as examining the different meanings of the word in German. The second and longest section is dominated by an interpretation of his main literary example, a story by E.T.A. Hoffmann, *The Sandman*. This section concludes with an eclectic catalogue of further cases of the uncanny. Then in the final section Freud qualifies some of his remarks by attempting to draw some distinctions between the uncanny in fiction and the uncanny in reality.

Keeping in mind that Freud contradicts himself more than once in the essay, we can try to isolate some of his main claims. Freud returns regularly to a basic definition of the uncanny as what is perceived when something supposedly familiar in fact appears strange and unfamiliar. Equally, the reverse can be an instance of the uncanny: when something unfamiliar strikes one as familiar. In the uncanny, then, it is difficult to distinguish what is known from what is unknown. Freud reveals that this collapsing of opposites also occurs at the linguistic level, for the dictionary definitions of *unheimlich* and *heimlich* (homely) tend to merge: '*heimlich* is a word the meaning of which develops in the direction of ambivalence, until it finally coincides with its opposite, *unheimlich*'.[12] So, while *heimlich* should imply everything that is safe, cosy, secure and friendly, its meanings also encompass what is frightening, obscure and secret. The other definition Freud seizes upon is Schelling's: '"*Unheimlich*" is the name for everything that ought to have remained ... secret and hidden but has come to light.'[13] Both of these versions of the uncanny come to bear on Freud's reading of *The Sandman*.

According to Freud, the hero of that novella regularly encounters childhood memories that he has repressed. The memories are of a fear of having his eyes torn out by the sandman, a bogeyman of children's stories. Freud effortlessly equates this anxiety about losing one's eyes with the fear of being castrated. In the Freudian schema, the threat of castration happens to young boys, who, in the face of the threat, renounce their love for their mothers and then repress the memory of the threat in order to take up their place in society. A repressed idea may always return, though, and when it does it is at once unfamiliar (because it has been successfully banished from the conscious) and familiar (because it has been experienced before). It is, literally, something that 'ought to have remained secret and hidden but has come to light'. If Freud left matters here, the uncanny would be bound to strike us as a crude and limited concept. Not the least of its shortcomings is that it seems to apply exclusively to men. However, he carries on and lists many more uncanny things that appear to go beyond the scope of the castration explanation. For example, although he dismisses Jentsch's idea that the uncanny is produced by 'doubts whether an apparently animate being is really alive', he returns rather too often to the problem of undecidability between the animate and inanimate.[14] In addition, he cites doubles, telepathy, the repetition compulsion and the return of animistic conceptions of the universe as yet more instances of the uncanny. There appears to be an irresolvable tension in Freud's essay between the drastic reductiveness of the castration thesis on the one hand and the proliferation of kinds of uncanniness on the other.

One way of addressing this tension is through a reformulation of the theory of the castration complex. Rather than simply thinking of castration as a threat to a physical organ, it can be used as a way of describing the relationship of all human subjects to their culture. Culture is castrating in the sense that it subjects us to a set of prohibitions and symbolic codes that we do not choose. This experience of being a 'subject' is felt through entry into language, a symbolic order that precedes us and that presents us with a series of differences (including sexual difference) which we must abide by. Most subjects resign themselves to this state of affairs and contrive to forget, or repress, this fact of symbolic castration, eventually imagining themselves to be autonomous, unique. The uncanny, then, is that moment when we are faced with the fundamental fact of our identities, when we are reminded that we are not in fact natural, spontaneous individuals but subjects of a culture. Travellers often have this experience, and the term for it is 'culture shock'. Strangely enough, culture shock tends to be much more powerful for people returning home. In foreign countries, you can build up a notion of your own uniqueness based on your difference from those around you, only to confront on your return a disturbing familiarity at the heart of your cherished distinctiveness. Freud himself puts his finger on this paradoxical state of affairs when he writes 'the dictionaries we consult tell us nothing new, perhaps only because we ourselves speak a language that is foreign'.[15] The uncanny marks the subject's confrontation with its own internal division, its strangeness to itself.

This location of the uncanny at the level of language – or the *sign* – by Freud gives us another way to account for the ambiguities and contradictions of his essay. The post-structuralist commentators on 'The "Uncanny"' argue that what is at stake in the essay is no less than psychoanalysis's vexed relationship to artistic or fictional work. Many if not most of Freud's examples come from fiction, but generally he is not interested in the complexities of fictional form, contenting himself instead with thematic or content-based readings. For Freud, Hoffmann's story illustrates the psychoanalytic truth of the castration complex. This truth is beneath the surface of the text, which Freud does not allow to distract him. Derrida says that this method of analysis, which 'makes the text into a form of expression [and] reduces it to a signified theme', is characteristic of Freud's texts on art and literature prior to 1919–20, but that with 'The "Uncanny"' something else happens.[16] Freud may desire 'an originary, central, or ultimate signified' for both the uncanny and

35

Hoffmann's tale, but at the same time he is

> here more than ever attentive to undecidable ambivalence, to the play of the double, to the endless exchange between the fantastic and the real, the 'symbolized' and the 'symbolizer', to the process of interminable substitution.[17]

He wants to look 'through' the fictional text to an ultimate signified, but everything he knows about the uncanny makes him vacillate, suspends him on the edge of undecidability.

Home

The Homecoming has had its fair share of pre-1919 Freudian treatment. Precisely because it is so 'mysterious', it has invited attempts to decipher it, to provide an explanation for the actions of its characters. Why does Max at turns eulogize and heap abuse on his dead wife, Jessie, and then administer similar treatment to his visiting daughter-in-law, Ruth? Why does Ruth agree to leave her husband, Teddy, and choose to stay with his father and brothers in the dual capacity of prostitute and substitute mother? How can we account for the calculated abuse Lenny levels at his father and at Ruth? There must be something behind all this, critics say, and psychoanalysis is the methodology *par excellence* for revealing latent depths. The story of Oedipus, who unwittingly killed his father and slept with his mother, was Freud's favourite myth, and so it has proved with psychoanalytic critics who have relentlessly discovered this narrative lurking beneath fictional or dramatic situations of every stripe. In the case of *The Homecoming*, Martin Esslin arrived at this conclusion early, interpreting the play as a wish-fulfilment dream, whereby the sons Lenny and Joey succeed in their ambition to sleep with their mother (Ruth, who stands in for Jessie); and subdue their father. According to Esslin, the symbolic murder of Max and dream of sexual union with the mother is realized in the final tableau of the play.[18] More recently, M. W. Rowe has read the play as a perfect illustration of the thesis put forward by Freud in 'The Most Prevalent Form of Degradation in Erotic Life'. In this reading, Lenny's predilection for 'abnormal' rather than 'genuine' sexual object choice and Teddy's total capitulation to his family's proposals are indicative of neurosis on the part of both characters. This neurosis can be traced back to certain repeated structures within the family's history. After this diagnosis Rowe even prescribes a course of action designed to ensure a more 'healthy' sexuality for Teddy!

Esslin and Rowe, and other psychoanalytic interpreters of the play,[19] repeat the strategy of Freud when he claims that the loss of eyes in *The Sandman* is directly equivalent to castration. They all make of the fictional or dramatic work an *exemplary* instance of a psychoanalytic lesson which precedes the work itself. They might as well state the psychoanalytic argument and bypass the play altogether, so intent are they on finding the content they desire – what Derrida calls an 'originary, central, or ultimate signified'. Invariably, to do this, they must make the dramatic text say something it does not say, at least not in any 'manifest' way, to borrow another psychoanalytic term. Just as castration is not mentioned explicitly in *The Sandman*, neither the Oedipus complex nor neurosis actually come up in *The Homecoming*. This is not to say that those thematic readings are to be ruled out of court entirely; but to assert them inevitably obliterates the uncanniness of the play – that is, it closes down the radical ambivalence at work in *The Homecoming*.

Although *The Homecoming* is not on the surface 'about' Oedipal desire or neurosis, it is quite manifestly about the *heimlich*. The title of the play alerts us to this fact, and like the titles of many of Pinter's earlier plays – *The Room, The Birthday Party, The Caretaker, The Basement, Tea Party* – it carries connotations of intimate physical spaces or cosy familiar events. A homecoming implies both an absence and a return. Someone needs to have left a home in order to have a homecoming, and so inevitably the place returned to is also no longer strictly speaking that person's home. Homecomings are opportunities for renewing acquaintance with a locale and with the people who inhabit that locale. Because a homecoming is necessarily preceded by a period of separation, it is an occasion to measure the changes (if there are any) that have taken place in the intervening time. People may have died or been born, married or divorced; buildings may have been built or destroyed, houses or rooms renovated. If 'home' has changed since it was left, the term 'homecoming' is literally inaccurate, because the place is not identical to the home that was left. In this case, then, a homecoming can be a moment for reminiscence and nostalgic reflection on the way things were. Needless to say, Pinter's play does not fall easily into this familiar pattern of the homecoming, partly because the social and geographic location of the play is less than precise.

Nevertheless, Teddy, whose titular homecoming it putatively is, goes through the returnee's motions by checking whether or not his room is as he left it:

> TEDDY: I'll just go up ... have a look.
>
> *He goes up the stairs, stealthily.*
> *RUTH stands, then slowly walks across the room.*
> *TEDDY returns.*
>
> TEDDY: It's still there. My room. Empty. The bed's there.[20]

Teddy never really gets beyond this blandest and most commonplace of possible reflections on the current state of what was supposedly once *heimlich* to him. A little later he asserts that 'Nothing's changed. Still the same', and nothing in the play conclusively proves or disproves this confident claim.[21] What is worth remarking on is the stage direction for Teddy's ascent of what are familiar stairs for him: '*stealthily*'. Stealth is appropriate for someone who does not belong, or who at the very least wishes to keep his actions secret – hardly the disposition of someone at home.

The title of the play appears to be somewhat misleading, since there are hardly any of the usual formal trappings of the homecoming. Indeed, Lenny, the first to encounter Teddy, greets him as if he had never left. In Act Two, some of the formal language of homecoming is uttered by Lenny and Max. In a long speech in which he chastises Teddy for becoming 'less forthcoming', Lenny produces some of the clichés reserved for returning elder sons:

> Your family looks up to you, boy, and you know what it does? It does its best to follow the example you set. Because you're a great source of pride to us. That's why we were so glad to see you come back, to welcome you back to your birthplace.[22]

And just before Teddy departs without his wife, Max apes the conventions of saying farewell at the end of a homecoming; Teddy responds in kind:

> TEDDY: Yes. Well, bye-bye, Dad. Look after yourself.
>
> *They shake hands.*
>
> MAX: Thanks, son. Listen. I want to tell you something. It's been wonderful to see you.
>
> *Pause.*
>
> TEDDY: It's been wonderful to see you.

MAX: Do your boys know about me? Eh? Would they like to see a photo, do you think, of their grandfather?

TEDDY: I know they would.[23]

These types of exchanges cannot but appear as though within inverted commas, because of the scenes that frame them. For every clichéd and sentimental assertion of family values there is a stage image or passage of dialogue which contradicts it. As with Freud's definitions of *hoimlich* and *unhoimlich*, where the meanings of the two cross over and tend towards ambivalence, in *The Homecoming* everything to do with the home and with the familiar tends to dovetail towards what is alien and unfamiliar.

The play achieves this uncanny effect whereby *heimlich* and *unheimlich* run together through a series of stark juxtapositions. It is typically Max who is the source of these juxtapositions, as he tends to be the character most likely to summon up idealistic homilies about the family and express violent feelings towards his family within the same breath. In the curtain scene to Act One, Max '*hits* JOEY *in the stomach with all his might*', then strikes Sam '*across the head with his stick*', whereupon he addresses Ruth and then Teddy:

MAX: Teddy, why don't we have a nice cuddle and kiss, eh? Like the old days? What about a nice cuddle and kiss, eh?

TEDDY: Come on, then.

Pause.

MAX: You want to kiss your old father? Want a cuddle with your old father?

TEDDY: Come on, then.

TEDDY moves a step towards him.

TEDDY: Come on.

Pause.

MAX: You still love your old Dad, eh?

They face each other.

TEDDY: Come on, Dad. I'm ready for the cuddle.

MAX begins to chuckle, gurgling.

He turns to the family and addresses them.

MAX: He still loves his father![24]

Max speaks in a language of tenderness and intimacy dramatically at odds with the violence that has come before. Even if Max acts as

The Homecoming, Royal Shakespeare Company, 1965. *From left*: Michael Bryant (Teddy), Vivien Merchant (Ruth), Terence Rigby (Joey) and Paul Rogers (Max)

though nothing had occurred, the audience cannot help but read in tandem the contrary things it has just been shown. And even without the preceding display of unfatherly and unbrotherly love, Max's suggestion to Teddy carries much doubt with it. An offer of 'cuddles and kisses' generally implies the relationship between an adult and a child, and although it is the grown man, Teddy, who is to be the recipient of the cuddle, it is Max who 'gurgles' like a baby. And of course, Teddy's repeated 'Come on' could be read as a prelude to fisticuffs just as well as acquiescence to a fatherly kiss. Some of this ambivalence will necessarily be resolved by the actors' choices of delivery, but a certain hesitation between *heimlich* and *unheimlich* is bound to remain. The final ideal of family life uttered as a curtain line may provoke amusement if played comically, but it also resonates with Teddy's earlier 'Nothing's changed. Still the same.' It might be tempting to interpret such episodes as satire on hypocrisy within the traditional family unit. However, satire requires a well-defined object, and in this play it is almost impossible to locate an external reality which the family refers to.[25]

A homecoming is a return, and Freud has a few things to say about returns in 'The "Uncanny"'. More specifically, he notes that if an event or situation is repeated involuntarily, it tends to produce an uncanny feeling. He writes,

> it is only this factor of involuntary repetition which surrounds what would otherwise be innocent enough with an uncanny atmosphere, and forces upon us the idea of something fateful and inescapable when otherwise we should have spoken only of 'chance'.[26]

This observation is a useful gloss on the 'Come on' Teddy repeats four times in the passage just analysed. If he had said it once, or even just twice – the second time for emphasis – it might not have raised as many doubts regarding its meaning. In fact Freud's comment on repetition might account for the uncanny language in almost all of Pinter's plays where characters regularly engage in dialogue that returns to where it began rather than progressing forward. There are in addition, two notable repetitions, or returns of the same thing, at the level of plot in *The Homecoming*. Max alerts Teddy and us to one of them: 'TEDDY: We've got three boys, you know. / MAX: All boys? Isn't that funny, eh? You've got three, I've got three.'[27] Having three boys is in itself 'innocent enough', as Freud says, but when Teddy repeats the pattern of an already uncanny

41

family, it is a bit 'funny'. How many other aspects of this family are destined to be repeated in the spectral family so far removed in America?

The other repetition is not so directly remarked upon by any of the characters. This time the repeated situation involves Ruth, who is to take the place of Jessie, the dead mother of Teddy, Lenny and Joey. Jessie, according to what we can piece together about her, was both a mother to the boys and a prostitute earning income for the family. It is this dual role that Max and Lenny devise for Ruth and to which she agrees with certain amendments. Max explains how Ruth will be a direct substitute for Jessie:

> Since poor Jessie died, eh, Sam? We haven't had a woman in the house. Not one. Inside this house. And I'll tell you why. Because their mother's image was so dear any other woman would have ... tarnished it. But you ... Ruth ... you're not only lovely and beautiful, but you're kin. You're kith. You belong here.[28]

Ruth, who is not returning to the house, but coming there for the first time, is in fact treated as if she had already been there before: 'You belong here'. In the case of this repetition, what is repeated is not 'innocent enough'. In fact, Jessie's sexual history has been threatening to emerge at various points throughout the play, and it does so shortly after the negotiations with Ruth are complete, when Sam reveals that 'MacGregor had Jessie in the back of my cab as I drove them along.'[29] This might be an illustrative instance of Schelling's definition of the uncanny: something 'that ought to have remained secret and hidden but has come to light'. Sam's collapse immediately after his revelation would appear to confirm its seriousness, but the cool negotiations leading up to it and the disinterested response of the rest to his fainting fit seem to obviate its impact. What is uncanny about Ruth's repetition of Jessie's role is not the recurrence of something frightening but the recurrence of something quotidian, something everyday.

Sexual difference and the uncanny

The doubling of Jessie and Ruth raises questions about the links between the uncanny and sexual politics in *The Homecoming*. Two early readers of the play convincingly claim that the homecoming of the title is not Teddy's but Ruth's. Irving Wardle writes, 'The play's title refers to [Ruth], not to Teddy. It is no homecoming for him;

whereas she (even distrusting her probably untrustworthy statement that she was born nearby) is instantly on home ground.'[30] Martin Esslin concurs: 'At the end of the play Ruth again rules the household. This is the "homecoming" of the title. It is not Teddy who has come back home – after all he left after one day – but the mother who has returned.'[31] While Wardle and Esslin are right to claim that the homecoming may also be Ruth's, they surely make a mistake in eliminating Teddy as a possibility, as if it were an 'either/or' situation. In a play in which so much is undecidable, the question of whom the homecoming 'belongs to' must also remain open. The two critics base their claim on an unproblematic notion of home, of the *heimlich*. Wardle says that Ruth is 'instantly on home ground', as if this were something secure and stable (although his qualifying parenthesis betrays rather more doubts); and Esslin equally treats the word 'homecoming' as if it were something unequivocal and finite. Everything else in the play leads us to distrust the cosiness, safety and security of 'home', so how can Ruth be identified with it with such certainty? And even if she does 'belong here', as Max asserts, how can we know what that means when the *heimlich* so easily bleeds into the *unheimlich* in the play?

The critics unconsciously take up the position of Max in trying to assert the proper domestic function for Ruth. In his efforts to place her definitively in the house, Esslin imputes to Ruth a set of motives not directly available from the play:

> Having failed in her marriage, Ruth is in a state of existential despair, a deep accidie, which is both fully understandable and completely motivates her behaviour. She has tried to fight her own nature and she has been defeated by it. Now she yields to it, and surrenders beyond caring.[32]

According to Esslin, then, not only is a woman's place in the home (serving her family as a prostitute) but it is also 'in her nature'! Here is a last gasp reassertion of nature in the face of the uncanny. The uncanny, remember, is that moment when the illusion of the natural is shattered by the return of the repressed of culture. The basic, initiating division made by culture is sexual differentiation, and it is a division that these critics, along with Max and sometimes Lenny, struggle to assert as given in nature. They do this by affirming the traditional ideology of home and hearth as a feminized space. In *The Homecoming* this 'home truth' is rendered uncanny by the constant doubts cast on everything to do with the home, but also by the sudden shift to the technical language of contracts made by Ruth at the moment when she is negotiating her new position. It is almost as if she is quoting directly from a business manual when she says 'All aspects of the agreement and conditions of employment would have to be clarified to our mutual satisfaction in the presence of witnesses'.[33] Far from being natural, in this model gendered subjectivity is arrived at through legal constraints and due process.

One of the reasons it is so difficult to make claims about Ruth's 'motivations' – as if she had psychological depth – has to do with her physical presentation on the stage in performance. In many ways she resembles a favoured figure of gothic fiction, the automaton. Peter Hall, the director for the first production of *The Homecoming* at the Aldwych theatre, has said: 'I believe it mandatory to do as few moves in a Pinter play as possible.'[34] Whereas straight naturalist drama strives for animation on stage, creating movements for its actors which signify to the audience 'real life', a Pinter play is more likely to be dominated by stillness. Consequently, the stage directions indicating movements in the play are few and far between. In a play of few dynamic actions, Ruth is possibly the stillest of the characters. In her first scene, while Teddy '*walks about*', her directions are the static '*She does not move*', '*RUTH stands*' and '*RUTH sits*'; and in the following scene with Lenny the pattern repeats itself, with Lenny moving back and forth to the sideboard while Ruth stands still or simply sits.[35] When she is asked to change position in these scenes, the directions on both occasions are specific about her pace: '*slowly walks across the room*', and '*walks slowly into the room*'.[36] The implication of this slowness and stillness is that there is something mechanical about Ruth, that she is not fully animate. This is not to say that she is an automaton, but that her way of inhabiting the stage may raise uncertainties about the distinction between the animate and inanimate.

According to Jentsch, who wrote on *The Sandman* before Freud, the source of the uncanny in that story lies in doubts about whether the automaton-doll Olympia, idealized love object of the protagonist Nathanael, is in fact alive. Freud dismisses Jentsch's speculation outright in his haste to diagnose Nathanael's castration complex, and as subsequent critics have repeatedly pointed out, he thereby passes over women in his analysis. Jane Marie Todd proposes another reading: 'Olympia is a caricature of the ideal woman: silent, powerless, docile. It is only when, having lost her eyes, she is exposed as an automaton, that the "tea circle" realizes how this ideal is achieved.'[37] In *The Homecoming*, if Ruth embodies in some ways an ideal woman for the family, the play's way of presenting her, suspended in uncertainty, mitigates any firm belief that she is somehow real or natural. She is not an automaton, but there is enough automatism about her to cast suspicion on the truth of the gender roles she adopts. Ruth is, of course, a double for Jessie, and as Sarah Kofman points out, once again commenting on Freud,

> The double is neither living nor dead ... By creating what he hopes are immortal doubles, man tries to conceal the fact that death is always already present in life. The feeling of uncanniness that arises from the double stems from the fact that it cannot but evoke what man tries in vain to forget.[38]

An uncanny stage

Freud has been criticized, even by his post-structuralist admirers and inheritors, for not being an expert enough literary critic in 'The "Uncanny"'. In his reading of Hoffmann he paraphrases large parts of the story, excluding the elements that do not suit his analysis, and he has scant regard for the fine detail of narrative strategy. In particular, he fails to comment on how the use of the epistolary form and the interventions by the narrator necessarily affect the reading process.[39] Outside post-structuralist debate, most subsequent discussion of the uncanny has centred on prose fiction and, more specifically, on gothic and fantasy novels. In this work, Freud's neglect of form has been redressed, and a great deal of attention has been paid to how the uncanny is an effect created through textual effects as well as thematic ones. *The Homecoming*, however, is not a piece of prose fiction. Is the 'uncanny' equally valuable as a term of analysis for theatre and drama? Do theatre and drama pose particular formal problems for the uncanny which we ignore at our peril? This reading has attempted as far as possible to avoid the pitfalls of the thematic psychoanalytic reading which seeks clinical truths in the content of a play, but it has not thus far had very much to say about *The Homecoming* as a play. The comments on the moves given to Ruth on stage indicate that the theatre specifically is responsible for some of the uncanniness of the play. It can be argued even further, though, that the play's use of theatrical conventions is intimately tied up with its uncanny effect.

Pinter's plays have been notoriously difficult to categorize in terms of dramatic genre or tradition. However, they do at one level subscribe quite closely to the trappings of realist drama. Katherine Worth has noted 'his commitment to the proscenium stage ... Exceptionally, almost uniquely among the playwrights of the New Wave, he seems to feel no pull towards an open stage, mixed forms, improvisation'.[40] For the audiences of 1965, then, Pinter's plays were at least framed in a manner they were accustomed to. Stephen Lacey outlines more elements which place Pinter in the realist tradition: 'all the markers of theatrical naturalism are present in performance – the box-sets, curtains, fourth-wall illusionism, the "realistic" lights and costumes'.[41] We might add that the play takes place in that most recognizable of realist settings, the domestic sphere. Countless plays taking families as their subject matter had crossed the British stage in the twentieth century and many more would follow. At the time when Pinter was starting to find some success as a playwright, in the late 1950s and early 1960s, the New Wave of realist drama examining lower-middle-class and working-class domestic environments was in full swing; and as Stephen Lacey points out, in Pinter as in the New Wave, 'the settings were uniformly lower-class and contemporary.'[42] Indeed, in the opening scenes of *The Homecoming* one can identify resemblances between the bickering of Max and Lenny and equivalent scenes of domestic strife in *Look Back in Anger* or *The Wesker Trilogy*.[43] Max even embarks on a classic well-made play style of exposition within the first moments of the play: 'I used to knock about with a man called MacGregor. I called him Mac. You remember Mac? Eh?'[44] What could be more conventional?

The Homecoming is presented in a familiar theatrical style, a style still very much hegemonic in 1965. It is the accumulation of uncanniness, of undecidable moments, over the course of the play which renders this familiar form unfamiliar. *The Homecoming* does not overturn dramatic conventions or throw them out, but rather presents its audiences with the shadows of them. When the curtain opens it may present a 'cavernous set', but it is still a recognizable domestic interior. It manages to make strange and alien what is most familiar, dramatically speaking. Freud said that 'we ourselves speak a language that is foreign'. It is foreign because we do not speak it as a matter of course, but learn it. We then manage to forget or repress this fact and convince ourselves that we are masters over language because it is so familiar to us. As Elizabeth Wright says, '[t]he familiar, the *heimlich*, is the result of the apparently successful orderings we have made of the world'.[45] Realism as a theatrical convention has been one apparently successful ordering of the world. It is also bound by a set of conventions – a language – which an audience must learn and then contrive to forget that it has learned. The disquiet that audiences feel at *The Homecoming* is a sign that this stage language is still foreign to them.

It is dangerous to draw too many broad-reaching conclusions about audiences' subjective reactions to *The Homecoming*, since there are no reliable measuring devices for such ephemera. We do have as documents the 'uneasy' impressions registered by the earlier critics of the play. Later critics tend to be more relaxed and confident of the academic distance they can gain in relation to this and other early Pinter plays that also made the familiar proscenium arch an alien piece of architecture. This familiarity with Pinter may be foolishness on their part, but it may also indicate that Pinter is not as uncanny as he used to be. What was familiar in 1965 may no longer be so thirty-five years later. There are still traditional proscenium arch plays with box-sets and actors speaking naturalistically, but this mode of theatrical presentation no longer dominates a stage that has seen a proliferation of theatrical styles in the intervening years. This is so much the case that it is difficult to identify an obviously 'familiar' set of conventions or to claim that audiences are learning a single stage language. Having said that, Pinter's plays may still be uncanny for audiences brought up on a cinema still dominated by naturalist conventions. And there is always that American Air Force colonel.

Notes

1 Harold Pinter, *The Homecoming* [1965], in *Plays: Three* (London: Methuen, 1978), pp. 29–30.
2 Philip Hope-Wallace, 'Feeling cheated' [1965], in Michael Scott, ed., *Harold Pinter: The Birthday Party, The Caretaker and The Homecoming: A Casebook* (Basingstoke: Macmillan, 1986), p. 197.
3 R. F. Storch, 'Harold Pinter's happy families' [1967], in Arthur Ganz, ed.,

Pinter: A Collection of Critical Essays (Englewood Cliffs, N.J.: Prentice-Hall, 1972), pp. 145 and 146.

4 Bert O. States, 'Pinter's *Homecoming*: the shock of nonrecognition' [1968], in Ganz, *Pinter*, pp. 147–60, pp. 149, 152 and 159.

5 Martin Esslin, *Pinter: The Playwright* (London: Methuen, 1982 [1970]), pp. 127, 128 and 138.

6 Katherine Worth, 'Pinter and the realist tradition' [1972], in Scott, *Harold Pinter*, pp. 30, 32 and 35.

7 Simon Trussler, 'A case against *The Homecoming*' [1973], in Scott, *Harold Pinter*, p. 184.

8 M.W. Rowe, 'Pinter's Freudian homecoming', *Essays in Criticism* 41:3 (1991), p.189.

9 Sigmund Freud, 'The "Uncanny"' [1919], in *Art and Literature, Penguin Freud Library*, vol. 14, trans. James Strachey, ed. Albert Dickson (Harmondsworth: Penguin, 1985), p. 340.

10 Freud, 'Uncanny', p. 340.

11 Derrida's 'The double session' first appeared in *Tel Quel* in 1970. The three enigmatic footnotes are on pages 220, 248 and 268 of *Dissemination* [1972], trans. Barbara Johnson (London: Athlone Press, 1981). The fascinating sequence of readings which follows is Hélène Cixous, 'Fiction and its phantoms: a reading of Freud's *Das Unheimliche* (the "uncanny")' [1972], *New Literary History* 7 (1976), 525–48; Samuel Weber, 'The sideshow, or: remarks on a canny moment', *Modern Language Notes* 88 (1973), 1102–33; Sarah Kofman, 'The double is/and the devil: the uncanniness of *The Sandman* (*Der Sandmann*)', in *Freud and Fiction* [1974], trans. Sarah Wykes (Cambridge: Polity, 1991), pp. 119–62; Neil Hertz, 'Freud and the Sandman', in *Textual Strategies: Perspectives in Post-Structuralist Criticism*, ed. Josué V. Harari (Ithaca: Cornell University Press, 1979), pp. 296–321. Julia Kristeva also develops a thematics or poetics of the uncanny in *Strangers to Ourselves*, trans. Leon S. Roudiez (New York and London: Harvester Wheatsheaf, 1991).

12 Freud, 'Uncanny', p. 347.

13 Freud, 'Uncanny', p. 345 (emphasis as in original).

14 Freud, 'Uncanny', p. 347.

15 Freud, 'Uncanny', p. 341.

16 Derrida, *Dissemination*, p. 248.

17 Derrida, *Dissemination*, p. 268.

18 Esslin, *Pinter*, pp. 143–45.

19 See, for instance, Lucina P. Gabbard, *The Dream Structure of Pinter's Plays: A Psychoanalytic Approach* (Rutherford, NJ, and London: 1976) and Marc Silverstein, *Harold Pinter and the Language of Cultural Power* (Lewisburg, PA: Bucknell University Press, 1993).

20 Pinter, *Homecoming*, p. 37.

21 Pinter, *Homecoming*, p. 38.

22 Pinter, *Homecoming*, p. 81.

23 Pinter, *Homecoming*, p. 95.
24 Pinter, *Homecoming*, pp. 58–60.
25 Elin Diamond has made a case for Pinter's plays as parodic, although her emphasis is on *The Collection* above all. Elin Diamond, 'Parody play in Pinter', *Modern Drama* 25:4 (1982), 477–88.
26 Freud, 'Uncanny', p. 360.
27 Pinter, *Homecoming*, p. 66.
28 Pinter, *Homecoming*, p. 91.
29 Pinter, *Homecoming*, p. 94.
30 Irving Wardle, 'The Territorial Struggle' (1971), in Scott, *Harold Pinter*, p. 170.
31 Esslin, *Pinter*, p. 143.
32 Esslin, *Pinter*, pp. 144–5.
33 Pinter, *Homecoming*, p. 93.
34 Peter Hall, 'Directing Pinter: an interview with Catherine Itzin and Simon Trussler' [1974], in Scott, *Harold Pinter*, p. 49.
35 Pinter, *Homecoming*, pp. 36–7.
36 Pinter, *Homecoming*, pp. 37, 43.
37 Jane Marie Todd, 'The veiled woman in Freud's "Das Unheimliche"', *Signs* 11:3 (1986), p. 525.
38 Kofman, 'The Double', p. 148.
39 See in particular the readings of Kofman and Hertz.
40 Worth, 'Pinter and the realist tradition', pp. 31–2.
41 Stephen Lacey, *British Realist Theatre: The New Wave in its Context, 1956–1965* (London and New York: Routledge, 1995), p. 142.
42 Lacey, *British Realist Theatre* p. 141.
43 I owe this point to Andrew Stott.
44 Pinter, *Homecoming*, p. 24.
45 Elizabeth Wright, 'The Uncanny and Surrealism', *Modernism and the European Unconscious*, ed. Peter Collier and Judy Davies (Cambridge: Polity Press, 1990), p. 265.

3

Hamlet games – Stoppard with Lyotard

A weightless pair

Rosencrantz and Guildenstern are Dead (1967) and *The Postmodern Condition* (1979) have at least two things in common. Neither is the first work of its author, but both first brought their authors wider prominence: Tom Stoppard's play provided his breakthrough on the London stage after unheralded radio and television pieces, and Jean-François Lyotard's work for the Conseil des Universités of the government of Quebec, sub-titled *A Report on Knowledge*, is still his best known and most referenced book in the anglophone world, in spite of the numerous volumes of philosophy and cultural criticism he wrote before and after it. Along with their wide popularity and exposure, the play and the 'report' also share something of a poor reputation among those in the know. Stoppard experts tend to prefer the more dense literary and philosophical allusiveness of *Jumpers, Travesties* and *Arcadia* to the *jeu d'esprit* which is *Rosencrantz and Guildenstern*, perhaps because the former allow for rather more exegesis and scholarly apparatus than the latter. Meanwhile, Lyotard aficionados and proper philosophers alike will sneer at *The Postmodern Condition* for its accessibility or its lack of rigour and point you instead to *Libidinal Economy* or *The Differend*. There may be some reverse snobbery at work here, where there is an inverse relationship between popular and critical acclaim, but it is probably true that *Rosencrantz and Guildenstern* and *The Postmodern Condition* constitute 'lightweight' Stoppard and Lyotard. This alone does not necessarily guarantee that the two will make good traveling companions, but I will take it as a good omen. This chapter will, therefore, embrace, rather than disdain, the purported insubstantiality of its protagonists.

'Protagonists', as it turns out, are precisely what both *Rosencrantz and Guildenstern* and *The Postmodern Condition* are short on. The main conceit of Stoppard's play is that it is about two figures who are patently *not* protagonists: Rosencrantz and Guildenstern are very minor characters from *Hamlet*, attendant lords summoned to 'glean what afflicts' the Prince of Denmark, a task they comprehensively fail to accomplish before being unceremoniously put to death in England through Hamlet's own machinations. What if, *Rosencrantz and Guildenstern* asks, the audience were to follow, during the course of *Hamlet*, these two supernumeraries rather than the 'main' action of Shakespeare's play and its troubled hero? Could two peripheral characters placed centre stage take on the mantle of heroism, their little lives and deaths matching the proportions of Hamlet's? The answer, except for the most optimistic or blinkered viewer, must be *no*. Far from trying to rescue Rosencrantz and Guildenstern from obscurity, Stoppard's play aims to puncture the tragic pretensions of the play from which it poaches and, indeed, the whole tradition of tragedy with its trappings of fate, nobility, pity and terror. If Hamlet is the very imprint of the modern hero, tormented by the vagaries of subjectivity, Stoppard's Rosencrantz and Guildenstern may be models for a postmodern heroism, which is, of course, no heroism at all.

Among its main theses, *The Postmodern Condition* puts forward the claim that the 'great hero' of previous epochs is no longer a credible figure in the postmodern period which we currently inhabit, a period which was gaining momentum at the time *Rosencrantz and Guildenstern* was first staged (at the Edinburgh Festival in 1966). According to Lyotard, the loss of the hero goes hand in hand with the decline of several other mainstays associated with narrative: 'The narrative function is losing its functors, its great hero, its great dangers, its great voyages, its great goal.'[1] Lyotard is not exactly talking about Hamlet here. His coordinates are more continental European politics and philosophy of the eighteenth and nineteenth centuries than early modern English humanism. However, with slight modifications, his insights can be made to apply to the situation Stoppard's Rosencrantz and Guildenstern find themselves in. Set adrift in a narrative not their own, Rosencrantz and Guildenstern, those non-protagonists, appear to be lacking all the narrative 'functors' Lyotard mentions. Rather than facing great dangers, they gamble and play word games; rather than embarking on great voyages they remain static as the action of *Hamlet* swirls past them; and rather than seeking great goals, they complain of lacking any real 'direction'. If anything ails them, they could be said to be suffering from the postmodern condition. But 'suffer' is probably the wrong term, because, to follow Lyotard, one of the key features of the postmodern condition is a disinclination to mourn the loss of narrative and its functors. The period of mourning, he says, is over.

What follows, then, will assess the extent to which *Rosencrantz and Guildenstern* registers the postmodern condition, with special attention to whether or not this 'condition', should it indeed exist, is lamented or not.

The postmodern condition

To the less than eagle-eyed reader, it may come as something of a surprise that *The Postmodern Condition* enjoys such high currency in literary and cultural studies, since it is, on the face of it, primarily about science. And when it is not specifically about science it is more generally commenting on the state and future of the University as an institution. If nothing else, Lyotard showed disturbing prescience on this issue, for his forecasts of 1979 bear a striking resemblance to the average British university of 2001. He wrote about science and universities because the task he had set himself, or the task set for him by the Quebec government, was to report on the current status of knowledge, circa 1979 – no small undertaking. Knowledge, he concludes, is not what it used to be. It is not what it used to be because of the rapid 'computerization of society', which has transformed the way that information or knowledge is stored and transmitted. There are profound knock-on effects for science, as well as philosophy, the discipline which in the past had set down the guidelines for the operations of science. So far, so unpromising for understanding a modern play about Renaissance courtiers. After an attentive reading of Lyotard's text one might be justified in wondering whether its ubiquity in discussions about literary and cultural postmodernism is based entirely on highly selective quotation. Indeed, *The Postmodern Condition* does yield some tasty one-liners, such as the one about narrative and its 'functors', among some rather heavy-going matter about telematics, paradoxology and thermodynamics. It would be a shame not to invoke the famous passages, but it is also worthwhile exploring the overall thesis of the text.

Lyotard's most notorious claim, and the one with the greatest relevance in this context, is that the postmodern period is marked by an 'incredulity toward metanarratives', or, to put it another way, that '[t]he grand narrative has lost its credibility'.[2] To grasp Lyotard's point here, it is necessary first to see how he contrasts science and narrative in their relationships with knowledge. Scientific knowledge is, for the most part, 'denotative', in the sense that it usually comes down to verifiable or falsifiable statements about particular facts of nature. 'Water boils at 100 degrees centigrade' – to take an extremely simple example – is a denotative statement subject to proof by the scientist and therefore guaran teed as knowledge. Narrative, on the other hand, is not so easily subject to proof: it is difficult to tell whether a story is true or false, and therefore narrative presumably comes a poor second to science in the production and transmission of knowledge. But Lyotard protests that 'what is meant by the term *knowledge* is not only a set of denotative statements, far from it. It also includes notions of "know-how", "knowing how to live", "how to listen" ... etc.', and it is these forms of 'competence' for which narrative is particularly well suited.[3] For instance, an anecdote told interminably by an older relative may be tedious, and it may not even be 'true', but it may also transmit crucial cultural knowledge or, to use an old-fashioned word, wisdom.

Not only do narrative knowledge and scientific knowledge bear on different subjects, contends Lyotard, they also have different ways of 'legitimating' themselves. Before scientific knowledge can be accepted, it must be submitted to the rigours of a complex apparatus of proof and argumentation; it must create a consensus within a community of peers. Narrative has no such scruples, since it contains a self-legitimation within its own utterance: 'narrative knowledge does not give priority to the questions of its own legitimation ... it certifies itself in the pragmatics of its own transmission without having recourse to argumentation and proof'.[4] In other words, a story skilfully and seductively told needs no additional supports. But the scientist is not about to allow the cavalier attitude of narratives to pass unquestioned: 'He classifies them as belonging to a different mentality: savage, primitive, underdeveloped, backward, alienated, composed of opinions, customs, authority, prejudice, ignorance, ideology.'[5] Scientific knowledge and narrative knowledge, then, are incompatible and at odds with each other. But this antagonism between science and narrative is not the end of the story, for, ironically, science almost inevitably resorts to narrative in its efforts to know and make known its own truths. This is what Lyotard calls the 'return of the narrative in the non-narrative'.[6] As it turns out, narrative becomes instrumental in the very legitimation of science.

Science does not resort to any old narrative for its legitimation. Lyotard identifies two main 'narratives of legitimation' that emerge from the eighteenth and nineteenth centuries and it is these two he dubs the 'grand narratives'. They are the grand narratives of *emancipation* and *speculation* or, alternatively, of freedom and knowledge. The first emerges from France and its revolutionary legacy, whereas the second is German and has philosophical rather than political origins. The hero of the narrative of emancipation is the People, and the State frequently invokes this narrative and this subject 'under the name of "nation", in order to point them down the path of progress'.[7] The hero of the narrative of knowledge is not necessarily any individual or group, but rather the 'spirit' of speculation. Two very different ideas of science and the university derive from the two narratives. The narrative of emancipation sees science as the tool of liberty – science for all – whereas the narrative of speculation thinks more in terms of science for its own sake, the accumulation of knowledge as a good in its own right. What concerns us here is not so much what this means for science as the ways in which these two grand narratives have had much wider cultural consequences. They are 'metanarratives' because they are supposedly at the foundations of all other narratives: their basic structure should be discernible in all other stories from the early nineteenth century onwards. Certainly, we could test this hypothesis by examining any number of novels or plays from the period. No doubt a majority of them could be made to conform to either one or the other of the grand narratives, since so many fictions involve the protagonist's gradual movement towards emancipation from some constraint or other, or towards enlightenment from ignorance. And even if that movement ends in failure, the structure would still be implied as an ideal. However, we can leave the hypothesis untested, because in the postmodern condition, the two grand narratives have supposedly lost their credibility and are no longer invoked.

To live in the postmodern condition is to live in a period of 'delegitimation', when the organizing, master narratives no longer hold sway. Although Lyotard is reluctant to give proof of the decline of grand narratives or explain the causes for their decline, we are entitled to ask what he thinks will succeed or has already succeeded them. One of his answers has received a great deal of attention from commentators: in lieu of the grand narratives, we will have instead only little ones (*petits récits*). There is a nice symmetry about this substitution, but Lyotard only mentions the *petit récit* once, and near the end of *The Postmodern Condition*.[8] It is in fact language games which he sees proliferating in the place of the grand narratives with great goals. Instead of great goals, there are only contingent 'moves' within various language games, each of which is discrete from the others and obeys its own rules. Even science, it transpires, has always been a kind of language game, allowing certain sorts of utterances and suppressing others in the course of its development. The 'players' in these games are in competition with one another and delight 'in the endless invention of turns of phrase, of words and meanings'.[9] Which brings us to those inveterate gamers, Rosencrantz and Guildenstern.

Defunct grand narratives

Lyotard does not say that the grand narratives vanish altogether in the postmodern condition. He claims that they are treated with 'incredulity'. This is certainly the case in *Rosencrantz and Guildenstern*. The play flirts with both grand narratives as possible trajectories for the hapless courtiers but ultimately dismisses their viability. Taking them one at a time: 'speculation' is one of the favoured activities of Guildenstern in particular, and he engages in pseudo-philosophizing from the outset of the play in an apparent attempt to gain his bearings. Slightly alarmed by 76 consecutively tossed coins landing on their heads, he resorts to a proven mathematical formula, the law of probability:

> GUIL: [...] (*Flips a coin.*) The law of averages, if I have got this right,
> means that if six monkeys were thrown up in the air for long
> enough they would land on their tails about as often as they
> would land on their—
> ROS: Heads. (*He picks up the coin.*)
> GUIL: Which even at first glance does not strike one as a particularly
> rewarding speculation, in either sense, even without the
> monkeys.[10]

Guildenstern's hesitant 'if I have got this right' and his remark that the speculation is not 'particularly rewarding', in combination with the monkeying example, establish a keynote for any such 'deep' inquiries for the rest of the play. Efforts to grasp conceptually the universe – to gain a knowledge of its workings – through careful reasoning and logical argument, are doomed to failure and are, frankly, a trifle silly. Soon after, Guildenstern as much as admits that his faith in the speculative spirit is contingent rather than absolute: 'GUIL: The scientific approach to the examination of phenomena is a defence against the pure emotion of fear.'[11] That the horizons of the pair's knowledge are severely restricted becomes something of a running joke as the play proceeds. They are consistently in the dark about the goings-on around them, quite literally so at the beginning of Act Three on the boat. The grand narrative of knowledge, were the play to follow its prescribed path, would see the pair moving from this obscurity into some form of clarity, into enlightenment about their circumstances. They do, of course, ask innumerable plaintive questions about the nature of their own existence, but these questions go unanswered, because there is no self-knowledge to be had at the end of that road: as we know, when it comes to the subjectivity of these two, there is no there there. The lofty pretensions of speculation are shown to be no more than another word game, played more or less well by Rosencrantz and Guildenstern. But more on games later.

The grand narrative of emancipation also makes a cameo appearance in *Rosencrantz and Guildenstern*. At the end of Act Two, Rosencrantz makes a move to leave the stage, an action neither of them have appeared capable of heretofore. Guildenstern gives him a look of admonition:

ROS: He [Hamlet] said we can go. Cross my heart.
GUIL: I like to know where I am. Even if I don't know where I am, I like to know that. If we go there's no knowing.
ROS: No knowing what?
GUIL: If we'll ever come back.
ROS: We don't want to come back.
GUIL: That may very well be true, but do we want to go?
ROS: We'll be free.
GUIL: I don't know. It's the same sky.[12]

This exchange alludes to Vladimir and Estragon's abortive attempts to depart the stage in *Waiting for Godot*, another play fully aware of the waning force of metanarratives.[13] As in that play, the proposed departure comes to naught in the end, although in this case the two characters, unlike Vladimir and Estragon, do in fact exit the stage, even if with low expectations. Is Guildenstern simply resigned to his chains, unwilling to surrender their relative security in the face of the promise of freedom? He sees little difference between freedom and un-freedom: 'It's the same sky'. Is this an evasion, a refusal to grasp emancipation when offered, or is it a cool acceptance that liberation is a chimera? Whichever reading we choose to impose, there is little doubt that heirs of Danton and Robespierre, Marx and Engels, these two are not. Even when, at the opening of the next scene on the boat, Guildenstern speaks optimistically of their chances of escape from their circumstances, his language is couched in qualifications: 'One is free on a boat. For a time. Relatively.'[14]

Rosencrantz and Guildenstern does not do away with Lyotard's two grand narratives; on the contrary, it invokes them knowingly: both speculation and emancipation are mooted as possible teleologies. The play seems to be saying that, bankrupt though they may be, grand narratives still haunt us: we turn to them as a familiar and automatic language.[15] In this instance, though, they are only resurrected to be mocked, since there is no question that they offer credible solutions to the dilemmas faced by Rosencrantz and Guildenstern. They are, in effect, quoted, ironically and playfully, as reminders to the audience of what is no longer really believable. As far as stories go, they are just two more among many. The same cannot necessarily be said about the third 'master plot' that guides events in *Rosencrantz and Guildenstern* – *Hamlet*.

From master plots to language games

Hamlet is not, strictly speaking, a grand narrative. Even loosely speaking, it probably isn't one. However, the attitude of *Rosencrantz and Guildenstern* towards Shakespeare's play tells us a great deal about narrative in the postmodern condition. *Hamlet* is the metanarrative of *Rosencrantz and Guildenstern*: it operates at a level above that of Stoppard's play and it dictates everything that happens to the two courtiers. Well, not everything, since there are large portions of time when they are not participating in *Hamlet*, but when they do, they may not deviate from the path laid out in 1600. No matter how bemused they are by the actions of Ophelia, Hamlet, Claudius and Gertrude, they step into line with a comic automatism when their cues come up. Much of the humour of the play derives from the juxtaposition of the formal language of the tragedy and the demotic speech of the very twentieth-century Rosencrantz and Guildenstern; and it is pretty clear that the rhetoric of tragedy comes off worst in the encounter. An early critic of the play put it like this: 'Script is destiny ... [T]heir context is not blank; it is *Hamlet*. If the two men are caught in a universal dilemma, they are also trapped in a script ... [They are] victims ... of the story-line.'[16] There may be a danger that in using words like 'trapped' and 'victims' the overall light-heartedness of the play will be lost, but there is a sense in *Rosencrantz and Guildenstern* that the plot of Hamlet is almost tyrannical in its demands. The meta-narrative allows for no exceptions; all elements must eventually come under its sway.

If Rosencrantz and Guildenstern interrogate the primacy of the metaplot even while they abide by it, the Player endorses its validity without question:

> PLAYER: Between 'just deserts' and 'tragic irony' we are given quite a lot of scope for our particular talent. Generally speaking, things have gone about as far as they can possibly go when things have got about as bad as they reasonably get. (*He switches on a smile.*)
>
> GUIL: Who decides?
>
> PLAYER: (*Switching off his smile.*) Decides? It is *written*. [...] We're tragedians, you see. We follow directions – there is no *choice* involved. The bad end unhappily, the good unluckily. That is what tragedy means.[17]

It is moments like these in his plays which have lead some critics to accuse Stoppard of a weak liberalism. In a perceptive if slightly harsh article about Stoppard's early plays, Philip Roberts sums up the position: 'His initial heroes ... are all trapped within a hostile mechanistic world which is at odds with individual aspiration.'[18] The implication is that Stoppard is on the side of the harried individual against any form of collective organisation, and indeed, Stoppard has more than once stated his antipathy towards leftist politics.[19] But we already know that the term 'hero' must be approached with caution when it comes to postmodern Rosencrantz and Guildenstern; and behind the idea of 'individual aspiration' (invoked negatively by Roberts) lurks no doubt the grand narrative of emancipation which the play discredits anyway. Perhaps there is another way of reading the Player's emphatic statement on tragedy. Tragedy is *the* privileged dramatic mode, he implies. Its formula is rigid – 'the bad end unhappily, the good unluckily' – and its conclusions inevitable. Given the wider context of the play and the various potshots taken at the pompousness of *Hamlet*, might the point not be that one form of story (tragedy), one playwright, and one play in particular, are given far too much weight within (anglophone) culture? Rather than lamenting the lot of the little man, of the poor individual, isn't *Rosencrantz and Guildenstern* displaying suspicion about the primacy of any single story and displacing it from its cultural centrality by turning it inside out, like a sock?

There is no doubting that *Hamlet* has legitimacy on its side. The canonical status of Shakespeare, the playwright's position within the culture industry and the constant performance and filming of the plays ensure that *Hamlet* needs no special legitimation. This is a fact that *Rosencrantz and Guildenstern* happily exploits, since its success depends upon a certain level of knowledge in its audience of things Shakespearean. At the same time, the play is sceptical about the automatic recognition from which it benefits. The parasite distrusts the special status of its host, calling into question the processes of legitimation leading to this status. It does so through pastiches of the tragic style and through ironic recapitulations of Hamlet's tribulations:

> ROS: [...] He's depressed! ... Denmark's a prison and he'd rather live in a nutshell; some shadow-play about the nature of ambition, which never got down to cases, and finally one direct question which might have led somewhere, and led in fact to his illuminating claim to tell a hawk from a handsaw. (*Pause.*)
> GUIL: When the wind is southerly.
> ROS: And the weather's clear.[20]

Rosencrantz and Guildenstern is not alone in doing this in recent years. Edward Bond's *Lear* reworks *King Lear* (a play in many ways about the legitimation of authority) from a highly critical perspective, and Angela Carter's last novel, *Wise Children*, goes to great lengths to mix illegitimate Shakespeare with the more familiar legitimate one.[21] This more general suspicion of the culturally legitimate would seem to confirm Lyotard's claim that the postmodern moment is marked by a 'crisis in legitimation' whereby the traditional narratives of legitimation are no longer operative. He says, 'the postmodern condition is as much a stranger to disenchantment as it is to the blind positivity of delegitimation. Where, after the metanarratives, can legitimacy reside?'[22] After the demystification of the Bard, this is the question Rosencrantz and Guildenstern must set out to answer.

Hamlet's princely status confers upon him an automatic legitimacy that comes to royalty. However much he questions himself, he enjoys enough special privileges not to be immediately questioned by others when he acts in madcap fashion. The sovereign authority of his father may have been usurped by Claudius, but the exhortations of the ghost give ample justification for Hamlet's murderous inclinations. For Rosencrantz and Guildenstern there are no such guarantees to vouchsafe their actions. They have no regal prerogatives: they are merely attendant lords, distant from the sources of power. As such, they are condemned to reacting to situations as they arise, and Stoppard cleverly reworks their few, forgettable, lines from *Hamlet* to look like pragmatic and contingent responses, rapid improvisations in circumstances which are out of their hands.

Rosencrantz and Guildenstern is alive to its characters' tenuous hold on legitimacy and shows them actively seeking legitimation by one means or another. If you lack legitimacy, one obvious strategy is to turn for endorsement to those forces or structures which do possess legitimacy. In *Hamlet*, Rosencrantz and Guildenstern are entrusted with a letter from the King of Denmark, Claudius, to the King of England, where they are bound. The letter calls for the immediate execution of Hamlet, whom they are conducting across the sea. Hamlet swaps the letter for one calling for the execution of the bearers of the letter, and this is how Rosencrantz and Guildenstern meet their end in Shakespeare's play. In Stoppard's version of events, Guildenstern endows the letter with a talismanic quality:

GUIL: Everything is explained in the letter. We count on that.
ROS: Is that it, then?
GUIL: What?
ROS: We take Hamlet to the English king, we hand over the letter
— what then?
GUIL: There may be something in the letter to keep us going a bit.[23]

The seal of the King is a seal of legitimacy; in this case, unfortunately, it legitimates their deaths. But without the letter, they would have no grounds to be received at all, and it is between such rocks and hard places that those lacking legitimacy find themselves.

The letter from Claudius shows how legitimacy is tied up with documents and texts, signatures and seals. Lyotard, on the other hand, places special emphasis on the role of narrative in legitimation. How can simply telling stories bestow a quasi-legal status on acts or positions? Well, take, for instance, an institution like marriage: to be legitimate, it requires all the proper documents to be signed and lodged with the civic authorities. But imagine a marriage that was only a set of signatures on paper, that was unable to give an account of itself in the form of a tale of romance, proposal, wedding, and so on? And it is not only in the eyes of society that a story must be told about a marriage (to take one example) in order to confer on it legitimacy. Is it by chance that immigration officials quiz potential new citizens of a country on the history of their relationship with their spouse or spouse-to-be? By ordering events in time and space, narration gives materiality and justification to them. To take a completely different example, think of the much maligned National Lottery in the United Kingdom. It could be said that both its successes and failures have hinged on its ability to tell a convincing story about itself. In a country uneasy with gambling, the National Lottery has had to invoke grand narratives in order to justify emptying the pockets of its less fortunate citizens. What, after all, is a 'good cause', if not the handmaiden of progress and therefore part and parcel of both grand narratives: emancipation (swimming pools for all) and the advance of knowledge and culture (opera for some)? This explains why the bi-weekly draws, which are what interests everyone, must be accompanied by earnest and uplifting accounts of money well spent in community centres throughout the nation.

Unlike an average marriage or the National Lottery, Rosencrantz and Guildenstern seem singularly incapable of fashioning a coherent story about themselves, and this is half their problem. Severely handicapped by their limited roles in the master plot, they never get much further than the most abrupt and inconclusive of narratives:

ROS: That's it—pale sky before dawn, a man standing on his saddle
       to bang on the shutters—shouts—What's all the row about?!

> Clear off!—But then he called our names. You remember
> that—this man woke us up—
>
> GUIL: Yes.
> ROS: We were sent for.
> GUIL: Yes.[24]

In Rosencrantz's account of how they arrived where they are, there
are many hesitations or pauses – marked by the dashes – indicating
that even this very basic rendering is by no means secure. What is
more, the tale in miniature does not get any further; instead, the
two simply repeat it in various forms, the failings in their collective
memory outdoing its powers of recall throughout the play. To the
question 'what's your story?', they are constitutionally unable to
give a reply, which has clear consequences for their self-legitimation, since dysfunction in narration means a failure to locate themselves in space and time. The fascination of the play with such a
predicament in legitimation is what marks it out as postmodern, in
Lyotard's sense of the term.

For Lyotard, legitimation need not come through narrative,
although it has traditionally done so. These days, it is more likely to
arise from the immediate circumstances of two interlocutors than
through any outside guarantee:

> That is what the postmodern world is all about. Most people have
> lost the nostalgia for the lost narrative. It in no way follows that they
> are reduced to barbarity. What saves them from it is their knowledge
> that legitimation can only spring from their own linguistic practice
> and communicational interaction.[25]

Earlier in *The Postmodern Condition*, Lyotard gives more detail about
what he means by 'their own linguistic practice'. Borrowing from
Wittgenstein, he claims that the social bond is built on 'language
games':

> In the ordinary use of discourse – for example, in a discussion
> between two friends – the interlocutors use any available ammuni-
> tion, changing games from one utterance to the next: questions,
> requests, assertions, and narratives are launched pell-mell into battle.
> The war is not without rules, but the rules allow and encourage the
> greatest possible flexibility of utterance.[26]

It can be confusing when Lyotard on the one hand disparages the
legitimating power of narrative and on the other includes narrative

in his list of 'ammunition'. This is not a mistake but a deliberate move on his part: rather than dispense with narrative altogether, he makes it only one language game among many. Now, Rosencrantz and Guildenstern may struggle with narrative legitimation, but they are rather good at all forms of games, many of them linguistic. In the course of the play, we see them betting on tossed coins, playing the game of questions, playing guess which hand the coin is in, role-playing the parts of Hamlet and the English King, and of each other, for that matter. In fact, they come across as extraordinarily flexible when compared with the text of *Hamlet* which guides them. It could even be said that all they do when not participating in *Hamlet* is play one form of game or another. And even tragedy is a game for them: as Guildenstern says, 'it's a matter of asking the right questions and giving away as little as we can. It's a game'.[27] Unfortunately, it is one game they are not very good at. In any case, while they are playing each game, the master plot is not important: the narrative stops and the gaming itself takes priority. And, as Lyotard says, games legitimate themselves – they have a set of self-contained rules, and the onus is on the players to invent within those rules or bend them as best they can. There is, of course, a character called the Player in the play, but it is Rosencrantz and Guildenstern who display the greatest skill.

It might be argued that Lyotard's emphasis on language games as constitutive of the social pushes material reality too far into the background; that games, after all, are only games in the long run, and that Rosencrantz and Guildenstern must already occupy a privileged position in order to play. While Lyotard is very much the post-structuralist in his tendency to see reality as constituted by language rather than the other way around, he does not overlook the possibility that someone might refuse to play a language game or might try to silence another player. He calls such an event 'terror' and says that it 'lies outside the realm of language games, because the efficacy of such force is based entirely on the threat to eliminate the opposing player, not on making a better "move" than he'.[28] Would it be an exaggeration to suggest that *Hamlet* (or Hamlet) exerts just this sort of terror on Rosencrantz and Guildenstern, not only refusing to play, but eliminating the opponents? Or are their deaths just another move in the game called *Rosencrantz and Guildenstern are Dead*?

First coda (on mourning)

Guildenstern is adamant that death cannot be played at, scorning the Player for theatricalizing it: 'you cannot *act* it [...] [N]o one gets up after *death* – there is no applause – there is only silence and some second-hand clothes, and that's – *death*'.[29] At the end of this speech, to punctuate his point, Guildenstern drives a knife into the throat of the Player, who promptly dies in convincing fashion, before rising again to receive the applause of his troupe and reveal that the knife has a trick blade. Even death, he has illustrated, is a game. Death cannot be ignored in this comedy, since the fate of the characters is inscribed alongside their names from the very outset, in the title. However, the self-conscious theatricality of *Rosencrantz and Guildenstern* does not allow for their deaths, or death in general, to be taken seriously. And if death is not taken seriously, if it is approached with a lightness of heart, then there is presumably no need for mourning. There are some who would call this dis-avowal, or even denial, but it may be a characteristically *comic* denial, rather than one specific to Stoppard, since comedy, unlike tragedy, generally averts the catastrophic ending in favour of playfulness.

In one of the few places in *The Postmodern Condition* where he addresses artistic production, Lyotard speaks of it as a tool of mourning. He says that artists and philosophers in turn-of-the-century Vienna (Musil, Krauss, Loos, Hofmannsthal, Schönberg, Wittgenstein) recognized the decline of grand narratives and the 'splintering' of the social into ever more language games. Rather than ignoring the advance of delegitimation, they took it upon themselves to face up to it and mourn it. The best definition of mourning comes from another turn-of-the-century Viennese, Freud, who describes it this way in 'Mourning and melancholia':

> [It] is regularly the reaction to the loss of a loved person, or to the loss of some abstraction which has taken the place of one, such as one's country, liberty, an ideal ... We rely on it being overcome after a certain lapse of time, and we look upon any interference with it as useless or even harmful.[30]

Freud's account is instructive, and even prescient, for he effectively identifies the goals of both grand narratives among the abstractions potentially lost and therefore to be mourned.

If it is 'useless or even harmful', as Freud puts it, to interfere with the process of mourning, then Lyotard's next claim is even more interesting. With regard to the loss of meta-narratives, he announces, 'We can say today that the mourning process has been completed. There is no need to start all over again.'[31] Lyotard is fond of breaking down language into the kinds of utterance they constitute, and it is worthwhile turning his method on his own text. Lyotard's two sentences are both denotative, in the sense that they

> place ... the sender in the position of 'knower' ... [,] the addressee is put in the position of having to give or refuse his assent, and the referent itself ... demands to be correctly identified and expressed by the statement that refers to it.[32]

However, it could be argued that implicit in the second sentence is also another kind of utterance, a prescriptive one, along the lines of 'Stop mourning!' The Viennese did the job well enough and now it can – should – end, he seems to be asserting (assertions also fall under his list of 'ammunition' available in language games). If Freud is right, such an interference in the process of mourning is fruitless and even dangerous, although Lyotard would probably insist that his statement is descriptive rather than prescriptive. The question of whether or not to mourn the passing of the metanarrative is not an idle one, because it is one way of separating modernists (still in mourning) from postmodernists (past mourning).

Lyotard may be asking the impossible by demanding (or describing) the end of mourning, but it would appear that *Rosencrantz and Guildenstern* at least agrees with him. Given its treatment of its metanarrative, there is little sense in that play that the loss of the grand narrative would be regretted. In this context, it is worth pointing out that *Hamlet*, although generically usually described as a tragedy, is also a 'mourning-play', or in German, a *Trauerspiel* (where there is a death at or before the beginning which haunts the whole play), a genre dealt with at length by Walter Benjamin in *The Origin of the German Tragic Drama [Trauerspiel]*, a text which also examines *Hamlet*.[33] The melancholy young prince spends the greater portion of the play grieving for his father and planning his revenge. In this way he resembles those vociferous critics of the postmodern such as Terry Eagleton, who view Lyotard as a latter-day Claudius, poisoning the grand narratives before their time.[34] It is perhaps best to leave him and others to carry on the work of mourning. Who is to say, for instance, that the spectre of emancipation is not still worth discoursing with?

Second coda (on theatricality)

This chapter has tended thus far to concentrate on the conceptual content of *Rosencrantz and Guildenstern* rather than its theatrical qualities. Lyotard actually mentions theatre once in *The Postmodern Condition*, but only to deny its difference, which is somewhat surprising given his usual attentiveness to alterity. Theatre comes up in a discussion of Plato's *Dialogues*, which Lyotard claims contains the first attempt on the part of philosophy to legitimate science through narrative. Lyotard wants to show how science always relies on its supposed competition in the knowledge game, narrative, for its legitimation, and in making his case he is somewhat hasty in his distinctions:

> The legitimation effort, the *Dialogues* of Plato, gives ammunition to narrative by virtue of its own form: each of the dialogues takes the form of a narrative of a scientific discussion. *It is of little consequence here that the story of the debate is shown rather than reported, staged rather than narrated* ... Scientific knowledge cannot know and make known that it is the true knowledge without resorting to the other, narrative, kind of knowledge, which from its point of view is no knowledge at all. (My emphasis)[35]

Almost the first thing that a student of theatre learns, following Aristotle, is that theatre is *not* primarily a narrative form, but one dominated by action.[36] Instead of the narration of a story, we are given a theatrical presentation of it. The consequences of this difference are hardly minor, and Lyotard is too abrupt in collapsing the staged into the narrated. His final point is probably not compromised: science cannot legitimate itself on its own, but must resort in the *Dialogues* to another kind of knowledge. But is Lyotard too quick to assume that that other kind of knowledge is simply 'narrative'? Can we speak of the transmission of knowledge through the theatrical rather than the narrated? Is knowledge any different if it is staged, shown and acted out, than if it is narrated? Why does Lyotard so automatically subsume the theatrical under the narrated, as if the former were no more than a by-product of the latter? Are there ways in which the theatrical is not simply a faithful amanuensis to narrative but at times a direct hindrance to the relentless progression of plot? In *Rosencrantz and Guildenstern*, for instance, the endless theatrical digressions of the lead pair – coin tossing, role-playing, trouser-dropping, slapstick, audience-baiting, barrel-hopping – distract us from the plot: in the interstices of *Hamlet* they inhabit, is it not theatre which, temporarily, usurps narrative?

Notes

1 Jean-François Lyotard, *The Postmodern Condition: A Report on Knowledge*, trans. Geoff Bennington and Brian Massumi (Manchester: Manchester University Press, 1984 [1979]), p. xxiv.
2 Lyotard, *Postmodern Condition*, pp. xxiv and 37.
3 Lyotard, *Postmodern Condition*, p. 18.
4 Lyotard, *Postmodern Condition*, p. 27.
5 Lyotard, *Postmodern Condition*, p. 27.
6 Lyotard, *Postmodern Condition*, p. 27.
7 Lyotard, *Postmodern Condition*, p. 32.
8 Lyotard, *Postmodern Condition*, p. 60.
9 Lyotard, *Postmodern Condition*, p. 10.
10 Tom Stoppard, *Rosencrantz and Guildenstern are Dead* (London: Faber and Faber, 1967), p. 10.
11 Stoppard, *Rosencrantz and Guildenstern*, p. 13.
12 Stoppard, *Rosencrantz and Guildenstern*, p. 70.
13 'ESTRAGON: Well, shall we go?/VLADIMIR: Yes, let's go./*They do not move.*' Samuel Beckett, *Waiting for Godot* (London: Faber and Faber, 1956), p. 54. The same lines are repeated at the end of Act Two, with the speakers reversed.
14 Stoppard, *Rosencrantz and Guildenstern*, p. 74.
15 It should be noted that not everyone thinks that emancipation is bankrupt, and Lyotard has come under fire from many sides for dismissing this ideal in particular. For an even-handed treatment of the concept of emancipation today, see Ernesto Laclau, *Emancipation(s)* (London: Verso, 1996).
16 William Babula, 'The play–life metaphor in Shakespeare and Stoppard', *Modern Drama* 15:3 (1973), p. 279.
17 Stoppard, *Rosencrantz and Guildenstern*, p. 59.
18 Philip Roberts, 'Tom Stoppard: serious artist or siren?', *Critical Quarterly* 20 (1978), 86.
19 Most notoriously in a bad-tempered conclusion of an interview with *Theatre Quarterly*: 'Ambushes for the audience: towards a high comedy of ideas' *Theatre Quarterly* 4:14 (1974), 3–17.
20 Stoppard, *Rosencrantz and Guildenstern*, pp. 41–2.
21 Edward Bond, *Lear*, in *Plays: Two* (London: Methuen Drama, 1978); Angela Carter, *Wise Children* (London: Chatto & Windus, 1991). See Kate Chedzgoy, *Shakespeare's Queer Children* (Manchester: Manchester University

Press, 1996) for discussions of both Carter and Shakespeare in terms of cultural legitimacy.

22 Lyotard, *Postmodern Condition*, pp. xxiv–xxv.

23 Stoppard, *Rosencrantz and Guildenstern*, pp. 76–7.

24 Stoppard, *Rosencrantz and Guildenstern*, p. 15. Ros's 'then he called our names' is what we might call interpellation, since it is only at this point in the mini-narrative that the two 'recognize' themselves. See Chapter 5 on *Comedians* and Althusser for an in-depth discussion of this term.

25 Lyotard, *Postmodern Condition*, p. 41.

26 Lyotard, *Postmodern Condition*, p. 17.

27 Stoppard, *Rosencrantz and Guildenstern*, p. 31.

28 Lyotard, *Postmodern Condition*, p. 46.

29 Stoppard, *Rosencrantz and Guildenstern*, p. 90.

30 Sigmund Freud, 'Mourning and melancholia', in *On Metapsychology, Penguin Freud Library*, vol. 11, trans. James Strachey, ed. Angela Richards (Harmondsworth: Penguin, 1984), pp. 251–2.

31 Lyotard, *Postmodern Condition*, p. 41.

32 Lyotard, *Postmodern Condition*, p. 9.

33 Walter Benjamin, *The Origin of German Tragic Drama*, trans. John Osborne (London: NLB, 1977)

34 See, for instance, Terry Eagleton, *The Illusions of Postmodernism* (Oxford: Blackwell, 1996). Joining Eagleton at the funeral: Alex Callinicos, *Against Postmodernism: A Marxist Critique* (Cambridge: Polity, 1989) and Christopher Norris, *What's Wrong with Postmodernism?: Critical Theory and the Ends of Philosophy* (London: Harvester Wheatsheaf, 1990).

35 Lyotard, *Postmodern Condition*, p. 29.

36 It is precisely this bias towards action over narration which Brecht aimed to overturn in his epic, Non-Aristotelean theatre. See for instance, Bertolt Brecht, 'A short organum for the theatre', in *Brecht on Theatre*, trans. & ed. John Willett (London: Methuen, 1964), pp. 179–205.

4

After Orton, before Foucault

Which side are you on, Joe?

Less than a decade separates the writing of *What the Butler Saw*
(1967) and the publication of the first volume of *The History of
Sexuality* (1976); there is just a seven-year gap between the first
production of Joe Orton's last play (1969) and the first volume of
Michel Foucault's trilogy. The distance is minimal, and yet one
cannot help feeling the enormous chasm of events that divides the
two works. Intervening are the *événements* of 1968, the moonwalk,
the escalation and end of the Vietnam War and the end of theatre
censorship, to mention only a few developments. Perhaps most relevant to Orton and Foucault, though, is the flowering, in this period,
of the sexual revolution. It is difficult to fix a date for this revolution
– there is no Bastille Day for sexual emancipation – but many would
agree that it comes sometime soon after Orton's death in August
1967. In other words, although Orton lived through and participated in the rumblings of disquiet that heralded the revolution – the
moment known as 'the permissive sixties' – he did not survive to
enjoy the shackles of oppression being finally thrown off.

We know where Foucault stands on the question of sexual liberation. Writing immediately in the wake of a rupture which made
possible his ground-breaking work, he is sceptical and suspicious
about the achievements of the revolution. With Orton, on the other
hand, we can only speculate, reconstructing for him a perspective
on future events based on the traces he left behind. There are
obvious dangers in such retroactive prognostication, but this has
not deterred commentators. Broadly speaking, there have been two
ways of judging Orton's position on a period whose beginnings
he only tasted. Some regard Orton's plays as overt challenges to
the sexual conformities of his day and therefore figure Orton as an
advance guard of the revolution, a sort of fifth columnist among the
sexual conservatives. There is, however, an equally convincing case
that plays like *What the Butler Saw* are so firmly wedged in the

closet that they have nothing positive to offer a progressive sexual politics, and indeed, that Orton, far from being a radical in formation, was quite happy to remain in the closet without directly confronting the sexual powers that were.

Jonathan Dollimore and Alan Sinfield represent well the two poles of opinion on Orton and *What the Butler Saw*. Dollimore dubs the style of Orton's farce 'a kind of delinquent and black camp' and argues that 'In *What the Butler Saw* sexuality, like language, becomes decentred and therefore radically contingent: it escapes continually from medical and legal attempts to define and regulate it.'[1] Orton is clearly placed on the side of sexual liberation here: not only is sexuality '*radically* contingent', but it '*escapes* continually' in his play. In Dollimore's essay – an account of changing meanings of sexuality in Britain from 1945 to 1970 – Orton and *What the Butler Saw* occupy a pivotal point in the argument: whereas other writers of the 1950s and 1960s approached sexuality tentatively, either treating homosexuality as an illness or indulging in 'legitimate transgression', Orton goes much further in his stylistic challenge. Sinfield is not so sure. He contrasts Orton unfavourably with the gay playwrights who thrived in the more open atmosphere after the abolition of stage censorship in 1968. Sinfield admits that *Entertaining Mr Sloane* (1964) and *Loot* (1966) were daring for their time, but that with *What the Butler Saw*, Orton was falling behind: 'In 1969, for many people, the concern in *Butler* with adultery and nakedness was merely quaint.'[2] From Dollimore to Sinfield, then, we have moved dramatically from 'radical' to 'quaint', from avantgarde to retrograde.

It is not that Sinfield has low expectations of Orton. As much as he critiques *Butler* for what it does do, he reproaches it for what it fails to do, particularly in light of the sexual revolution which could already be heard rumbling on the horizon. Sinfield claims that Orton effectively ignored the developments of his time: 'In his diaries Orton shows virtually no interest in other gay plays, or in the new "fringe" companies, or in moves to abolish stage censorship, or even in the legalization of male homosexuality.'[3] Here is the crux of Sinfield's charge against Orton: as a male homosexual living in a time when the status of the homosexual in British society was highly contested and about to change in the eyes of the law,[4] Orton did not do nearly enough for the cause.

Orton was out of step with [the] reforming tendency; he refused nature, depth, and sincerity at least partly because, although he felt an intuitive opposition to the prevailing sexual ideology, he had difficulty conceiving a positive view of the homosexual.[5]

Orton was not in the habit of distributing 'positive views' of anybody, but Sinfield certainly has a point. *What the Butler Saw* may be about nothing other than sex, but it is a play populated for the most part by heterosexuals, while homosexuality and bisexuality are decidedly on the margins of events. The debate between Dollimore and Sinfield is not easily resolved, but on the face of it at least, *Butler* is hardly a theatrical manifesto for the Gay Liberation Front.[6]

Almost inevitably, both Dollimore and Sinfield allude in passing to Michel Foucault in their essays. So influential is Foucault's *History of Sexuality*, and so forceful its arguments, that two writers taking up contrary positions on Orton feel it appropriate to invoke the French theorist for their side. Certainly, 'Foucault with Orton' seems a felicitous and attractive match-up for this chapter, but it remains to be seen whether the historian and the playwright occupy the same, or opposite camps in the twentieth-century disputes over sexuality. To start with, since Foucault was at best ambivalent about the ideology of the sexual revolution he was (indirectly) writing about, perhaps it is wiser to delay judging Orton solely in terms of a conflagration he was not to experience. Coming after the revolution, Foucault has the clear advantage of hindsight, but perhaps it is also worth considering what advantages Orton accrued by coming before it.

Repression – confession

Farce has always been cruel to married couples, but it usually finds a way to reconcile them (uneasily) at its conclusion, and *What the Butler Saw* is no exception. In Orton's play, the tormented twosome is the Prentices, whose marital difficulties are summed up in some early repartee:

> MRS PRENTICE (*with a brittle laugh*). My trouble stems from your inadequacy as a lover! It's embarrassing. You must've learnt your technique from a Christmas cracker. (*Her mouth twists into a sneer.*) Rejuvenation pills have no effect on you.
> PRENTICE (*stuffily*). I never take pills.
> MRS PRENTICE. You take them all the time during our lovemaking.

71

The deafening sound of your chewing is the reason for my never having an orgasm.
DR PRENTICE *is stung by her remarks. He approaches closer.*
PRENTICE. How dare you say that! Your book on the climax in the female is largely autobiographical. (*Pause. He stares.*) Or have you been masquerading as a sexually responsive woman?
MRS PRENTICE. My uterine contractions have been bogus for some time![7]

The Prentices use a peculiarly technical vocabulary in their spat, in a sort of sly pastiche of the manner of popular books on sexuality in the period. For instance, Masters and Johnson's *Human Sexual Response*, published in 1966, tried earnestly to dispel myths about female sexuality and explain the complexities of the female orgasm.[8] It is this earnestness that *Butler* exploits and mocks. The main point seems to be that the problems in the Prentice marriage can be traced to the bedroom. Their sex life – or lack of one – is apparently the source of all their antagonisms, antagonisms which are only resolved at the end of the play when they realize that their marriage has not been entirely sterile after all, for Geraldine and Nick are both their children – progeny of a fleeting, but passionate, encounter in a linen cupboard. Mrs Prentice is a full-blown stereotype of a frigid yet secretly sexually ravenous woman, and Dr Prentice's sexual frustration manifests itself in the attempted seduction of Geraldine, the single indiscretion which precipitates the snowball of confusions and complications characteristic of farcical plotting. The revelations at the play's conclusion – that the Prentices had always had the potential for fruitful sexual relations – suggest that if only this pair had rediscovered the delights of the linen cupboard at the Station Hotel, all the play's madcap misunderstandings might have been averted. In this admittedly naïve reading, sexual energies stymied in one place will bubble up mischievously and chaotically elsewhere, such is their power and potency. Orgasms are denied at one's peril, so the argument would go. It is an argument which relies heavily on what Michel Foucault calls the 'repressive hypothesis'.

Perhaps the most important achievement of *The History of Sexuality* is the calling into question of the 'repressive hypothesis'. Foucault does not name names, but one of the main proponents of the repressive hypothesis was Herbert Marcuse, counter-cultural guru of the 1960s. In *Eros and Civilization*, Marcuse argued that

Reason and capitalist modes of production conspire in a regime of productivity that represses the 'sex instinct'. According to Marcuse, in industrial society sexuality is rigidly restricted to a narrowly reproductive function, while non-reproductive sexuality is labelled as perverse:

> The societal organisation of the sex instinct taboos as perversions practically all its manifestations which do not serve or prepare for the procreative function ... The perversions thus express rebellion against the subjugation of sexuality under the order of procreation, and against the institutions which guarantee this order.[9]

Sexuality, in Marcuse's model, is powerful, and a potential challenge to any established order, which consequently sets up a series of prohibitions against it. This is why liberation from capitalist society must go down the road of sexual liberation. Marcuse's thesis has gained wide popular currency, and sex is commonly thought of as something that is silenced or restricted by conventional morality but that nevertheless persists under the surface, waiting to escape. Imagine a protest orgy staged in the boardroom of an international conglomerate, and you get a sense of the way the 'repressive hypothesis' envisages the struggle between unproductive pleasure and instrumental reason. Or think of an equivalent instance in *What the Butler Saw* where it is implied that Winston Churchill, great British Statesman, had a penis, and possibly a large one. What could be more subversive?

Foucault objects to the repressive hypothesis on two counts. He is very doubtful that there is any naturally occurring secret core of sexuality that is waiting to be released. On the contrary, he thinks – with many other cultural relativists – that sexuality has no existence outside of its historically and culturally changing circumstances. More importantly though, Foucault casts doubt on the assumption that sex has been silenced in modern Western culture. The story is a familiar one: the prudish Victorians, with their strict bourgeois morality, pushed sex out of sight, confining it to the privacy of the conjugal relation. Above all, it was not to be spoken about. Foucault turns this persistent myth on its head, claiming that far from being silenced, sex has been spoken about more and more since the eighteenth century. There may have been prohibitions on the discussion of sex in certain quarters – over the Victorian dinner-table perhaps – but Foucault argues that people have nevertheless been increasingly

73

urged to speak about sex in specially designated places and under specific conditions. These conditions were not unlike the Catholic confessional, which originally trained its attention on married couples and demanded to know every detail of their transgressions, insisting that they put their desires into words. Secular institutions which gradually replaced the church – education, medicine, psychiatry – adopted the model of the confessional and its subjects were encouraged to bring their sex into language: 'Rather than a massive censorship, beginning with the verbal proprieties imposed by the age of Reason, what was involved was a regulated and polymorphous incitement to discourse.'[10]

The Marcusian argument is that power represses sex, that power is a force of negation. Foucault, on the contrary, suggests that power is productive, that it is eager to generate discourses on sex:

> more important was the multiplication of discourses concerning sex in the field of the exercise of power itself: an institutional incitement to speak about it, and to do so more and more; a determination on the part of the agencies of power to hear it spoken about, and to cause it to speak.[11]

The thesis that the 'establishment' does its best to stamp out any form of sexuality not oriented towards procreation is misleading. If anything, power is dedicated to finding out more about the so-called perversions. In the nineteenth century, sex became more and more a medical and then a psychiatric matter. Sex was conceived of no longer in terms of sin but in terms of pathology. And in this transition, something peculiar happened: 'normal' heterosexual sex was allowed to retreat into relative privacy, while 'perverts' – homosexuals, of course, but also 'Krafft-Ebing's zoophiles and zooerasts, Rohleder's auto-monosexualists; and later, mixoscopophiles, gynocomasts, presbyophiles, sexoesthetic inverts, and dyspareunist women', to name but a few – came under increasing scrutiny.[12] Far from being silenced in the Victorian period, sexuality – and 'abnormal' sexuality in particular – was rendered feverishly into knowledge. 'The machinery of power that focused on this whole alien strain did not aim to suppress it, but rather to give it an analytical, visible, and permanent reality.'[13] Each new and more bizarre case history extracted from confessing individuals could be written up and published, eventually generating a huge body of pseudo-scientific work known as 'sexology'.

Not a prohibition and censoring of sex, then, but an 'incitement to discourse' and a zeal for 'analysis, stocktaking, classification, and specification'[14] mark the Western attitude to sex from the eighteenth century. And what is more, sexualities not only multiply and diversify in this period but also become the very key to individual identities. Whereas certain sexual acts – like sodomy – were once considered sinful aberrations potentially performed by anyone succumbing to temptation, one's sexual proclivity now became an index of one's soul. In a famous and oft-quoted passage, Foucault describes the invention of homosexual identity in the late nineteenth century: '[the] homosexual became a personage, a past, a case history, and a childhood, in addition to being a type of life, a life form ... Nothing that went into his total composition was unaffected by his sexuality. It was everywhere present in him.'[15] Our sexuality, then, saturates our being, and it is visible and legible in every tiny detail of our appearance. Foucault's suspicion of sexual liberation must be understood in light of this historical welding of sexuality and identity, because in many of its forms sexual liberation may simply continue rather than impair the workings of power.

Gagged?

In terms of theatrical performance, followers of the repressive hypothesis would tend to focus their attention on censorship of the stage, while Foucault would be inclined to downplay this side of things. This is not to say that Foucault denies the existence of censorship, just as he does not deny that historically, there have been restrictions placed on sexual activity and what may be said about sex; but he objects to what he sees as an overemphasis on censorship:

> Let there be no misunderstanding: I do not claim that sex has not been prohibited or barred or masked or misapprehended ... nor do I even assert that it has suffered these things any less from that period on than before. I do not maintain that the prohibition of sex is a ruse; but it is a ruse to make prohibition into the basic and constitutive element from which one would be able to write the history of what has been said concerning sex starting from the modern epoch.[16]

For the record, before the Theatres Act of 1968, the Lord Chamberlain, who operated independently of courts and parliament, read advance copies of all scripts and granted or withheld licences for any plays performed commercially on the British stage. The censor's red pen went through swearing (for instance, 'Piss off' in Pinter's *The Caretaker*),[17] critical representations of religious figures and living political figures, scenes of nudity (unless the naked bodies were stationary) and, notoriously, any mention of homosexuality. Nicholas de Jongh has ably chronicled the loosening of controls on the representation of homosexuality from 1958 onwards, and there is no need to repeat his work here.[18] After the lifting of censorship, the theatre critic Kenneth Tynan was one of the first to take advantage of the relaxed conditions with the staging of his revue, *Oh! Calcutta!* (1970), which featured for the first time full frontal nudity. The reviewer of the piece in *Plays and Players* announced solemnly the dawning of a new age of openness, post-repression:

> *Oh! Calcutta!* ... crashes the barrier once and for all ... [I]t is a bold and triumphant attack on the taboos which have hedged in the Western theatre for centuries, not only by celebrating the human body, but by laughing at the activity which that body, in a 'cultured' society, has come to regard as its most unspeakable pastime.[19]

Culture, in this Marcusian articulation, renders sex unspeakable, and the guardian of culture – the Lord Chamberlain – previously ensured that sex stayed quiet; but now, with the lifting of censorship, taboos can be tackled, and honesty will prevail. Such, we can presume, was the progressive sentiment about sex on stage at the moment of *What the Butler Saw*.

Whether or not *What the Butler Saw* would have passed the Lord Chamberlain is debatable, but also, thankfully, irrelevant, since the play was staged only after the end of censorship.[20] In a diary entry, though, Orton implies that his play is specifically designed to give offence:

> Kenneth, who read *The Observer*, tells me of the latest way-out group in America – complete sexual licence. 'It's the only way to smash the wretched civilization,' I said, making a mental note to hot-up *What the Butler Saw* when I came to re-write. 'It's like the Albigensian heresy in the eleventh century,' Kenneth said. Looked up the article in the *Encyclopedia Britannica*. Most interesting. Yes. Sex is the only way to infuriate them. Much more fucking and they'll be screaming hysterics in next to no time.[21]

The tendency, when quoting this passage, is to leave out the references to Kenneth Halliwell's erudition and the fact that the idea of 'complete sexual licence' comes from a respectable Sunday newspaper. Well-placed ellipses allow for a much punchier call to arms than does the image of Orton with his nose in the *Encyclopædia Britannica*. In many ways, though, Orton echoes the sentiment of the *Plays and Players* reviewer: civilization, or culture, is intrinsically at odds with sexual activity, which either 'crashes' (*Plays and Players*) or 'smashes' against it. This is only half of Marcuse's thesis, of course. In *Eros and Civilization* he claims that since Freud we have incorrectly associated the free-play of the sexual instincts with the dissolution of civilization, whereas, he suggests, the careful cultivation of Eros can actually be the sound basis of a better civilization – not for him any smashing or crashing. In any case, Orton is not as specific as the *Plays and Players* reviewer – he does not claim that simply speaking about sex will *liberate* anything, or that the breaking of taboos is automatically progressive. He probably wanted to do no more than *épater les bourgeois*. If we leave aside Orton's striking but inconclusive statement and concentrate instead on the play, we will find that it is in no obvious way an affirmation of a previously *negated* sexuality; on the contrary, what it hilariously and relentlessly dramatizes is how sex is constantly exhorted to speak about itself, to stop being unspeakable.

Tell me everything

RANCE. You may speak freely in front of me.[22]

Three characters are asked to undress during *What the Butler Saw*. Although each in turn hesitates at Dr Prentice's request, first Geraldine, then Nick and finally Sergeant Match remove their clothing. In the first instance, Prentice is hoping to seduce an unsuspecting Geraldine; the subsequent undressings are Prentice's attempts to cover up the misunderstandings occasioned by the first one. This allows for much comic business as naked characters and their clothes must be hidden behind curtains, in a wastepaper basket, in a vase. Farce relies heavily on such structures of concealing and revealing, and therefore as a form lends itself well to the topic of sex and sexuality, which, according to Foucault, have been subjected to a double imperative to remain silent *and* to expose themselves. Dr Prentice's advances on Geraldine must be hidden, and yet every attempt to stifle them leads to some other indiscretion – real or imagined – being revealed. Whatever his ulterior motives, the joke is that Prentice can insist that anyone undress on medical grounds, however far-fetched: 'And kindly remove your stockings. I wish to see what effect your step-mother's death had upon your legs', he says to Geraldine.[23] When his wife discovers him with the naked-save-drawers Nick, Prentice claims 'My investigations upon his clothed body would be strictly "unscientific" and, inevitably, superficial.'[24] There are two assumptions being sent up here: that a doctor has a neutral scientific eye and that certain psychological truths can be read on the naked body. Dr Prentice does not really believe the various medical explanations he gives. They are merely expedient, 'like "open sesame" – a formula for gaining entrance',[25] and he takes advantage of his prerogative as a doctor – able to legitimately command anyone to undress to gain access to some 'truth' of their body – for his own ends.

Things start going very wrong for Prentice when Dr Rance arrives, because Rance, unlike Prentice, not only speaks the language of psychiatry, but appears to believe it as well. In fact, he is a perfect caricature of the sexologists whom Foucault identifies as the main culprits of the late nineteenth-century 'incitement to discourse', the urging of 'perverts' to confess to their nature. There are three things worth noting about Rance's approach to his psychiatric duties: first, the insistence with which he seeks confessions from all and sundry; second, his tendency to equate mental illness with perversion in a form of sexual pathology; and third, his constant invocation of case studies he has written and the book he might write on the basis of his extraordinary findings in Prentice's clinic.

Rance operates on the assumption that all patients and potential patients have something to hide concerning their sexual nature; equally, he assumes that they secretly want to admit to the desires they harbour. Like a policeman, he seeks to get to the truth of the matter by extracting an admission from the source. Unlike a policeman, though, he does not consider his patients to be guilty of crimes, even though their mental illness may require them to be incarcerated. Historically, we might say that (abnormal) sex has gradually shifted in status from sin to crime to illness. Rance arrives at this final point, although he is by no means consistent, since he lapses occasionally into the language of morality (the play suggests that psychiatry is only a cover for moralizing tendencies dressed up in modern gear). For the most part, though, he maintains a 'scientific' stance. His cross-examination of Geraldine, whom he takes for a boy (she is wearing Nick's hotel uniform), reaches its climax with her desperate admission:

> GERALDINE: I can't go on, doctor! I must tell the truth. (To DR RANCE.) I'm not a boy! I'm a girl!
> RANCE (to DR PRENTICE). Excellent. A confession at last. He wishes to believe he's a girl in order to minimize the feelings of guilt after homosexual intercourse.[20]

As Foucault says of modern confession,

> It is no longer a question simply of saying what was done – the sexual act – and how it was done; but of reconstructing, in and around the act, the thoughts that recapitulated it, the obsessions that accompanied it, the images, desires, modulations, and quality of pleasure that animated it.[27]

Rance is not so much interested in the fact that Geraldine had homosexual sex (which of course she hadn't) as in the intricate psychological ramifications of this act, and it is these deep-seated motivations which he is most intent on extracting from her. This is particularly the case when he turns his attentions to Dr Prentice, whom he suspects of a truly polymorphous sexuality. But his success at eliciting confessions begins to overwhelm him when Nick, unsolicited, appeals to him:

> NICK (with a groan). Oh, doctor, I'm obsessed by feelings of guilt. I have to make a confession.
> RANCE. You must ring for an appointment. I can't listen to confessions off the cuff.[28]

Confession may be coerced, as in the case of Geraldine, but it holds pleasures as well, and the listener may soon find a queue of willing penitents at his door.

Rance's diagnosis of Geraldine turns relentlessly on the idea that sexual perversion occupies the same horizon of experience as mental illness – that is, that sexual appetites and activities have their seat in psychological processes and, by association, in the very identity of the patient in question. He saves his most exorbitant theories for Dr Prentice, whose case history is spectacularly nuanced:

> DR RANCE. [...] The demands of a nymphomaniac wife and patient, coupled with those of his torrid secretary, prove too much for his

sanity. He turns, in his anguish, to assaulting young boys. Retaining, however, some vestiges of normal feelings, he persuades his minions to dress in women's clothes. This explains his desire for female garments. As his neurosis matures we'll better be able to decide whether he intended his boys to impersonate wife, patient or secretary.[29]

Rance's enthusiasm for making sex (as psychosis) speak is matched by the magnitude of his misapprehension of events in Prentice's clinic. However, the play implies that his drive to seek out sexual pathology is not entirely motivated by scientific impulses. He announces to Mrs Prentice the depth of her husband's case as something to celebrate: 'As a transvestite, fetishist, bi-sexual murderer Dr Prentice displays considerable deviation overlap. We may get necrophilia too. As a sort of bonus.'[30] Necrophilia is a 'bonus', because everything that Rance encounters in the asylum is more meat for his '"documentary type" novelette' on Prentice.[31]

Almost as soon as he arrives, Rance sees in Geraldine a publishing opportunity. Her case, he says, has 'the bizarre quality that makes for a fascinating thesis', and he is quick to announce that hers is 'a text-book case'.[32] An apparently massive textual or discursive apparatus supports the existence of sexual deviance, and Rance is eager to contribute to and enlarge it. He sees Prentice as a valuable specimen whose case will add much to the literature on perversion: 'My "unbiased account" of the case of the infamous sex-killer Prentice will undoubtedly add a great deal to our understanding of such creatures.'[33] *What the Butler Saw* lampoons Rance as a representative of sexual psychiatry cashing in on what are really lurid tales dressed up as case histories; but the play does capture a key point about the construction of sexuality: not only is sex pathologized and set up as the source of identity, but it is also turned into a body of knowledge. When knowledge about sex is generated by countless textbooks on the question, then sex enters the realm of truth – sex is expected to tell the truth about itself. Rance may appear an oppressive figure, labelling every other character with sexual desires they do not feel, but he is in no conventional way *repressive*. On the contrary, what he does is produce *more* sex in the clinic than there was to begin with. To understand this, we must adopt Foucault's model of knowledge: 'Sexuality must not be thought of as a kind of natural given which power tries to hold in check, or as an obscure domain which knowledge tries gradually to uncover. It is a name that can be given to a historical construct'.[34] If anything, *What the Butler Saw* is contradictory on this matter: on some occasions it asserts that sex is a natural given, barely suppressed everywhere; and yet in the antics of Rance we see sex as a contingent construction of knowledge, the product of just so many textbooks.

A sex that does not speak its name

Jonathan Dollimore argues that the attitude towards Rance and Prentice in *What the Butler Saw* reflects a phenomenon of the 1960s, the anti-psychiatry movement:

> In the sixties the psychiatry that had developed after the war was, like the family, attacked: it was perceived as a form of social policing which, with the aid of pseudo-scientific categories, mystified socially desirable behaviour as natural, and undesirable behaviour as the result of abnormal psychosexual development.[35]

R.D. Laing, one of the main proponents of anti-psychiatry, did not give up on the idea of madness, but suggested that a more sympathetic approach be taken to it, whereby the therapist 'draws on his own psychotic possibilities'.[36] Dollimore thinks that Laingian ideas inform *What the Butler Saw* but that Orton's play parts ways with Laing by rejecting a notion of the true self. We could take this even one step further and read the play as a parody of not only the powers of post-war psychiatry, but also of the well-meaning 'anti-psychiatry' that tries to comprehend madness. In his diaries, Orton describes madness as a sort of fad of the late 1960s:

> I thought how fashionable madness is at the moment. The film Marat/Sade is just out. Of course it's the perennial fascination of most people with watching lunatics ... [A] director and actors re-create a madhouse in a theatre. Let's look at mad people. At queer people ... Kenneth H. said, 'In *What the Butler Saw* you're writing of madness.' 'Yes,' I said, 'but there isn't a lunatic in sight – just the doctors and nurses.''[37]

There are not even any nurses in sight, so Orton must be talking about an earlier draft of the play. More importantly, in this diary entry, Orton displays an awareness that mental illness and 'queerness' occupy the same horizon of meanings in the perceptions of contemporary audiences. He is clearly contemptuous of his audi-

What the Butler Saw, National Theatre, 1995. *From left*: Richard Wilson (Dr Rance), Nicola Paget (Geraldine Barclay) and Debra Gillett (Mrs Prentice)

ence, and *What the Butler Saw* is meant as a slap in the face for those eager to see madness on show. Disappointment awaits any audience member who expects an earnest portrayal of mental deterioration. However 'mad' the farcical plotting of *Butler* may be, Orton is very definite on this matter: 'there isn't a lunatic in sight'. Or any queer people, we could add. With the exception of the apparently bisexual Nick, all the other characters are, consciously at least, heterosexual.

Madness without lunatics? Madness without queers? What is *What the Butler Saw* trying to achieve? Alan Sinfield claims that Orton showed little interest in the struggles of homosexual politics, but in this diary entry, at least, Orton displays an instinctive knowledge of the forms of power that work on sexuality. In the moment of writing of *What the Butler Saw*, a very specific public opinion about homosexuality had coalesced. It was based on 'progressive' arguments dating back to the late nineteenth and early twentieth centuries, when socialists like Edward Carpenter and Havelock Ellis had argued that sexual deviance could be explained and understood in terms of medical science and not criminality. Jeffrey Weeks claims that the Wolfenden report in Britain in the late 1950s saw the more general acceptance of the 'medical model' of homosexuality. He reports that 'by 1965, 93 per cent of those polled in an opinion poll saw homosexuality as a form of illness requiring medical treatment' and cites a Roche Laboratories leaflet that stated: 'In a discussion of homosexuality, psychiatrists would probably agree unanimously on at least one point: the belief that the homosexual is a sick person.'[38] Once homosexuality was recognized as a kind of mental illness, it was obviously subjected to various forms of treatment and 'cure'. Weeks catalogues measures as drastic as castration and as 'humane' as hypnotherapy; he also mentions 'aversion therapy' as a method of treatment occasionally employed through the 1960s: 'it consists of making people nauseous and inflicting electric shocks on them while viewing pictures of same-sex people to whom they are attracted.'[39] When we know that this method was employed in the 1960s, it gives a special resonance to Rance's query about Geraldine's case – 'Have you tried shock treatment?'[40] Given this widespread tendency in the 1960s to place homosexuality under the gaze of psychiatric medicine, the strategy of *What the Butler Saw* to exclude 'lunatics' and 'queer people' begins to look rather more deliberate.

Rightly or wrongly, Orton perceived his audiences in the commercial theatre – where, after all, his plays found favour – as conservative and (mainly) heterosexual, and for good measure, probably as part of that ninety-three per cent polled in 1965.[41] Their 'perennial fascination' for 'watching lunatics' would, therefore, be well satisfied by theatre that linked homosexuality with illness. By declining to show any lunatics or sexual deviants, *What the Butler Saw* frustrates the audience's appetite and gives them instead characters with insatiable appetites of their own for hunting out sexual deviance and mental illness. This strategy must be understood in the context of what Nicholas de Jongh calls the 'pity for perverts' style of play which began to appear when the Lord Chamberlain reduced controls on the stage-depiction of homosexuality in 1958:

> there were predictable vistas of homosexuals suffering not quite manfully, and inspiring a limited, superior form of pity from disapproving audiences. Strangely it was the commercial West End stage, and not the Royal Court theatre, that took advantage of the Lord Chamberlain's modest relaxation of the total ban on plays about homosexuality.[42]

If we follow Foucault, a lifting of prohibitions and loosening of controls does not necessarily mark the end of the workings of power. It could be that the new freedoms to speak about homosexuality on the stage constituted an 'incitement to discourse' and a bringing into vision of this illness. If this is the case, the silence about homosexuality maintained by *What the Butler Saw* can be read as something other than the continued closeting of Orton. If, in the late 1960s, it had become relatively acceptable for homosexuality to speak about itself on stage; if, indeed, it was urged to do so by 'progressive' voices and by the vogue for madness, then *Butler* deliberately thwarts such a drive to render sex audible and visible. It is not a straightforward silence, though, since the play relentlessly shows how sex is solicited by the agencies of power.

A note on power

One of the most notoriously difficult and controversial aspects of Foucault's later work is the theory of power he proposes. It is often easier to understand the model of power he displaces than the one he puts in its place. He claims that modern thinking continues to be dominated by the 'juridico-discursive' model of power. This model dates from the eighteenth century and focuses on sovereignty and constitutionality, where the role of the law-giver is paramount. In this conception, power is centralized in a person or an institution; it is wielded by an authorized force. Even if this force is not a king, it is a model that still imagines power in terms of sovereign force. But Foucault thinks that power has stopped working this way: the idea that power is thus centralized 'is utterly incongruous with the new methods of power whose operation is not ensured by right but by technique, not by law but by normalization, not by punishment but by control'.[43] He suggests we need an 'analytics' of power rather than a theory, and such an analytics would address 'a power bent on generating forces, making them grow, and ordering them, rather than one dedicated to impeding them, making them submit, or destroying them.'[44] In other words, the idea of power as a sovereign force tends to emphasize *repression*, while Foucault insists that power operates on sexuality productively, not through negation or prohibition.

It is hard to know where power resides in *What the Butler Saw*. Prentice's clinic is private, and his examination of Geraldine is not to be 'under the Health Scheme', yet Rance appears to have jurisdiction over him: 'I represent her Majesty's government. Your immediate superiors in madness.'[45] Rance exercises this authority freely, ordering other characters to be committed, sedated or confined to strait-jackets; but he gives the overriding impression that he operates independently of reason or any known laws. The hapless Sergeant Match is the other representative of external authority in the play. Although he does not even begin to approach the caricature of brutal police violence found in Inspector Truscott in Orton's *Loot* (1966), he is nonetheless subjected to merciless satire for his incompetence and dimness as he searches for the missing private parts of Winston Churchill's statue. Power then, in the form of government or sovereign force, is invoked by the play as a dangerous and potentially corrupt institution off stage. On stage, the power vested in doctors by medical expertise is subjected to the same level of ironic exposure. If this is all the play has to say about power, then it is hardly novel, because farce has always delighted in placing figures of authority in compromising positions and showing up their vices and weaknesses.

If we look at it another way, perhaps farce has always known something about power that power's theorists have failed to grasp. Farce has little respect for power as that thing exercised by the law-giver. If anything, the characters in farce tend to be powerless over their own fates, subject instead to the relentless forces of situation and plot. This is the case in *What the Butler Saw*, where the attempts by Prentice and Rance to direct events are swept aside by the circumstances they find themselves plunged in. Their medical authority counts for very little, and Prentice in particular finds that his prerogatives as a doctor disappear as he comes more and more under the scrutiny of the medical science over which he is meant to be master. Foucault also warns us not to overestimate the powers of the doctor over the patient, because power is distributed between these two in a *relation* rather than residing simply with the former:

> We must not look for who has power in the order of sexuality (men, adults, parents, doctors) and who is deprived of it (women, adoles-cents, children, patients) ... The nineteenth-century grouping made up of the father, the mother, the educator, and the doctor, around the child and his sex, was subjected to constant modifications, con-tinual shifts. One of the more spectacular results of the latter was a strange reversal ... ultimately it was in the relationship of the psychi-atrist to the child that the sexuality of adults themselves was called into question.[46]

If *What the Butler Saw* achieves anything, it is to draw our atten-tion away from those whose sexuality has been increasingly been scrutinized (women, homosexuals, patients) and refocuses it on those who supposedly wield power over sex (doctors, the police). In doing so, it recognizes that sexuality is caught up in networks of power and knowledge, but that power is not the special privilege of a sovereign few. A year earlier, in *Discipline and Punish*, Foucault explained how in the Panopticon, the position of the prison guard is not above power, but it is wholly implicated in its structures. In the institution of modern sexuality, the psychiatrist occupies a similar position to the prison guard – as much an object in the networks of knowledge as the purported subject of that knowledge. *What the Butler Saw* does not critique the power of the psychiatrist, then, but relocates the psychiatrist as a less than omnipotent figure in the map of sexuality.

Notes

1 Jonathan Dollimore, 'The challenge of sexuality', in Alan Sinfield, ed. *Society and Literature 1945–1970* (New York: Holmes and Meier, 1983), p. 80.

2 Alan Sinfield, 'Who was afraid of Joe Orton?', *Textual Practice* 4 (1990), p. 269. For a recapitulation and amplification of these ideas, see Alan Sinfield, *Out On Stage: Lesbian and Gay Theatre in the Twentieth Century* (New Haven and London: Yale University Press, 1999).

3 Sinfield, 'Who was afraid?', p. 267.

4 The Sexual Offences Act of July 1967 decriminalized male homosexual activities in private for adults over the age of twenty-one in England and Wales, with certain restrictions (the armed forces).

5 Sinfield, 'Who was afraid?', p. 270.

6 In this debate on Orton's sexual politics, Sinfield is supported by Simon Shepherd, *Because We're Queers* (London: GMP, 1989), and Mark Lilly, 'The plays of Joe Orton', in *Gay Men's Literature in the Twentieth Century* (Basingstoke: Macmillan, 1993), pp. 168–79. More or less in Dollimore's camp are John Lahr, *Prick Up Your Ears: The Biography of Joe Orton* (London: Penguin, 1978), Christopher Bigsby, *Joe Orton* (London and New York: Methuen, 1982) and Maurice Charney, *Joe Orton* (Basingstoke: Macmillan, 1984).

7 Joe Orton, *What the Butler Saw*, in *Orton: The Complete Plays* (London: Eyre Methuen, 1976), pp. 371–2.

8 William H. Masters and Virginia E. Johnson, *Human Sexual Response* (New York: Bantam, 1980 [1966]).

9 Herbert Marcuse, *Eros and Civilization: A Philosophical Inquiry into Freud* (London: Allen Lane, 1969 [1955]), p. 49.

10 Michel Foucault, *The History of Sexuality: Volume 1, An Introduction*, trans. Robert Hurley (London: Penguin, 1981 [1976]), p. 34.

11 Foucault, *History of Sexuality*, p. 18.

12 Foucault, *History of Sexuality*, p. 43.

13 Foucault, *History of Sexuality*, pp. 43–4.

14 Foucault, *History of Sexuality*, p. 24.

15 Foucault, *History of Sexuality*, p. 43.

16 Foucault, *History of Sexuality*, p. 12.

17 This, and other 'oddities and absurdities' of the Lord Chamberlain's decisions, can be found in Paul O'Higgins, *Censorship in Britain* (London: Thomas Nelson, 1972), pp. 90–99.

18 Nicholas de Jongh, *Not in Front of the Audience: Homosexuality on Stage* (London and New York: Routledge, 1992) and *Politics, Prudery and Perversion* (London: Methuen, 2000).

19 Helen Dawson, '*Oh! Calcutta!* at the Roundhouse' (Sept 1970), in Peter Roberts, ed., *The Best of Plays and Players: Volume 2: 1969–1983* (London: Methuen Drama, 1989), p. 36.

20 The Lord Chamberlain was still active when Orton was writing *What the Butler Saw*, and there is much speculation in his diaries about whether the play would pass the censor unscathed. The brandishing of Winston Churchill's penis was subject of the most discussion and thought unlikely to pass. In the end, Ralph Richardson, who played Dr Rance in the post-censorship production in 1969, insisted that the display of the dead Prime Minister's body part should be forbidden. See John Lahr, ed. *The Orton Diaries* (London: Methuen, 1986), pp. 35–6, 231–2, 249–50, 252, 256.

21 Orton, *Orton Diaries*, p. 125.

22 Orton, *What the Butler Saw*, p. 376.

23 Orton, *What the Butler Saw*, p. 366.

24 Orton, *What the Butler Saw*, p. 397.

25 Orton, *What the Butler Saw*, p. 404.

26 Orton, *What the Butler Saw*, p. 413–14.

27 Foucault, *History of Sexuality*, p. 63.

28 Orton, *What the Butler Saw*, p. 432.

29 Orton, *What the Butler Saw*, p. 424.

30 Orton, *What the Butler Saw*, p. 428.

31 Orton, *What the Butler Saw*, p. 424.

32 Orton, *What the Butler Saw*, pp. 378–9, 383.

33 Orton, *What the Butler Saw*, p. 427.

34 Foucault, *History of Sexuality*, p. 105.

35 Dollimore, 'The challenge of sexuality', p. 67.

36 R. D. Laing, *The Divided Self* (Harmondsworth: Penguin, 1965), p. 34.

37 Orton, *Orton Diaries*, pp. 114–15.

38 Jeffrey Weeks, *Coming Out: Homosexual Politics in Britain from the Nineteenth Century to the Present*, rev. edn (London: Quartet Books, 1990), p. 30.

39 Weeks, *Coming Out*, p. 31.

40 Orton, *What the Butler Saw*, p. 378.

41 In the planning stages for the production of *What the Butler Saw*, its director, Oscar Lewenstein, suggested that it might have to play at the Royal Court Theatre. In his diaries, Orton writes, 'I'm not keen on this. I think a short tour and straight into the West End.' *Orton Diaries*, p. 250.

42 de Jongh, *Not in Front of the Audience*, p. 119.

43 Foucault, *History of Sexuality*, p. 89.

44 Foucault, *History of Sexuality*, p. 136.

45 Orton, *What the Butler Saw*, pp. 367, 376.

46 Foucault, *History of Sexuality*, p. 99.

5

Jokes and their relation to interpellation – Griffiths with Althusser

Ideology on the mind

CHALLENOR: [...] Had a sort of ... earnestness about it I didn't much take to. You know, as if you were giving a sermon. One thing you've gotta learn, people don't learn, they don't want to, and if they did, they won't look to the likes of us to teach 'em.[1]

Bert Challenor is a sort of recruiting officer for club comics, and in this scene from Act Three of Trevor Griffiths' *Comedians* he gives his frank assessments – from a cool commercial perspective – of the acts he and the audience have observed in Act Two. He goes through each act in turn, distributing praise, criticism and advice to the would-be comics who have just performed to a bingo audience in East Manchester. When he finishes, he selects two of the acts for enlistment in the Comedy Artists and Managers Association. It is the routine of Mick Connor that Challenor finds too much like a 'sermon', and he conveys the lesson to Connor in no uncertain terms. According to Challenor, Connor's fatal mistake is to attempt to change the way the audience think, to make them examine the ideas they have about the Irish, rather than simply confirming pre-existing stereotypes. Stand-up comedy is no place for such progressive instruction. In Act One, addressing the budding comics just before their try-out spots, Challenor had already invoked the opposition between religion and comedy, warning them: 'We're not missionaries, we're suppliers of laughter.'[2] In a play which has no easily identifiable hero, Bert Challenor is clearly the villain of the piece. As a representative of London interests and commercial imperatives, he is seen to be imposing his 'Southern' values on a set of trainee Manchester comedians honed in an altogether different style of comedy promoted by their somewhat priestly teacher, Eddie Waters. Although the Waters method does not appear to win the day in *Comedians*, Challenor's approach is clearly shown to be politically bankrupt, even if it is financially lucrative.

If *Comedians* has a thesis it is that, far from being innocent spurs to laughter, jokes are inextricably tied up with the fabric of a society's beliefs. Or, to put it another way, jokes are *ideological* through and through. It is, of course, precisely this assumption which Challenor disputes in his evaluation of Connor's 'sermonizing'. He does not use the term 'ideology' at any point, and he is by no means a Marxist, but ever since Marx's early writings, like *The German Ideology*, religion has been recognized as the instance of ideology *par excellence*. Challenor's disparaging remarks about missionaries, those classic dispensers of ideology, leave no doubt about where he stands. By comparing Connor's act unfavourably with a sermon, Challenor implies that Connor has introduced ideology where there should be none. 'Ideology' is used here in the pejorative sense of the word – that is, ideology as doctrine, or an unnecessarily narrow set of beliefs. Most importantly, in this conception of the term ideology is a *consciously* held position.

But there are other senses of ideology than this popular one, and it is the French Marxist Louis Althusser, in his essay 'Ideology and ideological state apparatuses', who has done the most to complicate contemporary thinking on ideology. For instance, in the case of Challenor's insistence that on the one hand there are sermons (ideology) and on the other simply laughter (non-ideology), it is instructive to note Althusser's comments on such a position:

> those who are in ideology believe themselves by definition outside ideology: one of the effects of ideology is the practical *denegation* of the ideological character of ideology by ideology: ideology never says, 'I am ideological'.[3]

In *Comedians* Challenor's ideological opponent, Eddie Waters, provides an idea and ideal of comedy in direct contrast to Challenor's, but he actually shares Challenor's claim to be outside ideology. According to Waters, there are bad jokes which are ideological in the sense that they are motivated by bigoted or narrow beliefs, and then there are good jokes which are non-ideological because they express some form of 'truth'. For Waters the ideological joke is almost immoral; for Challenor the ideological joke makes no pragmatic sense because it won't sell. In both cases the one's idea of a good joke is the other's idea of an ideological one. No wonder it is so difficult to know whether one is inside or outside ideology.

Clearly, neither of these retired comedians had read Althusser, who wanted to rescue 'ideology' from its traditional pejorative meanings. Or, to be more precise, not from the pejorative meanings of the capitalists like Challenor but from the pejorative meanings of the more classically Marxist definitions. In one of his lessons to his students Waters says 'a true joke, a comedian's joke, has to do more than release tension, it has to *liberate* the will and the desire ... But when a joke bases itself upon a distortion ... and gives the lie to the truth so as to win a laugh and stay in favour, we've moved from the comic art and into the world of 'entertainment' and slick success.'[4] Waters' terminology is telling because the traditional Marxist analysis saw ideology as a 'distortion' of the real material conditions of men and women, and therefore as a lie to be exposed as such. For instance, in feudal European economics, Christianity, as the dominant ideology, would represent the exploited position of peasants in the hands of nobility to those peasants as the natural and harmonious state of nature, thus ensuring the continued reproduction of exploitative conditions. Peasants who accepted their lot through the distorting power of ideology were said to labour under 'false consciousness'. Waters relies very much on this theory of ideology as an 'illusion' or false representation in his analysis of jokes. He goes so far as to suggest that to tell the joke that 'gives the lie to the truth' is to comply with the dominant ideology of capitalism, where 'slick success' is the ideological sugar around the material pill of the exploitation of labour.

If we follow this line that ideology, as Marx put it, is no more than 'the phantoms formed in the human brain',[5] the false expression of humans' real material conditions, it is worth examining the 'real conditions' of the trainee comics themselves. They are, for the most part, on the wrong side of the exploiter–exploited equation of contemporary capitalism (circa 1975). Gethin Price drives a van for British Rail, Mick Connor works on a construction site, Ged Murray is a milkman and George McBrain is a docker, while Phil Murray is an aspirational white-collar worker (an insurance salesman) and Sammy Samuels owns his own club. In each case, with the possible exception of Samuels, the comics sell their labour for wages and any surplus profit from their work goes to their employers. Leaving aside for the moment the ideological content of the actual jokes they tell – and the play very carefully makes distinctions between them on this

basis – it can be argued that their very relationship to the comedian's art can be seen in classic ideological terms as a 'distortion' of
their real material conditions. Or, to use a closely affiliated word,
the students all see comedy as a potential 'escape' from their worka-
day worlds. This feeling is expressed most succinctly by Connor,
who simply states: 'I want to be famous. I want to be rich and
famous.'[6] Even Samuels, who is relatively prosperous, gives voice to
such a desire: 'I wouldn't be seen dead working in a club like mine,
I want the tops, I want TV, I want the Palladium.'[7] A false, and
ultimately vain, individualist ideology of success masks their true
conditions and prevents them from taking the only appropriate
action in a class society, that is, entering into the class struggle. This,
at least, is the conclusion reached by one of their number, Gethin
Price, who scorns the promise of material reward and brings class
conflict to the fore in his performance.

It is quite possible to read *Comedians* like this – in terms of the
traditional Marxist view of ideology as 'the system of the ideas and
representations which dominate the mind of a man or a social
group.'[8] However, there are aspects of the play which lead us to
believe that ideology does not just amount to what is in people's
heads, or, as Challenor would have it, what you can 'teach 'em'. It is
true that the play emphasizes the ideological 'content' of jokes, but
it also asserts that that ideological content cannot be separated from
the *practice* of joke-telling, from a set of established social rituals and
material situations. And this is where Althusser's essay 'Ideology and
ideological state apparatuses' becomes so valuable. In that essay
Althusser sets out to break down an age-old opposition between the
ideological and the material. Ideology, according to Althusser, is not
only 'the phantoms formed in the human brain'; on the contrary, 'an
ideology always exists in an apparatus, and its practice, or practices.
This existence is material.'[9] In addition, Althusser develops a term,
'interpellation', which helps to account for another major concern of
Comedians, the audience of a joke. For *Comedians* is as concerned
with the ideological implications for those who hear a joke as for
those who tell it.

A theatre of ideology

In a metaphor that is auspicious for this context, Althusser at one
point describes his account of ideology as 'my little theoretical

theatre'.[10] The theatrical metaphor appears more than once in 'Ideology and ideological state apparatuses' and is entirely appropriate to the theses put forward in the essay. It allows Althusser to move away from a theory of ideology as simply a set of beliefs, ideas, representations in people's minds and towards a theory that sees ideology as necessarily *acted out*, in the way a play has a physical manifestation on a stage. For the purposes of this chapter, three Althusserian insights will be examined: first, the distinction he makes between the repressive state apparatus (RSA) and the ideological state apparatuses (ISAs); second, the thesis that 'ideology is a "representation" of the imaginary relationship of individuals to their real conditions of existence'; and third, that ideology 'hails' or 'interpellates' individuals as *subjects*.

Distinction between RSA and ISAs

Althusser starts with the question that haunts all Marxists: if a capitalist system ruthlessly exploits the vast majority of those who participate in it, how does it continue to survive? Capitalism has a set of conditions of production and it must 'reproduce' those conditions of production to ensure its survival. Not only must it reproduce machines, buildings and raw materials but, more problematically, it must reproduce the labour power from which it extorts surplus value. Although the continued presence of labour power is partly guaranteed by wages, Althusser argues that *ideology* is also necessary. Ideology is part of a 'relatively autonomous' superstructure that includes Law and, crucially, the State.[11] Althusser accepts the Marxist claim that 'the State is a "machine" of repression, which enables the ruling classes ... to ensure their domination over the working class'.[12] However, he makes a vital modification to the Marxist theory of the State. While he agrees that the repressive forces at the beck and call of the State – the police, the courts, the prisons, the army – intervene on behalf of the interests of the ruling class, he claims that they do so only in the 'last instance'. The violent and expensive 'repressive state apparatus', as he calls it, is only a supplement to a proliferation of 'ideological state apparatuses', institutions that operate by ideology rather than violence.

Given that Althusser always emphasizes the material reality of ideology, it is appropriate that he sees it taking 'the form of distinct and specialized institutions.'[13] He gives a list of ISAs that includes the Church, the school system, the family, trade unions, the communications ISA (media) and the cultural ISA (literature, the arts, sports). Although these various apparatuses are relatively independent of each other and of the State, the 'unity of the different ISAs is secured ... by the ruling ideology, the ideology of the ruling class.'[14] Althusser then proposes that the dominant ISA in modern capitalist societies (circa 1970) is the educational ideological state apparatus. The school is instrumental in the reproduction of capitalist relations of production because its ideology is the 'ruling bourgeois ideology: an ideology which represents the School as a neutral environment purged of ideology'.[15] Schools, in other words, are usually viewed in the way Challenor (and Waters) view good jokes. Althusser does not (just) mean that teachers are indoctrinating students into belief in the legitimacy of capitalism but that by its processes and practices – setting pupils 'on the path to the freedom, morality and responsibility of adults' – the school is ideological.[16]

Take, for example, the ideal of the university, as that institution which dispenses (neutral) knowledge or trains its students in indispensable skills. We imagine the university as an institution that is relatively independent of state control, a space for the pursuit of ideas outside the prerogatives of a dominant capitalist culture. Although this picture is accurate up to a point, a university is not only a seat of learning. As an institution, it works on the basis of a series of rituals and practices, a machinery without which it could not exist. To take only one such practice: examinations. This familiar and 'obvious' procedure makes actors of both students and lecturers, who are both expected to play their part and for the most do so with only cursory complaint. Students sit nervously but docilely in endless rows of desks and lecturers patrol or monitor or sleep. Althusser would say that it is here, in the most 'obvious' and taken for granted activities, that the theatre of ideology plays itself out because it is here that subjects are made. In this case, the subjects produced are responsible individuals capable of thinking independently and taking care of themselves – the bourgeois ideal! If they were to refuse to stay at their desks, or fail to turn up in the first place, that would be another matter – the disciplinary mechanisms of the university would have to come into play. That this happens so rarely is testimony to the success of the mechanisms of ideology. But this begins to move us from the stage of ideology – the ISA – towards its *mise-en-scène*.

Ideology as representation of imaginary relationship to real conditions

Althusser adjusts the traditional concept of ideology in an oft-quoted phrase: 'What is represented in ideology is therefore not the system of the real relations which govern the existence of individuals, but the imaginary relation of those individuals to the real relations in which they live.'[17] He distinguishes this position from two prior ones which he rejects. The first is what we might call the 'conspiracy theory' of ideology – the idea of a 'small number of cynical men who base their domination and exploitation of the "people" on a falsified representation of the world which they have imagined in order to enslave other minds'.[18] The second position, attributed to Feuerbach and the early Marx, is already there in the first quotation – ideology as a distorting representation of men's real conditions, a distortion that comes about because of the material alienation men live in. Althusser's adjustment is delicate one. He introduces two key terms: 'imaginary' and 'relation'. If we take the latter first, we see that Althusser gently displaces the pejorative sense of ideology as *simply* an illusion, that is, a mystified expression of real relations. In his schema ideology is no longer a direct, if distorted, version of real conditions but rather a 'relation to' those real conditions.

The use of the term 'imaginary' is crucial because it introduces (a half-hearted) Lacanian psychoanalysis into ideology critique. Jacques Lacan's best-known discussion of the imaginary is in the essay 'The mirror stage as formative of the function of the I', where he argues that a small infant in front of a mirror experiences a jubilant moment of (mis)recognition as it sees its uncoordinated body as reassuringly whole.[19] Lacan's argument is that the mirror stage returns throughout the life of adults, those decentred and split subjects who continually (mis)recognize their own integrity and unity in the various mirrors available to them. Althusser's implication is that ideology functions through imaginary identifications, giving subjects a mirror in which to (mis)recognize themselves as unified, autonomous individuals. This Lacanian turn by Althusser is half-hearted because, as Terry Eagleton points out, Althusser leaves out large chunks of Lacan, particularly his notion of a scandalous desire which upsets the easy symmetry of the imaginary.[20] But the introduction of 'recognition' moves us usefully on to the third salient feature of Althusser's theory.

95

Ideology 'interpellates' individuals as subjects

'[A]ll ideology hails or interpellates concrete individuals as concrete subjects.'[21] For Althusser, ideology addresses individuals, and individuals are the ultimate destination of ideology. The individual who recognizes her or himself as addressed by and in ideology is a subject. He gives the example of a policeman shouting 'Hey, you there' to someone in the street. If the person thus hailed turns around (or starts to run), a recognition of subjectivity has taken place in the form of 'Yes, it's me'. 'Subject' is an ambivalent word because it can mean both an autonomous, free position and a position of subjection to a greater force. Althusser deliberately uses it in both senses at the same time. That is, ideology, a force of subjection, recruits us as free, individual subjects. 'Interpellation' is the word for this moment of paradoxical subjection. It is a necessary new word to distinguish what happens in ideological 'hailing' from, say, coercion, since interpellation does not make people do what they do not want to do but, rather, is that moment when they find themselves faced with the 'obvious'. A good subject (and most of us are) will recognize the obvious as such and accept the subject position therein delimited. There is nothing inevitable about this process, and occasionally a bad subject will resist. The ideological state apparatuses are there to ensure that the obviousness of our subject position is continually drummed into us by providing for us practices and rituals where we act out our subjectivity materially.

Back to school

From Ibsen to contemporary situation comedy modern drama has been above all else preoccupied with the family ISA. They may not consciously think of it as an ideological state apparatus, but the writers of domestic comedy, modern tragedy, kitchen sink drama and soap operas all take the family unit as their main dramatic material. These families may be more or less secure, more or less stable; they may be in crisis or they may be taken for granted as a neutral backdrop, but they are omnipresent. A retroactive stock-taking of twentieth-century drama would force us to conclude that, for better or worse, the family was the most important social formation (ISA) of the period. This is a fact that is looked upon with some dismay by many left-leaning playwrights. Such an over-emphasis on the private world of domestic relations obscures the fact that the family is only one of the social formations we inhabit, and by no means the most important. We are also political animals, they would argue, and participate in a public world that includes many institutions (the workplace in particular) which are independent of the family. Feminist critics and playwrights have objected to this sort of argument on the grounds that it sets up a false opposition between the private and the public, and they claim that the family is also, fundamentally, a site of political struggle, as Althusser indicates by calling it the second main ISA of the modern era.[22] In any case, this apprehension on the part of left-wing playwrights of the 1960s and 1970s led them to write plays that left the domestic sphere behind and explored how people relate to institutions other than the family. *Comedians* is just such a play.[23]

Comedians is clearly located in the milieu of the educational ISA. The opening stage description tells us that the trainee comics' night classes take place in a secondary school *'Built 1947 in the now disappearing but still familiar two-storey style'.*[24] The date is not neutral but very specifically signifies the beginnings of a new ideology of education put into place by the Labour government, whose post-war settlement included the expansion of secondary education to include all British youth. Whereas previously such further education was mainly limited to the bourgeois classes and their betters, the post-war secondary school attempted to take in as subjects all classes. The sardonic stage directions which follow imply that this ideology never really reached its intended fruition. What we find instead is a decaying institution: *'a dozen chipped and fraying desks ... with green blackboard unwiped from the day's last stand beyond. ... Cupboards of haphazard heights and styles line the walls, above which the dogged maps, charts, tables, illustrations and notices warp, fray, tear, curl and droop their way to limbo.'*[25] Waters' students, the putative beneficiaries of this new educational dispensation, would have passed through this subject-making process ten years or so previously. As ISAs go, it appears to have been pretty ineffective if this exchange between the Murray brothers is anything to go by: 'PHIL: Yes, I learnt it at school. / GED: Oh they dint teach us like that. They taught us spittin'. And peein' up walls ...'[26] The education system tried its lacklustre best to enlist them as subjects, but the implication is that they were not an appropriate destination for its ideology. Phil informs the audience that he and his brother passed through the 'secondary modern' system. As Arthur Marwick explains, 'The route to better jobs and to higher education was through the grammar schools; the secondary modern school was the route to the traditional working-class occupations.'[27] It must be assumed that the school which is the setting for Acts One and Three is a secondary modern one and that its decrepit state is a reminder of the failure of a post-war ideology of inclusion.

It is not secondary modern but another kind of education that is dramatized in *Comedians*. The training comics are all participating in adult or further education, in night classes that are relatively autonomous of the state; the comics are, by association, in the same boat as '*the followers of yoga, karate, cordon bleu cookery, "O" level English, secretarial prelims, do-it-yourself, small investments and antique furniture*'.[28] The witty juxtaposition of incongruous courses of study should not blind us to what they also have in common. The syntax of the sentence indicates that it is not just yoga which has 'followers' but that the qualifier extends all the way down the line to 'antique furniture', taking in, by implication, the would-be comics as well. It is normally religions or political parties that have followers, but if education of any sort has an ideological function, why not followers of do-it-yourself or card-carrying cordon-bleuists? In a secular world where the ideals of widened participation in democracy and education seem to have failed, an ideology of self-improvement fills the void, and all the would-be comics are living that individualist ethos by training in what is, after all, a notoriously individualist theatrical mode. The concert secretary who resumes the interrupted bingo at the end of Act Two summarizes succinctly the doctrinal form of this ideology when he calls out the first ball: 'Always look after ... Number One.'[29] Like all successful ideology, this one presents itself as 'obvious' and is supported by a whole set of practices, of which night school is only one.[30]

Although the self-improving comics are dismissive about the values of traditional education, the traces of interpellation are still at work. A classic instance of what we might call the (mis)recognition[31] of subjectivity is played out in the physical responses of the comics to the entry of their teacher, Eddie Waters: '*There's a small but discernible reaction in the others, a regression to childhood responses ... The others break and begin drawing the desks and chairs into roughly parallel sides of a hollow square*.'[32] What brings about this semi-orderly set of actions if not ideology, the ideology that runs like a current between student and teacher? 'The others' refers to all the students save one, Gethin Price, who is an exception throughout the play. We are led to believe that, unlike the others, he is not a 'good' subject, that he resists the 'hailing' by ideology. Gethin's problematic relation to the educational ISA is spelt out in a story he tells about his youth in Act One: 'I thumped a teacher [...] She called us a guttersnipe [...] They sent me to a psychologist.'[33] Althusser says that ISAs function primarily by ideology but occasionally need, like RSAs, to use violence when subjects like Gethin resist too much. Psychology and medical science probably hover somewhere between the repressive state apparatus and ideological state apparatuses. In any case, we are led to understand that Gethin's tale about striking a teacher is analogous to his resistance to Waters' attempts to interpellate his students with his brand of humanist comedy. It would be a mistake, though, to see Gethin simply as the illustrative 'bad' subject in *Comedians*. He is, after all, the 'teacher's pet', and the final scene of the play, a kind of verbal report card, sees him almost querulously seeking the approval of his teacher: 'Did you like what I did? I'm asking.'[34] It is in fact these contradictions within Gethin's relation to ideology that inevitably make him the central problem of the play.

Hey you!

If the instant of ideology is the act of recognition – the answer 'Yes, it's me' to the policeman's 'Hey, you!' – it is significant that *Comedians* starts with a hesitation over recognition. The caretaker enters the classroom to find Gethin Price alone, shaving, face covered in foam, presenting the image of a clown and foreshadowing his performance in Act Two. Taken aback, the caretaker asks 'Are you in here?'[35] Rather than simply explaining his presence, Gethin does the clown's typical 'Who, me?' double-take before '*finally*' admitting yes. Of course, what the caretaker means is not 'Are you in here?', which, outside of metaphysical speculation, has an obvious answer, but 'Are you supposed to be in here?' – that is, in a night class. The answer again is yes, and a certain amount of exposition follows. It is typical of Price, though, to hesitate or prevaricate at the most 'obvious' level of recognition like this, and it sets the tone for his character throughout the play. He does it again later in the act – to the irritation of Sammy Samuels, who counters effectively with 'You know perfectly well that I mean you'. In other words, Gethin's hesitations are not really a failure of recognition that he is being addressed (you-d), but rather a playful, roundabout recognition through feigned failure of recognition.

Much of comedy in fact derives from the kind of deliberate misrecognition practised by Gethin. Another example arises on Connor's first entrance. He arrives in the classroom doorway soaking wet, wearing a terrible suit, buttonhole crumpled. McBrain sees him and says 'Oh, Christ', to which Connor – pretending that McBrain's oath addresses him directly rather than the room in general – replies 'Almost my son. Try again.'[36] Comedy exploits every double meaning it can lay its hands on, usually taking the less 'obvious' meaning in order to generate the misunderstandings so conducive to laughter. In each case, then, a deliberate misrecognition, like Price's frequent double-takes, is in fact a tacit recognition. The comedian's humorous 'It's not me' can only be brought about by a prior 'Of course it's me'.[37] It could be argued that, in Price's case, the situations in which he chooses to deploy this sort of 'recognition in misrecognition' form a challenge, a refusal to be positioned as a subject, or interpellated. On the other hand, he is in some ways paradoxically the closest to a 'good' subject of all the trainee comics. It is Price, after all, who follows the logic of Waters' teaching to the letter and is rewarded at the end with his teacher's grudging approval. This does not mean that he is passive or merely a subject of ideology, but since there is no outside of ideology, we might say that he has been successfully interpellated by another ideology. In the context of the play as a whole, this drama of contested interpellation makes the 'you' of 'Are you in here?' a problem rather than something self-evident and obvious. And, in *Comedians*, the problem of 'you' is above all addressed to the audience.

Hey who?

It may be the clown's prerogative to delay the instant of self-recognition, but something else is expected from the clown's audience. All theatrical performance relies on a relation between the stage and the auditorium or audience, and that relation changes according to the architecture of the theatre, the social make-up of the audience and the social or political context of the performance. It also changes with the 'mode of address' with which the stage greets the audience. Stand-up comics rely on a mode of address markedly different from that of much mainstream theatre. The great proportion of modern plays (*Comedians* included) do not speak directly to their audiences but instead operate within a closed dramatic world (behind an imaginary fourth wall if the set is a room) which the audience is lucky enough to look in on. Both the audience and the actors in such plays know very well that they occupy the same physical space, but for the course of the performance – until the curtain call at least – they usually agree to disregard this fact for the sake of the fictional events on stage. Stand-up comedy, on the other hand, works on the exactly opposite principle. The relation between audience and comic must be direct from the outset, and the comedian who makes out that the audience is not in the same space will surely fail.

Both theatrical scenarios are 'modes of address'. Just because a traditional play does not speak directly to the audience does not mean it is not speaking to the audience. That is to say, all theatrical performance 'hails' its audience. The question of 'modes of address' preoccupied an intensive and thorough-going English-language appropriation of Althusserian theories in the film journal *Screen* in the 1970s. The writers for *Screen* examined film spectatorship, focusing on how cinema provides its viewers with positions from which to apprehend the narrative of a film.[38] They took Brecht's critique of 'illusionist' theatre as a starting point and claimed that realist cinema in particular provides the spectator with a privileged viewing position. Catherine Belsey extended this analysis to what she called the classic realist text, stating that 'the conventional tenses of classic realism tend to align the position of the reader with that of the omniscient narrator who is looking back on a series of past events ... The text interpellates the reader as a transcendent and non-contradictory subject by positioning him or her as the unified and unifying subject of its vision.'[39] We could say that realist or illusionist drama also 'hails' its audiences as subjects in this way, making the spectator 'the unified and unifying subject of vision'. Of course, the Althusserian caveat that this is an 'imaginary' position still applies.

In stand-up comedy a rather different mode of address must be learnt and recognized. Whereas illusionist drama says 'Hey you!' without articulating the 'you' directly, the stand-up comic almost always utters the second-person (plural) in his or her act. Instead of standing behind a curtain that opens to reveal a scene separate from the audience, a comic generally stands in front of a curtain to indicate closeness to the audience. The comic is usually (though not always) alone and speaks to the crowd rather than to other characters. Of course, stand-up comedy is a notoriously precarious form of theatre because members of the audience can answer back, heckling when bored or simply inebriated. Because of this tenuous stage–auditorium relation, the comic must do everything possible to gain the favour of the audience, and one way to do this is to establish an intimacy with it. Mick Connor, the first comic on in the try-outs of Act Two, does this by asking 'Wuz yez ever foreigners, any of yez?'[40] He addresses them in the second person but hails them as potentially *different* from him and themselves. The way he says you – 'yez' – marks him as Irish and therefore different from this audience in a bingo hall in East Manchester (although of course Manchester has a large population with Irish ancestry). This is a mistake, at least according to Challenor, who criticizes Connor for his parochialism. Samuels and McBrain, who quickly adapt their acts to suit Challenor's tastes, also pepper their performances with intimate 'you's, even addressing individual members of the audience and thereby drawing them into the comic situation, implicating them as (willing) participants.

These two approaches are shown to us (the theatre, as opposed to the bingo, audience) merely as a prelude to Gethin Price's act – indeed, as foils to that act. The stage directions tell us that Price starts his act '*to himself, not admitting the audience's existence*', and he carries on in this mode for most of his performance.[41] For this refusal to acknowledge the audience Challenor chastises Price: 'You've got to speak to the audience, for God's sake.'[42] Challenor fails to realize that Price does in fact speak very intensely to an audience, one he provides for himself on stage: a pair of stage dummies dressed up in evening attire, looking as if they have just been to the theatre. They may be stand-ins for the real audience in the theatre at *Comedians*, or perhaps they are generalized representatives of the theatre-going middle classes. In any case, although Price hails the dummies directly in turn, it is clear that this hailing is ironic, even threatening. He speaks to the male dummy in the mode of masculine interpellation: 'Int this nice? I like a good chat. (*Intimate, man-to-man*.) Eh, I bet she's a goer, int she sunshine? She's got a fair pair of knockers on her too.'[43] The dummies, *obviously*, do not respond to Price's advances, and this is precisely the point: he speaks from a position – and correspondingly offers them a position to

occupy – which is not intelligible to them given the class antagonisms between them (Price is part-clown, part working-class 'bovver
boy' and Manchester United fan fresh from the terraces). As Janelle
Reinelt puts it:

> Price does not try to dissolve tensions of class, gender, and race by
> creating a humanist tolerance that merely camouflages the deep divi-
> sions of society. His piece articulates and attacks class privilege,
> creating the upper-middle class as a pair of unresponsive dummies to
> whom he is both solicitous and vicious.[44]

It is disastrous as comedy not because Price does not speak to the
audience but because he places his audience in a subject position
they cannot possibly recognize.

To understand further Gethin Price's comic strategy, it is worth
taking a closer look at jokes, the smallest units of the comic's art.
The listener to a joke is placed in a potentially difficult position.
With no escape, he or she must 'get' the joke, understand the prob-
able misdirection at the heart of it and then produce the goods that
confirm the success of the joke – laughter. Unfortunately, the joke
may not be funny, the listener may not understand, or the listener
may find the joke offensive rather than amusing – deathly silence
marks the temporary breakdown of the social situation the joke was
meant to lubricate. *Comedians* is probably more interested in jokes
that fail than in those that succeed. At the end of the play Price
points out to his teacher that he has not heard him crack a single
joke in three months.[45] This may be because Waters finds almost
every joke dangerously 'tendentious', to use Freud's word.

In *Jokes and their Relation to the Unconscious*, Freud examines the
structure of aggressive sexual jokes:

> a tendentious joke calls for three people: in addition to the one who
> makes the joke, there must be a second who is taken as the object of
> the hostile or sexual aggressiveness, and a third in whom the joke's
> aim of producing pleasure is fulfilled ... When the first person finds
> his libidinal impulse inhibited by the woman, he develops a hostile
> trend against that second person and calls on the ... third person as
> his ally. Through the first person's smutty speech the woman is
> exposed before the third, who, as listener, has not been bribed by the
> effortless satisfaction of his own libido.[46]

This is the sort of joke that Waters objects to most vociferously. It is also the kind of joke that Challenor approves of most heartily and which Samuels and McBrain resort to in their acts to impress the recruiter. As Challenor says of the second half of Samuels' act, there was no shortage of what Freud calls 'second persons': 'the wife, blacks, Irish, women, you spread it around'.[47] Another word for Freud's second person, the target of a joke's 'hostile trend', is the 'butt' of a joke. The butt is the necessary term that mediates a relation between the teller and the listener. A successful joke cements a bond between these two in which the butt acts as the glue; in other words, jokes are a way of establishing the borders of a social unit or community. In the case of a sexist joke, which Freud analyses and which abound in *Comedians*, a line is drawn around women; they are excluded in order better to mark the boundaries of a masculine community. Freud focuses on the libidinal gains (or losses) of tellers and listeners, but his analysis could equally well be understood in Althusserian terms. He says that the first person 'calls on the ... third person as his ally'. This could be rephrased as 'jokes interpellate the third person as a subject'. A sexist joke says 'Hey you!', you're a man and masculine in a patriarchal culture. You benefit from that culture. You are complicit in it. Laugh. Enjoy it.' And there is nothing to say that women cannot occupy this subject position as well, although the work of recognition is greater and more vexed. As Freud might say, this is no longer in the least a joke, but it tells us something about the social investments at work in humour, which is never innocent. A joke is a little ideological bullet, seeking out subjects for interpellation; and a joke has a materiality, which is its own utterance and reception. We are clearly a long way here from ideology as 'illusion', a term which cannot begin to account for the ideological work of a joke.

There is no shortage of jokes in *Comedians*. They are easy to spot, but their destination is more difficult to determine. That is, it is not clear whom they are hailing, or trying to recruit. One thing seems certain, though: the audience of *Comedians* will be hard pressed to laugh at the play's countless jokes. The play does its best to block the spontaneous ideological recognition of the jokes by the theatre audience. It achieves this denial through a proliferation of framing devices: everything prepares us to view the performances in Act Two from the 'outside', from a distance. Even before we see the routines, the first act is devoted to theories of comedy and analysis of jokes. We are not *told* how we should respond to jokes, but a dialectical debate about them is established between Waters and Challenor, and the audience has already been asked to think about jokes in this reflective, dialectical fashion before it hears them in Act Two. And then the jokes, although delivered directly to the audience in the theatre, miss their mark because intended for the fictional bingo audience. The audience of *Comedians*, in other words, views a stage performance that is normally divested of a fourth wall *through a fourth wall*: the jokes are there, but not for it. The contradiction can only distance the audience further from the jokes, inciting it, paradoxically, not to laugh, whether or not the jokes might provoke laughter under other circumstances. Furthermore, the audience of *Comedians* is urged to contemplate the additional implications of the inner spectators, Challenor and Waters, who flank the performers at tables on the side of the stage. The audience watches the watching of these two, who in turn represent alternative principles of reception. Finally, the middle-class audience finds itself transposed to the stage in the ultimate routine by Price, who abuses the audience by proxy in the form of the dummies.[48]

Laughter is effectively precluded by this multiple division and layering of levels of spectatorship. What then is left if we are denied recognition of these tele-jokes? Either we fail to clue in to these framing devices and laugh at the jokes anyway,[49] or our laughter is stopped up and we are set up at another level of recognition – the level of an audience trained in Brechtian 'distanciation', where the distance from the jokes and the laughter they are meant to elicit is precisely what we recognize (or fail to). Brecht famously offered cool distance (not 'alienation' – a poor translation of *Verfremdung*) as an antidote to the empathy elicited from the audience in illusionist drama. This does not mean that he stopped trying to recruit subjects from the audience. Far from it. He was actually trying to create new subjects by changing the mode of address of theatre, the way in which theatre interpellates its audience. In good Brechtian fashion, *Comedians* would have us give up our passive laughter and force us to take a position in the dialectical debate on jokes. But there is no simple taking sides because the final performance by Price refuses to submit to either Waters' or Challenor's versions, challenging and spurning them both and choosing confrontation and contradiction instead. His jokes all have 'butts', but he does not give the (fictional bingo) audience the jokes it wants; he does not attempt to establish a teller–listener bond. And from all this the audience of *Comedians* (not some real audience, part of which will fail to recognize the distancing frames and laugh willy-nilly at the jokes, but the one, in Althusser's terms, interpellated by the play's project) is kept at a distance: not an objective state of intellectual detachment, but, coming full circle, a distance in which its members must once again recognize themselves.

Laughter/leftovers

Even though they would seem to be an ideal micro-instance of ideology, Althusser does not have anything to say about jokes in 'Ideology and ideological state apparatuses'. Nor does he tell any, for that matter. This absence may be symptomatic of a crucial gap in Althusser's theory – a gap that is addressed by Freud, who is only obliquely interested in ideology. Althusser has nothing to say in his theory of subjectivity about *pleasure*, the yield of jokes marked by laughter. He explains beautifully the demands imposed by ideology on individuals when it makes them into subjects, but he does not take account of the rewards of subjectivity. If ideology makes subjects, inscribes them in a set of relations, it must also make these constraints worthwhile. The various ISAs – organized religion, schools, families – are ambivalent institutions for their members, providing enjoyment as well as limits. One of the elements Althusser lists under the 'cultural ISAs' is football. Football, that most successful subject-producer in late twentieth-century Britain, features in the acts of both Price and the Murray brothers. Ged Murray, dressed as a ventriloquist's dummy, declares: 'My dad said if he came home and found Colin Bell [a famous Manchester City striker] in bed with the old lady he'd brew him a cup of tea.'[50] The joke tells us that ideology generates perverse reactions or contradictions in its subjects, making them willing to make unheard of sacrifices to shore up their subject position.

The play *Comedians* shares with Althusser a blind spot over pleasure. What is the laughter of recognition at a joke if not pleasure? But *Comedians* only offers tele-pleasure, pleasure at a distance: it posits the possibility of pleasurable laughing, but then withholds it in favour of the more sober, less pleasurable recognition that there is always some stake in pleasure and that it is at someone's expense – the second person or 'butt' of the joke. Here is the difference from Brecht, whose mantra was 'educate *and* entertain'. Brecht may be thought of as a series of difficult theories, but anyone who has seen his plays performed with a lighter touch cannot but notice that they are full of gags and good tunes. Brecht saw the importance of inter-pellating his audiences and recognized that pleasure was the royal road to recruitment.[51]

The final joke of *Comedians*, the only one that Eddie Waters laughs at, is told by Mr Patel, who has been at the periphery of the action throughout:

A man has many children, wife, in the South. His crop fail, he have nothing, the skin shrivel on his children's ribs, his wife's milk dries. They lie outside the house starving. All around them, the sacred cows, ten, twenty, more, eating grass. One day he take sharp knife, mm? He creep up on a big white cow, just as he lift knife the cow see him and the cow say, Hey, aren't you knowing you not permitted to kill me? And the man say, What do you know, a talking horse.[52]

The deliberate misrecognition, taking a cow for a horse, allows the man in the joke to short-circuit his Hindu belief system, kill the talking cow and presumably feed his family. The joke is about the contradictions that arise when real conditions conflict with the inter-pellating powers of both the religious ISA (Hinduism) and the family ISA. The joke seems harsh, deriving humour from a situation of the greatest extremity, but many of the jokes in *Comedians* are like this, dealing with religion, family, football – all institutions that make subjects of us. The pleasure of such jokes often emerges thanks to the unique way in which jokes can articulate the contra-dictory and ambivalent relation we have to ideology, which at the same time subjects us *and* gives us pleasure. There may be no out-side of ideology, but neither is it a seamless totality. It has surpluses and remainders, none more eloquent than a burst of laughter.

Notes

1 Trevor Griffiths, *Comedians* (London: Faber and Faber, 1976), pp. 55–6.
2 Griffiths, *Comedians*, p. 33.
3 Louis Althusser, 'Ideology and ideological state apparatuses', in *Lenin and Philosophy*, trans. Ben Brewster (London: New Left Books, 1971), p. 163.
4 Griffiths, *Comedians*, p. 20.
5 Karl Marx, *The German Ideology*, in *The Portable Karl Marx*, ed. Eugene Kamenka (Harmondsworth: Viking Penguin, 1983), p. 169.
6 Griffiths, *Comedians*, p. 20.

7 Griffiths, *Comedians*, p. 24.

8 Althusser, 'Ideology', p. 149. Althusser attributes this position to the early Marx in particular.

9 Althusser, 'Ideology', p. 156.

10 Althusser, 'Ideology', p. 163.

11 Relatively autonomous from the material 'base'.

12 Althusser, 'Ideology', p. 131.

13 Althusser, 'Ideology', p. 136.

14 Althusser, 'Ideology', p. 142.

15 Althusser, 'Ideology', p. 148.

16 Althusser, 'Ideology', p. 148.

17 Althusser, 'Ideology', p. 155.

18 Althusser, 'Ideology', p. 154.

19 Jacques Lacan, 'The mirror stage as formative of the function of the I as revealed in psychoanalytic experience', *Écrits: A Selection*, trans. Alan Sheridan (New York: Norton, 1977).

20 Terry Eagleton, 'Ideology and its vicissitudes in Western Marxism', in Slavoj Žižek, ed. *Mapping Ideology* (London: Verso, 1994), p. 216.

21 Althusser, 'Ideology', p. 162.

22 See, for instance, Michele Barrett's *Women's Oppression Today*, rev. edn (London: Verso, 1988), where she argues that Althusser incorrectly privileges the educational ISA over the family ISA as the most powerful ideological institution in modern capitalist economies.

23 Television drama more often than not takes some version of the family as its subject matter or setting, but it is also fascinated by other institutions – the police, the hospital, the school, the courtroom. This is a tacit acknowledgment of their importance in framing and shaping contemporary subjectivity.

24 Griffiths, *Comedians*, p. 7.

25 Griffiths, *Comedians*, p. 7.

26 Griffiths, *Comedians*, p. 17.

27 Arthur Marwick, *British Society since 1945* (Harmondsworth: Penguin, 1982), p. 60. Of the 'eleven-plus' exams that decided whether a pupil would attend a secondary modern or a grammar school, Marwick adds, 'It also became apparent that middle-class children were far more likely to do well in the eleven-plus than working-class ones who came from a background where academic pursuits were not encouraged.' (p. 60) Althusser says that such *de facto* distinctions in schooling based on class are ideologically instrumental because each sort of student 'is practically provided with the ideology which suits the role it has to fulfil in class society'. 'Ideology', p. 147.

28 Griffiths, *Comedians*, p. 7. The play takes us through the student comics' final exam. I have chosen to call Challenor a 'recruiting officer' in allusion to Althusser's notion that ideology actively 'recruits' subjects. Alternatively, two of the best commentators on the play capture Challenor's relation to the educational ISA by dubbing him the 'external examiner'. Austin E. Quigley, 'Creativity and commitment in Trevor Griffiths's *Comedians*', *Modern*

Drama 24 (1981), p. 408; Janelle Reinelt, *After Brecht: British Epic Theatre* (Ann Arbor: Michigan University Press, 1994), p. 159.

29 Griffiths, *Comedians*, p. 51.

30 Thanks to Núria Triana-Toribio for pointing out to me the irony of the Individual Savings Accounts (ISA) introduced by the New Labour government in 1999, which share their acronym with the ideological state apparatuses. Although it is highly unlikely that members of Prime Minister Blair's financial think-tank are well read in Althusserian theory, it is nonetheless an excellent acronym for a banking option that encourages the British to rely less on state-funded pensions and more on their own frugality and self-preserving instincts.

31 Ideological recognition is always a (mis)recognition. The subject takes the moment as true and obvious, but, like the image the mirror gives back to us, the image ideology gives us is never fully authentic. It is contingent, imaginary.

32 Griffiths, *Comedians*, p. 11.

33 Griffiths, *Comedians*, p. 29.

34 Griffiths, *Comedians*, pp. 9, 61.

35 Griffiths, *Comedians*, p. 8.

36 Griffiths, *Comedians*, p. 10.

37 The comic potential of misrecognition is played out weekly in British celebrity quiz shows of the late 1990s like *Have I Got News For You*, *Never Mind the Buzzcocks* and *They Think It's All Over*. Regulars and guests are asked questions about current events, popular music or sport and, although they often know the correct answer immediately, they fall over themselves giving witty wrong answers. Occasionally an earnest guest will answer all the questions accurately and with a straight face, attempting to accumulate as many points as possible. They thereby miss the real point of the show. The winners are not the most knowledgeable but those who cleverly conceal their knowledge behind a screen of deliberate misrecognition.

38 Some of the main texts in this debate are Stephen Heath, 'Lessons from Brecht', *Screen* 15:2 (1974), 103–28; Heath, 'Narrative space', *Screen* 17.3 (1976), 68–112; Colin MacCabe, 'Realism and the cinema: notes on some Brechtian theses', *Screen* 15:2 (1975), 7–27; and MacCabe, 'Theory and film: principles of realism and pleasure', *Screen* 17:3 (1976), 7–27.

39 Catherine Belsey, *Critical Practice* (London: Methuen, 1980), pp. 77–8.

40 Griffiths, *Comedians*, p. 38.

41 Griffiths, *Comedians*, p. 49.

42 Griffiths, *Comedians*, p. 57.

43 Griffiths, *Comedians*, p. 49.

44 Reinelt, *After Brecht*, p. 159.

45 Griffiths, *Comedians*, p. 63.

46 Sigmund Freud, *Jokes and Their Relation to the Unconscious* [1905], trans. & ed. James Strachey (Harmondsworth: Penguin, 1976), pp. 143–4.

47 Griffiths, *Comedians*, p. 56.

48 Quigley has ably described the multiple levels of audience in Act II. 'Creativity and commitment', pp. 415–16.

49 I can only speak of my personal experience of a revival of *Comedians* at the Hammersmith Theatre in 1993 when the audience was divided in its reception of Act Two: pockets of the audience laughed at the sexist or racist jokes, while the rest maintained a stony silence.

50 Griffiths, *Comedians*, p. 43.

51 Janelle Reinelt correctly identifies the play as 'a kind of *Lehrstück*' (a Brechtian learning-play), but I disagree with her claim that 'the school and the examples [are] only too clear as "pleasurable learning" for the spectator'. *After Brecht*, p. 161.

52 Griffiths, *Comedians*, p. 67.

6

Towards a citational history – Churchill with Benjamin

Theory has been here

The plays of Caryl Churchill pose an interesting difficulty for the format of this book. The preceding chapters have operated on the premise that plays are introduced to theory for the first time and that the meeting will yield fresh insights about both. In the case of Churchill, though, the meeting has clearly already taken place, for her theatrical practice has consistently been informed by developments in theory. In contrast to Harold Pinter, who opens the introduction to his *Plays: One* with the words 'I'm not a theorist', Churchill's plays are decidedly theory-friendly.[1] For instance, in her introduction to *Softcops*, Churchill explains that she wrote it with Michel Foucault's *Discipline and Punish* in mind: '*Softcops* was written in 1978, after reading Foucault's *Surveiller et Punir*. It fitted so well with what I was thinking about that I abandoned the play I was groping towards and quickly wrote something that used Foucault's examples as well as his ideas.'[2] For Churchill, then, there is a necessity, even an urgency, in the collaboration between theatre and theory. *Cloud Nine* could very well have been composed with *The History of Sexuality* in one hand, and certainly it was influenced by academic and political debates about sexuality in the 1970s in Britain.[3] An early, unperformed Churchill play, *The Hospital at the Time of the Revolution*, is, according to Linda Fitzsimmons, '[p]artly based on Chapter 5 of [Frantz] Fanon's *The Wretched of the Earth*', an early text of post-colonial theory.[4] And the play for this chapter, *Top Girls*, is thoroughly informed by the insights of feminist theory and practice in Britain throughout the 1970s and 1980s.

Top Girls is also a history play of sorts, as many of Churchill's plays are history plays – of a sort. Like Foucault, whom she admires, Churchill's view of history hinges on *discontinuity*, and she is not afraid to commit the primary historical crime of mixing past and present. Her interest in discontinuity, in the way the line of history does not run straight and true, is often brought to the service of a feminist agenda. Therefore, both Foucault and feminist theory could be brought to bear in productive ways on Churchill's plays. However, the dialogue with Foucault has already been initiated by the plays themselves and, in any case, an earlier chapter in this book already links Foucault with Joe Orton.[5] Furthermore, Churchill, and *Top Girls* in particular, have already received a great deal of attention from feminist critics, and from more than one feminist perspective. As the introduction to this volume makes clear, feminist approaches to theatre and drama have generally been more fully developed than other explicitly theorized approaches. I propose, then, an earlier theoretical text which, before Foucault, thought of history in terms of discontinuity: Walter Benjamin's 'Theses on the philosophy of history', also translated as 'On the concept of history'. As will be seen, this text has the added advantage of making arguments that have, in retrospect, been amenable to feminist historiography.

The victor's time: Benjamin contra historicism

Preoccupied with the past, Caryl Churchill and Walter Benjamin are both historians – but neither are *historicists*. The distinction is crucial because it sets them apart from the dominant model of historical understanding, *historicism*. Paul Hamilton defines historicism thus: 'a critical movement *insisting* on the prime importance of historical contexts to the interpretation of texts of all kinds.'[6] 'Insisting' is a good choice of word by Hamilton because one of the characteristic moves of the modern historicist is to berate or chastise non-historicists for failing to 'historicize', for being 'unhistoricized'. An 'unhistoricized' or 'under-historicized' analysis of a play would be one that failed to place the play in its historical context. The danger in such a failure, according to the historicist, is that the analyst will misapprehend the play as somehow timeless and, therefore, universal in its meanings. Failing to historicize leads down a slippery slope at the end of which historical difference is sacrificed for eternal truths. (Although, as will be seen, the historicist conception of time, according to Benjamin, actually leads historicism into just what it purports to avoid: universal history.) So ubiquitous is the mantra of historicism that it has become almost like common sense, and it is difficult to imagine any form of history that does not give 'prime importance' to 'historical context'. Surely, history *is* historical context? No, reply Churchill and Benjamin, *historicism* is historical context, and context is not everything.

Much of Walter Benjamin's essay is a theoretical attack on the historicism of his time, as represented by Gottfried Keller and Leopold von Ranke; while *Top Girls* shows us what a non-historicist historical practice might look like. Nothing could be less historicist than the opening act of *Top Girls*, the celebration dinner party which brings five women from different historical moments together with one woman, Marlene, from the present. For the purposes of theatre, Pope Joan, Dull Gret, Lady Nijo, Patient Griselda and Isabella Bird are torn not only from their specific historical context but also from disparate and incompatible sources: painting (Gret), literature (Griselda), apocrypha (Joan) and 'real' history (Isabella and Nijo). Even the rest of the play, deceptively located in a more mundane world, opens up a decidedly un-historicist temporality in its reversal of chronology. The significance of Churchill's departure from traditional historicism can be helpfully illuminated by Benjamin's eighteen (plus two) 'Theses' on history.

Benjamin, a German Jew, composed the Theses in 1940 in exile in Paris, shortly before he died by his own hand on the Franco-Spanish border fearing that his escape from Nazi-occupied France had failed. This short, dense text is generally taken to be his last important piece of writing. The Theses are marked in complex ways by the desperate political circumstances in which they were written, and a good historicist would call attention to such contextual elements as the Nazi–Soviet pact and the failure of the Social Democrat opposition to the Nazis in Germany as determining factors in its main propositions about progress, redemption and memory. But, in the spirit of Benjamin's anti-historicism, no more will be said here about such factors.

Something must, however, be said about the distinctive style of the Theses, which are at some remove from conventional theoretical or academic discourse and closer to aphorism in their compression of insight into near fragments. The eighteen theses and two appendices are written in a prose bursting with astonishing figurative language: baffling parables, startling analogies, exorbitant metaphors and striking images punctuate this brief text, making it hard to discern the content for the audacity of the form. The theses do not lead logically from one to the next in a linearly developing argument, but, like a rebus, conceal a pattern of overlapping relations that make up an overall picture. Benjamin's style is often perplexing and does not make things easy for his readers, but it must be seen as part and parcel of his strategy to overturn some of the complacencies of the historicism he sets out to critique.

What, then, does Benjamin have against historicism? Briefly, he believes that historicism is based on a notion of 'homogeneous, empty time' (Thesis XIII), the possibility of historical closure and a naïve trust in progress, all of which inevitably lead 'the adherents of historicism' to 'empathize ... with the victor' consciously or not (Thesis VII).[7] The historicist thinks that the past should be understood in terms of the past, not in terms of the present, which would be anachronism, a great taboo of the historicist. To do this, Benjamin says, requires a certain form of melancholy. He paints a comic portrait of the sad historicist:

> To historians who wish to relive an era, Fustel de Coulanges recommends that they blot out everything that they know about the later course of history ... It is a process of empathy whose origin is the indolence of the heart, *acedia*, which despairs of grasping and holding the genuine historical image as it flares up briefly. Among medieval theologians it was regarded as the root cause of sadness ... The nature of this sadness stands out more clearly if one asks with whom the adherents of historicism actually empathize. The answer is inevitable: with the victor. And all rulers are the heirs of those who conquered before them. (Thesis VII)

According to Benjamin, the insistence on understanding a past text through its historical context arises from a melancholy desire to 'relive an era'; and to believe that you can successfully reconstruct an era in its entirety, give its *full* context, is to imagine that historical events can be safely consigned to the past *and* at the same time comprehended in their totality. But what really remains from the past to give us our picture of it? The only 'complete' picture can be derived from documents left behind by the rulers, or – as Benjamin, a sometime Marxist, envisioning history as a struggle between classes, calls them – the victors. These remainders, which Benjamin ironically dubs 'cultural treasures', 'owe their existence not only to the efforts of the great minds and talents who have created them, but also to the anonymous toil of their contemporaries' (Thesis VII). It is those who toiled anonymously who interest Benjamin, but the full context of their histories cannot be given because they come to us only in fragments out of a wider silence.

Benjamin is suspicious of the doctrine of historical progress. Living as he did under the shadow of Nazism, it is no wonder he doubted that human history was a constantly forward-moving tale. Progress for some – the victors – often means defeat for others: the oppressed classes. In a complex image, Benjamin imagines an 'Angel of History', who perceives the past as 'one single catastrophe which keeps piling wreckage upon wreckage and hurls it in front of his feet' (Thesis IX). But the Angel is prevented from contemplating the disaster which is history by a storm that blows him away from it: 'This storm irresistibly propels him into the future to which his back is turned, while the pile of debris before him grows skyward. This storm is what we call progress.' (Thesis IX.) Progress blinds us to the barbarism of the past, and progress, according to Benjamin, is what historicism subscribes to in its theory of time. The historicist sees history as an unbroken continuum of distinct time periods, each a moment of transition to the next. Benjamin rejects this tidy schema:

> A historical materialist cannot do without the notion of a present which is not a transition, but in which time stands still and has come to a stop. For this notion defines the present in which he himself is writing history. Historicism gives the 'eternal' image of the past; historical materialism supplies a unique experience with the past. (Thesis XVI)

Throughout the Theses historical materialism is offered as the alternative to historicism. In this case, discontinuity is offered in place of continuity.

Historicism is conservative precisely because it insists so strenuously on the pastness of the past. The historical materialist, however, refuses to endorse the notion that history is over or in any sense complete. For this reason the historical materialist does not hesitate to emulate the French revolutionary Robespierre, for whom 'ancient Rome was a past charged with the time of the now which he blasted out of the continuum of history' (Thesis IV). Robespierre's anachronistic appropriation of an earlier historical era, mocked by Marx in *The Eighteenth Brumaire*, constitutes just the sort of rupture Benjamin calls for. The past, then, is never entirely dead and can be seized for the purposes of the present. Change the past and you can change the future, Benjamin is almost implying. Certainly, he offers a crucial insight into the order in which historical events are given their meaning – that is, the reverse of what common sense dictates:

> Historicism contents itself with establishing causal connections between various moments in history. But no fact that is a cause is for that reason historical. It became historical posthumously, as it were, through events that may be separated from it by thousands of years. (Appendix A)

As Slavoj Žižek puts it, 'it was again Benjamin who – a unique case in Marxism – conceived history as a text, as series of events which "will have been" – their meaning, their historical dimension, is decided afterwards, through their inscription in the symbolic network.'[8] Benjamin's discovery – the retroactivity of historical meaning – is pertinent not only to the 'historical' dinner party scene of *Top Girls* but also to the reverse chronology of the latter half of the play.

A posthumous party: Churchill contra historicism

On the face of it, Marlene's extraordinary gathering of women from across the ages is just the sort of 'blasting' out of the 'continuum of history' that Benjamin advocates. It is almost designed to make the historicist shudder: a wild mixture of historical voices, all of them intelligible in the present even without their contexts. But the scene's main objective is not to offend any traditional historians in the audience (even historicists grant licence to fiction as long as it does not usurp their final authority). Instead, it supplies a 'unique experience with the past' (Thesis XVI) in the present. Dull Gret, Pope Joan, Isabella Bird, Lady Nijo and Patient Griselda are on stage to inform us about Renaissance painting, Catholic heresy, nineteenth-century travel, feudal Japan and feudal Europe only insofar as those historical conditions can be endowed with contemporary relevance. Together with Marlene, they make up what Benjamin might call a 'constellation'. The task of the historian is to establish such surprising and unique configurations of the past with the present: 'he grasps the constellation which his own era has formed with a definite earlier one' (Appendix A).

What constellation is formed between Marlene's era and those of the women she has invited to dinner? As with any good constellation, there is more than one way of perceiving the relations of the individual elements. A link which has often been remarked on is the way in which many of the women in their remarkable lives appropriated the garb, the language or the prerogatives of men. Although it is anachronistic to compare Gret's warlike disposition, Pope Joan's regal vestments and Latin-speaking and Isabella's adventures as a traveller, the play nevertheless encourages us to do so, and the characters themselves certainly do. Comparison, however, does not necessarily mean equivalence, and the differences in the women's remembrances are as productive as their similarities, the much commented on overlapping dialogue of the scene doing much to emphasize the dissonance of deliberate anachronism.[9] Anachronism is usually thought of as an error, but here the play pilfers from the past to throw into relief Marlene's success in the world of business. Like the invited guests, her position in the world is partly predicated on the adoption of a 'masculine' standpoint. Historical affinities are counterpoised with differences in a set of jarring juxtapositions without definitive resolutions.

A discussion about clothing gives some idea of the dialectical tension between historical difference and similarity the dinner party sets up:

JOAN: I dressed as a boy when I left home.*
NIJO: green jacket. Lady Betto had a five-layered gown in shades
            of green and purple.
ISABELLA: *You dressed as a boy?
MARLENE: Of course, / for safety.
JOAN: It was easy, I was only twelve. Also, women weren't /
            allowed in the library. We wanted to study in Athens.
MARLENE: You ran away alone?
JOAN: No, not alone, I went with my friend. / He was sixteen
NIJO: Ah, an elopement.
JOAN: but I thought I knew more science than he did and almost
            as much philosophy.
ISABELLA: Well I always travelled as a lady and I repudiated strongly
            any suggestion in the press that I was other than feminine.
MARLENE: I don't wear trousers in the office. / I could but I don't.[10]

Joan explains that she turned to transvestism as a means of accessing education, and Isabella, Nijo and Marlene respond in turn to her tale. Each response is curious and telling because each effectively misinterprets the meaning of Joan's male disguise. Nijo assumes that Joan's motivation was *romance* rather than the pursuit of learning

Top Girls, Royal Court Theatre, 1982. *From left*: Lindsay Duncan (Lady Nijo), Carole Hayman (Dull Gret), Gwen Taylor (Marlene) and Selina Cadell (Pope Joan)

('Ah, an elopement'). Isabella instinctively disapproves, seeing dangers in failing to at least pass as feminine in the Victorian public eye. Finally, Marlene invokes the world of work and the 1980s office, with its implicit dress codes. All three read Joan's story against their own historical epoch, effectively ignoring its original significance. This does not mean that the women are solipsistic and simply not listening to each other. On the contrary, it enacts brilliantly Benjamin's proposition that an event only becomes historical 'posthumously', by being given significance after the fact, in a subsequent era. This sort of retroactive interpretation occurs repeatedly during the dinner party, although when a woman from an earlier era comments on a later one she of course does so pre-humously.

Other patterns emerge from the constellation of women. Their understanding of religion and ideology, their experiences of pregnancy and childbirth and their relationships with their families overlap in some places and clash in others, forming a mosaic of historical juxtapositions. Within this network, Patient Griselda cuts a rather strange figure. Whereas the others have, to some extent or other, resisted the confining hold of the femininity of their day, Griselda has conformed to the most rigid of models and become the very model of wifely chastity and obedience. Lizbeth Goodman has argued persuasively that Griselda arrives late for the celebration because she would not have been capable of participating in the earlier debate:

> her arrival serves more generally to distract and even annoy the other characters, who react against her passivity and are incited to the drunken debauchery which characterizes the end of that scene. She is the unconscious spark which ignites their flame of indignation and drunken (rhetorical) rebellion.[11]

The odd one out, Griselda serves to gel the other five in solidarity against the trans-historical oppression of women. Perhaps Griselda is even there to punctuate the claim Marlene makes before her arrival. She toasts to the assembled women (minus Griselda): "'We've all come a long way. To our courage and the way we've changed our lives and our extraordinary achievements." *They laugh and drink a toast.*'[12] According to Marlene's rhetoric, then, the 'long way' they have come has Griselda at its starting point. The progress of women is measured by their distance from this stereotype of medieval literature who placidly accepted the cruelties meted out by her husband.

But *Top Girls* is as suspicious of progress as Walter Benjamin. It can escape no one who watches the second half of the play that Marlene is one of the 'victors' and that the events of the second half compromise the celebrations of the first scene. Marlene's promotion to managing director of the Top Girls employment agency is not an 'extraordinary achievement' but an isolated instance of individual advancement in a modern economy in which other women, such as her daughter, Angie, and her sister, Joyce, have not experienced the social progress she enjoys. How far the first scene is compromised depends on the critic – opinion varies widely. It is, after all, Marlene who has conceived of the fantasy meal and selected the guests. As with all victors, is she not trying to tell a tale of continuity where she is the logical endpoint of female success in the face of great adversity? Is she not simply parading these women as 'cultural treasures', whom we should 'view with cautious detachment' (Thesis VII) because they, like Marlene, were privileged in their time and 'owe their existence', like Marlene, to the 'anonymous toil of their contemporaries'?

While most agree on the retrospective hollowness of Marlene's triumphalist rhetoric, it is interesting how many interpreters of the play would disassociate the historical guests from the woman who has conjured them up. For instance, Geraldine Cousin echoes Marlene's toast when she asserts that 'overwhelmingly, the first scene is a celebration of achievement by women in the face of seemingly insurmountable odds'.[13] Lizbeth Goodman concentrates on the difficult practicalities of staging, and particularly filming, this scene, but in her collation of interviews with cast, director and playwright, Churchill's own opinion takes precedence: the playwright aimed to lure the audience into thinking of Marlene as a 'feminist heroine who had done things against extraordinary odds' but then question her as the play went on; of the other women she says: 'they were all people with extraordinary stories who were interesting to hear about'.[14] According to Churchill, then, Marlene's victory is undermined by our knowledge of the ordinary women she has left behind but the extraordinariness of her guests is not perceptibly tarnished.

Lisa Merrill and Harry Lane, on the other hand, tend to see the guests as a collective sign of Marlene's own self-deception and self-aggrandizement. According to Merrill, 'By attempting to equate Marlene's promotion at work with the extreme circumstances over-

come by the other five guests, Churchill renders Marlene's achievement petty and ludicrous', while Lane sounds veritably Benjaminian
when he says that the 'celebration is based on mystification of the
facts: that Marlene's promotion is in some way the end result of
a unified historical process of which all women have been part.
By implying that all women share in her success and by invoking
supposed historical antecedents Marlene valorizes herself.'[15] Finally,
Janet Brown expresses the greatest doubt about the 'achievements'
of Marlene's guests: she calls the dinner party 'Almost a parody of
feminist glorifications of women's community' and contends that
'the audience is asked to critique rather than celebrate [the] lives' of
these 'Role models from history and literature'.[16] And yet she also
thinks that the scene exceeds Marlene's intentions: 'Although
Marlene is the hostess and presumably "dreamed up" this party, it
rapidly escapes her control.'[17]

   If we follow Brown, it is possible to read the stories of the guests,
and their interaction around the table, as partly stage-managed by
their host and as partly resistant to her attempted historical appropriation. The residue of history is not neutral and unchanging but
must be fought over, *Top Girls* implies. As Benjamin puts it, '*even
the dead* will not be safe from the enemy if he wins' (Thesis VI).
Since history is only written posthumously (in the future: '*will not be
safe*'), the lives of the guests can be re-inscribed in Marlene's tale of
continuous female endeavour. However, this only works up to a
certain point, as Lane indicates, for Marlene's optimistic summary is
'at odds with her guest's stories of male subjugation and violence'.[18]
But it would be unwise to demonize Marlene as the 'enemy' or
the 'victor'. She is, rather, one beneficiary of the liberalization of
markets and an ideology of individualism at the very threshold of
the Thatcherite eighties. It is the historical achievement of *Top Girls*
to have wrested away the stories of those women from a tale of
triumphant individualism. In doing so it achieves what Benjamin
asks of history: 'to seize hold of a memory as it flashes up at a
moment of danger' (Thesis VI). The moment of danger is incipient
Thatcherism, blowing the strong wind of progress and asking us to
forget the wreckage that is left behind by rampant individualism.

   The variety of opinion on the dinner party scene attests to its
openness and reflects the variety of voices contained in the scene
itself. Its impact is further complicated by the latent, delayed meaning it continues to exercise for the duration of the play. As much as

we would like to read the celebration scene in isolation, the next two acts require us to assess it retrospectively, in light of what comes next. Just as the women's understanding of each other necessarily passes through the filter of historical difference, so the audience's impression of them is modified by subsequent events. Of course, some of these later events actually precede the party chronologically. The third act, set a year before the dinner party, underlines even further the posthumous strategies of *Top Girls*, while both it and the second act concentrate on the 'pile of debris' (Thesis IX) left in the wake of progress.

In Act One Marlene's toast to her guests encapsulates her thesis of the progress achieved by women. In Act Three she is given a line that articulates much the same position but from the vantage of anticipation: 'I think the eighties are going to be stupendous.'[19] The toast, which comes later chronologically, looks back, while this opinion, expressed earlier, looks forward. It initiates an argument between Marlene and her sister, Joyce:

JOYCE: Who needs them [men]?
MARLENE: Who needs them? Well I do. But I need adventures more. So on on into the sunset. I think the eighties are going to be stupendous.
JOYCE: Who for?
MARLENE: For me. / I think I'm going up up up.
JOYCE: Oh for you. Yes, I'm sure they will.
MARLENE: And for the country, come to that. Get the economy back on its feet and whoosh. She's a tough lady, Maggie. I'd give her a job. / She just needs to hang in there. This country
JOYCE: You voted for them, did you?
MARLENE: needs to stop whining. / Monetarism is not stupid.[20]

Some might say that exchanges like this – and the whole final act – load the dice far too heavily against Marlene. After all, the audience has already seen the future Marlene speaks so glowingly of, and it is not the rosy picture she paints. The toll taken by the 'stupendous eighties' has been painfully demonstrated in a series of sketches set in the Top Girls employment agency in Act Two. Indeed, Marlene and some of her fellow 'high fliers' – Nell and Win – have gained some emancipation in the workplace, displacing men from positions they once occupied by virtue of their sex alone, and we are encouraged to admire their vigour and ease. However, the interview scenes in the agency make it clear that many (most?) other working women who have imbibed the doctrine of individualism find that lack of training, or continued sexist practices, or age, block the realization of any ambition to go 'up up up'. Just as the narrative of progress in the dinner party scene has to be partly fabricated, so in the scenes which follow 'progress' is restricted to a select few, and it may even damage others.

The third act is more than a final comeuppance for Marlene, though. It presents the audience with the debris of Marlene's own past, debris that has been occulted or repressed by her narratives of progress; and, by reversing chronologies, it reaffirms the principle of historical time established by the anachronistic first scene. By presenting us with the past last, the play forces us to dwell on those things which a homogeneous, linear time would have us leave behind. Joyce, who has adopted Marlene's daughter Angie, scrapes by with 'four different cleaning jobs', the sort of employment available to women of her class and education.[21] Their parents, it emerges, were far from the idealized model of surrogate ancestors Marlene establishes in the first scene:

JOYCE: You say Mother had a wasted life.
MARLENE: Yes I do. Married to that bastard.
JOYCE: What sort of life did he have? / Working in the fields like
MARLENE: Violent life?
JOYCE: an animal. / Why wouldn't he want to drink?
MARLENE: Come off it.
JOYCE: You want a drink. He couldn't afford whisky.
MARLENE: I don't want to talk about him.
JOYCE: You started, I was talking about her. She had a rotten life because she had nothing. She went hungry.
MARLENE: She was hungry because he drank the money. / He used to hit her.
JOYCE: It's not all down to him. / Their lives were rubbish.[22]

The historicist, says Benjamin, 'recommends that [historians] blot out everything they know about the later course of history' (Thesis VII). *Top Girls* follows the opposite course. We cannot appreciate the significance of the past, it says, until we have seen into its future. Empathy for the past time is replaced by detachment and thought since the audience already knows what 'will have been'.

The most economical presentation on stage of 'what will have been' is Angie's blue dress. It makes its first appearance in Act Two scene two, in Joyce's backyard: 'ANGIE *comes out. She has changed into an old best dress, slightly small for her.*' Brick in hand, she tells Kit: 'I put on this dress to kill my mother.'[23] At this stage the dress has no special significance. It is only when it appears for the second time, *a year earlier*, that it belatedly makes its impact. Marlene gives it to Angie when she arrives in East Anglia for a visit: 'ANGIE: Thank you very much. Thank you very much, Aunty Marlene. *She opens a present. It is the dress from Act One, new.*'[24] An article of clothing that may have hardly been remarked on when first seen suddenly takes on a retroactive force, charged with all the investments Angie makes in her idealized aunt. For practical purposes of staging there are, of course, *two* dresses: one new, which fits the actress, and one worn, which does not. But even at the level of the narrative there are now two dresses, since historical continuity has been shattered, and we are compelled, once again, to look back to the future in our contemplation of the past.

Citation and montage

> The work has to develop to the highest degree the art of citing without quotation marks. Its theory is intimately related to that of montage. (Walter Benjamin, *The Arcades Project*)[25]

Traditionally, Caryl Churchill has not been associated with Walter Benjamin but with his good friend, Bertolt Brecht.[26] The discontinuities of *Top Girls*, the surprising temporal folds it opens up, can be accounted for in terms of Brecht's recommendations for an epic theatre as well as Benjamin's model of historical materialism. Just as Benjamin was suspicious of linear temporality in history, so Brecht distrusted the linear plot in theatre. The linear plot relied on suspense and therefore enlisted the desire of the spectator to find out what happened next rather than be astonished at what they were seeing right now. Empathy in an audience was as unproductive as empathy in the historian. He therefore proposed a plot that advanced in 'curves', an episodic plot, like the one in *Top Girls*.[27] Instead of continuous action, then, the action is interrupted. To understand the impact of interruption, it is worth turning to one of Brecht's finest commentators, Walter Benjamin:

We may go further here and recall that interruption is one of the fundamental methods of all form-giving. It reaches far beyond the domain of art. It is, to mention just one of its aspects, the origin of quotation. Quoting a text implies interrupting its context. It will readily be understood, therefore, that epic theatre, which depends on interruption, is quotable in a very specific sense.[28]

Benjamin goes on to explain how the actor in epic theatre generates quotable 'gestures'. He is therefore invoking the notion of quotation in a wider sense than the scholarly, textual one. Quotation is, rather, a general principle of composition much like montage, of which Brecht also made use.

It is worth noting that quotation has long been a strategy integral to Caryl Churchill's stagecraft. It has already been mentioned that *Softcops* and an early unperformed play work directly from the texts of Foucault and Fanon. *Light Shining in Buckinghamshire*, Churchill's play about the English Civil War, makes full use of the extant historical documents from that period, quoting directly, for instance, from Abiezer Coppe's *A Fiery Flying Roll* and condensing lengthy parts of the Putney debates. *Vinegar Tom*, meanwhile, in its exploration of witch-hunts, pilfers wholesale from 'a late medieval handbook on witches by Kramer and Sprenger, *Malleus Maleficarum* (*The Hammer of Witches*)'.[29] Of *Fen*, a play set in modern-day East Anglia, Churchill explains: '[it] is a play with more direct quotes of things people have said to us than any other I've written ... The murder story ... was taken from a newspaper cutting ... Most of what the ghost says is taken from a threatening letter written at the time of the Littleport riots.'[30] In *Top Girls*, meanwhile, Pope Joan's long drunken rant in Latin is in fact 'a fragment from Book II of *De Rerum Natura* (*On the Nature of Things*) by Lucretius'.[31] Churchill does not say whether other parts of *Top Girls* are direct quotations like this, but Nijo and Isabella are both writers, and Griselda comes from fiction, so all are subject to citation. And what is Dull Gret if not a sort of quotation in three dimensions of Brueghel's painting? Certainly, in her long outburst at the end of the dinner party nothing she says diverges substantially from the work of art that bears her name.

What implications for history does such constant quotation have? Does it make Churchill's history plays more authoritative or authentic because they are based on original documents? If the quotations

were acknowledged during the course of the play, perhaps; or if
Churchill's purpose were primarily documentary, which it is not.
They rather perform the role of 'interruption' that Benjamin finds at
work in epic theatre. They interrupt the linear flow of history from
which they are extracted because, as Benjamin points out, a quotation is always a *break* from a context. In this sense, history that
proceeds by the montage of quotations – textual and visual – is
unhistoricist. In Thesis III Benjamin gives a special status to such
history by citation: 'only a redeemed mankind receives the fullness
of its past – which is to say, only a redeemed mankind has its past
become citable in all its moments.' In some ways he is here giving
the theoretical justification for the historical method he uses in his
great unfinished history of the Paris arcades of the nineteenth
century, the *Passagen-Werk*, or *Arcades Project*, which consisted in
large part of disparate quotations placed in meaningful relationship
with each other.

Irving Wohlfarth and Sigrid Weigel have both usefully glossed
the meaning of quotation in the Theses and in Benjamin's work in
general. According to Wohlfarth, Benjamin believes his world is an
unredeemed one in which

> quotation stands for a kind of guerrilla warfare with the ruling
> culture, a quasi-anarchistic technique which explodes, and in every
> sense arrests, the continuity of texts, biographies, and periods – a
> continuity which merely reflects the inherited continuity of accumu-
> lated power relations and thereby serves as an ideological justification
> for 'progress' and the status quo. The function of quotation is to
> break up the unified, totalitarian blocks that conformist historio-
> graphy passes out as history.[32]

Quotation achieves the 'tiger's leap into the past' of Thesis XIV and
inaugurates a history of discontinuity, rather than of continuity and
progress. Weigel explains that Benjamin's practice of quotation
should be understood 'in the sense of invoking or summoning up
rather than ... making a scholarly reference' and adds that 'The quotation embodies as it were language as literature, broken out of one
discourse in order, as a fragment, to become part of another, different form of writing.'[33] Quotation is not in and of itself a challenge
to conformist history, but a certain practice of quotation can be, and
Weigel's account neatly illuminates Churchill's method. *Top Girls*,
and many of Churchill's other plays, break their quotations out of

one discursive context, making them into fragments and reordering them into another form of writing or, in this case, *mise-en-scène*. The fact that they are fragments is part and parcel of the project, which has no pretensions to totality but remains tentative and incomplete.

Weigel also sees many affinities between Benjamin's Theses and feminist historiography. It is worth quoting her at length as her comments could have been written directly about *Top Girls*:

> For a history of women – as for all historiography which does not share the perspective of the rulers, of the 'heirs of those who conquered before them' – Benjamin's historico-theoretical reflections offer a productive stimulus, not least because women have few moments or images from their past which they can quote, since in what has been handed down they have been largely 'forgotten' or repressed as subjects ... [M]yths, paintings, and other sources of the imaginary offer to the attentive reader a wealth of correspondences with the experiences and situations of present-day women – as is demonstrated by the quotations from historical and mythical women in those works of contemporary literature whose concern is not to show 'the way it really was', but rather to present literary thought-images, constellations of a female dialectic of enlightenment.[34]

Top Girls takes some of those 'few moments' from the past as part of a critical history which quotes not merely to recuperate or redeem but to question. Churchill does not 'invent' history. *Top Girls* is not entirely ahistoricist: the characters of the dinner party bring with them traces of their original contexts – dress, language, beliefs – that prevent historically different eras from being collapsed into each other. But it is instructive to compare a play like *Top Girls* with other feminist history plays, such as those of Pam Gems. Gems, like Churchill, is interested in famous women from the past, and the titles of her plays – *Piaf*, *Queen Christina*, *Camille* – reflect this. Like Churchill, Gems aims to rewrite the lives of these women from a feminist perspective, brushing away some of the myths that surround them. However, by concentrating on a single woman and locating her in her own era, recreating a context for her more or less, do these plays not encourage a certain empathy in the audience – that sadness so typical of the historicist? If members of the audience are encouraged to empathize with the (rewritten) past, may they not lose sight of 'the constellation which [their] own era has formed with a definite earlier one'?

Notes

1 Harold Pinter, 'Writing for the theatre', in *Plays: One* (London: Methuen, 1976), p. 9. Pinter goes on: 'I'm not an authoritative or reliable commentator on the dramatic scene, the social scene, any scene. I write plays, when I can manage it, and that's all.'

2 Caryl Churchill, *Plays: Two* (London: Methuen, 1990), p. ix.

3 Churchill freely admits quoting directly from theoretical texts, from interviews, from workshops with actors. To show how *Cloud Nine* engaged with contemporary debates about sexuality we need look no further than Clive's exchange about homosexual desire with Harry Bagley, the bisexual explorer: 'HARRY: It's not a sin, it's a disease. CLIVE: A disease more dangerous than diphtheria'. *Cloud Nine* in Caryl Churchill, *Plays: One* (London: Methuen, 1985), p. 283. This is a direct quotation from Jeffrey Weeks, *Coming Out: Homosexual Politics in Britain from the Nineteenth Century to the Present* [1977], rev. edn (London: Quartet Books, 1990), p. 23. Weeks, in his turn, was quoting from the prurient *Gloucester Journal*, circa 1967.

4 Linda Fitzsimmons, ed. *File on Churchill* (London: Methuen, 1989), p. 11.

5 In addition, Jane Thomas has already explored the links between Foucault and Churchill in 'The plays of Caryl Churchill: essays in refusal', in Adrian Page, ed., *The Death of the Playwright* (Basingstoke: Macmillan, 1992), pp. 160–85.

6 Paul Hamilton, *Historicism* (London and New York: Routledge, 1996), p. 2. Emphasis added.

7 Walter Benjamin, 'Theses on the philosophy of history' [1940], in *Illuminations*, ed. Hannah Arendt, trans. Harry Zohn (New York: Shocken Books, 1969), pp. 253–64. Because the Theses are so short and are widely anthologized, references will be made to the number of the thesis quoted rather than page numbers.

8 Slavoj Žižek, *The Sublime Object of Ideology* (London: Verso, 1989), p. 136.

9 Almost everyone who comments on *Top Girls* mentions the overlapping dialogue. One of the most rewarding and far-reaching recent discussions can be found in Lizbeth Goodman, 'Overlapping dialogue in overlapping media: behind the scenes of *Top Girls*', in *Essays on Caryl Churchill: Contemporary Representations*, ed. Sheila Rabillard (Winnipeg and Buffalo: Blizzard Publishing, 1998), pp. 69–101.

10 Caryl Churchill, *Top Girls*, in *Plays: Two* (London: Methuen, 1990), p. 62. In a note on layout Churchill explains: 'when one character starts speaking before another has finished, the point of interruption is marked /' and 'sometimes a speech follows on from a speech earlier than the one immediately before it, and continuity is marked *', p. 52.

11 Goodman, pp. 74–5.

12 Churchill, *Top Girls*, p. 67.

13 Geraldine Cousin, *Churchill: The Playwright* (London: Methuen, 1989), p. 95.

14 Goodman, p. 80.
15 Lisa Merrill, 'Monsters and heroines: Caryl Churchill's women', in *Caryl Churchill: A Casebook*, ed. Phyllis Randall (New York and London: Garland, 1988), p. 83. Harry Lane, 'Secrets as strategies for protection and oppression in *Top Girls*', in *Essays on Caryl Churchill*, ed. Rabillard, p. 63.
16 Janet Brown, 'Caryl Churchill's *Top Girls* catches the next wave', in *Caryl Churchill: A Casebook*, ed. Randall, pp. 127, 120.
17 Brown, p. 128.
18 Lane, p. 63
19 Churchill, *Top Girls*, p. 137.
20 Churchill, *Top Girls*, pp. 137–8.
21 Churchill, *Top Girls*, p. 136.
22 Churchill, *Top Girls*, pp. 138–9.
23 Churchill, *Top Girls*, p. 98.
24 Churchill, *Top Girls*, p. 121.
25 Walter Benjamin, *The Arcades Project*, trans. Howard Eiland and Kevin McLaughlin (Cambridge, MA, and London: Harvard University Press, 1999), p. 458.
26 See, most notably, Elin Diamond, *Unmaking Mimesis: Essays on Feminism and Theater* (London and New York: Routledge, 1997) and Janelle Reinelt, *After Brecht: British Epic Theater* (Ann Arbor: University of Michigan Press, 1994).
27 Bertolt Brecht, *Brecht on Theatre*, trans. & ed. John Willett, 2nd edn (London: Methuen, 1974), p. 37.
28 Walter Benjamin, *Understanding Brecht*, trans. Anna Bostock (London: New Left Books, 1973), p. 19.
29 Cousin, p. 37.
30 Churchill, *Plays: Two*, p. ix.
31 Diamond, p. 89.
32 Irving Wohlfarth, 'On the messianic structure of Walter Benjamin's last reflections', *Glyph* 3 (1978), p. 181.
33 Sigrid Weigel, *Body- and Image-Space: Rereading Walter Benjamin*, trans. G. Paul (London and New York: Routledge, 1996), pp. 13, 38.
34 Weigel, pp. 77–8.

7

Simulacra on Fleet Street – *Pravda* with Baudrillard

We lived once in a world where the realm of the imaginary was governed by the mirror, by dividing one into two, by theatre, by otherness and alienation. Today that realm is the realm of the screen, of interfaces and duplication, of contiguity and networks.

Jean Baudrillard[1]

Operator assistance

Who knows when Jean Baudrillard last went to the theatre? It can't have been very recently. It would be too hard to drag him away from his television set these days. Why bother going to a play, he might protest, in an age when 'there is no longer any such thing as an act or event which is not refracted into a technical image or onto a screen'?[2] Baudrillard is inordinately fond of declaring things obsolete, and the words 'there is no longer' occur alarmingly often in his writings, making him the theorist of 'disappearance'.[3] And there is no denying that theatre and the theatrical are on Baudrillard's disappearance hit-list. Not that he expends much time thinking about theatre (it no longer has the power to 'fascinate' – another favourite Baudrillard term); but, when he does mention it, he invariably does so in a tone of condescension verging on contempt. On this count, theatre is in good company. For instance, in *Simulacra and Simulation* he consigns three illustrious institutions to the historical dustbin in one fell swoop, announcing the end of the power of the university, 'an archaic feudalism ... whose survival is as artificial as that of barracks and theaters'.[4] In a hyperreal universe armies, education and theatres are operating on borrowed time, kept going on life support systems. One suspects that Jean Baudrillard would only be a willing collaborator in the project of this chapter if he were given the role of graveside orator. All this renders improbable, if not impossible, a fruitful encounter between his theories and Howard Brenton and David Hare's *Pravda: A Fleet Street Comedy*.

By now the reader should be familiar with the formula of this book. In each chapter a modern British play is read alongside a theoretical text. It is hoped that in each case the drama has been at least on an equal footing with the theory – that the latter has not been simply 'applied' to the former but that the two have entered into a sort of dialogue. Clearly, with 'Jean Baudrillard meets *Pravda*' this arrangement runs into difficulties. It is not so much that Brenton and Hare's *Pravda* does not share mutual ground with the thinking of postmodernism's most notorious guru. On the contrary, both reflect intensely on the workings and effects of that most modern of phenomena, the mass media. In fact, their diagnoses even overlap substantially. *Pravda* enacts theatrically the dizzying and delirious flight from reference and meaning of the mass media that is analysed so acutely by Baudrillard. It is just that Baudrillard would not see the point of framing the analysis of the culture of simulation within the primitive first-order simulacra of a theatrical performance. In addition, whereas Baudrillard is primarily preoccupied with the mass media as an image-producing machine, *Pravda* focuses on the rather more archaic business of print journalism – the old bourgeois public sphere. Baudrillard has had many provocative things to say about 'the news', things which are more than relevant to *Pravda*, but his insights are for the most part restricted to a world dominated by screens and not ink. Nevertheless, Baudrillard's own preferred medium is still the written word, so perhaps we can forge a tentative, if vexed, relation between this postmodern theorist and *Pravda*.

At this stage another obstacle arises. It has been the method of this book to pair a single, carefully delimited theoretical text with each play. Concentrating on a single text rather than the entire conceptual output of a thinker or movement has helped to focus the argument of each chapter as well as allowing the reader to consult both the theoretical text and the play without facing an enormous burden of reading. I have also adopted this strategy in the conviction that no set of theoretical concepts or methods can be abstracted from the textual forms in which they are articulated. It is not just the dramatic texts that need reading with the help of theory; the theoretical texts must be read as well. When we are forced to examine theoretical texts in detail – to actually *read* them – it is often the case that they do not say unequivocally what we would like them to say; formulas for reading cannot be extracted willy-nilly from what are inevitably complex and regularly contradictory pieces of writing.

Although in each case Freud, Lacan, Althusser and Foucault put forward challenging and coherent theses, I have also felt it necessary to test the limits of those theses at the very level of their inscription. With Baudrillard, though, we come up against a different type of animal.

I have chosen *Simulacra and Simulation* (1981) as the main Baudrillard text for this chapter, but I will be breaking the strict guidelines of this book by also making frequent reference to earlier and later writings within Baudrillard's œuvre, particularly *In the Shadow of the Silent Majorities* (1978) and *The Transparency of Evil* (1990). These texts reflect, respectively, on topics of immediate concern to *Pravda* – the masses and Evil – and I cannot resist quoting them as well. I feel justified in this because, in many ways, Baudrillard's books are not as distinct from each other as other thinkers' are. The same points appear again and again across his writings so that it quickly becomes possible to spot a Baudrillardian refrain. In some cases texts simply repeat previous ones wholesale: for instance, one chapter in *The Transparency of Evil* effectively reproduces a chapter from *Simulacra and Simulation*; and the essay *The Evil Demon of Images* is no more than a cut-and-paste job from *Simulacra and Simulation*, piecing together fragments from various parts of that book.[5] We can consider Baudrillard's work, then, as a sort of continuous text: quote from one part and you could be quoting from any part.[6] In fact, it is the very quotability of Baudrillard that makes him at once so appealing and so frustrating. He proceeds by aphorism rather than argument, shunning systematic analysis and the virtues of proof and counterproof, thetic statements and examples. He favours instead provocative declarations and sweeping generalizations unsupported by convincing empirical evidence ('there is no longer ...') and is therefore more difficult to summarize, and take seriously, than some of the other thinkers dealt with in this book. This is no reason to ignore him, but it does allow me to bend somewhat my rules of engagement.

From truth to simulation

Pravda: A Fleet Street Comedy is a satiric drama in epic style that charts the rise and fall of Andrew May, newspaper editor, and the rise and rise of Lambert Le Roux, newspaper proprietor. It also chronicles a turning-point in the history of British newspapers, some of whose ownership and control passed, in the late 1970s and early 1980s, from the English establishment into foreign hands. The play reserves special spite for the former, but it does not stint at savaging the latter. It dramatizes a struggle on Fleet Street between journalistic truth and fabrication, a struggle that is comprehensively won by the liars; but this is not the whole story. 'Pravda' is the Russian word for 'truth' and was also the name of the main newspaper of the communist Soviet Union. During the Cold War this title was viewed in the West with a good deal of irony since *Pravda* was widely thought to be little more than a propaganda sheet for the Soviet authorities. The existence of the ironically named Soviet organ of news information provided a useful foil for the Western press who, in contrast, could claim editorial freedom, factual reporting and investigative journalism free from political interference. Brenton and Hare challenge this standard conception of the gloriously free press of Western democracies by turning the ironic title *Pravda* on them, implying that great British institutions like *The Times* are not as far removed from their Soviet cousins as they make out.

A series of rhetorically impressive set pieces reinforces the impression that truth ('pravda') and its vicissitudes are at stake in *Pravda*. In a mock showdown on the moors near the end of the play Andrew confronts Le Roux, his erstwhile employer, with the damage that he and his newspapers (the *Victory* and the *Tide*) are doing to the fabric of the nation:

ANDREW: We want to be rid of you. Rid the whole country of you. This perpetual distortion of the truth. It has an effect. It's insidious. This contempt for balance. Facts! Because of you British people's minds are fogging ... clogging ... decaying ... silting up ... with falsehood.

[...]

LE ROUX: (*turns away*) Delusions! Does nobody see? What on earth is all this stuff about the truth? Truth? Why, when everywhere you go people tell lies. In pubs. To each other. To their husbands. To their wives. To the children. To the dying – and thank God they do. No one tells the truth. Why single out newspapers? 'Oh! A special standard!' Everyone can tell lies except for newspapers. They're the universal scapegoat for everybody else's evasions and inadequacies. (*He shouts at the top of his voice.*) It is a totally unworkable view of the world![7]

133

Andrew's faltering liberalism is no match for Le Roux's cynical *Realpolitik*, particularly since he too has been caught lying more than once during the play. At least Le Roux is consistent and has the charm to confess regularly to his ill deeds. He 'comes clean' again in the very last line of the play. Having reinstated Andrew as an editor – on the tabloid *Tide* rather than the broadsheet *Victory* – he stands triumphant in the newsroom and crows 'Welcome to the foundry of lies.'[8] The journalistic ideal of accurately representing daily events has been displaced entirely and the falsifiers have complete control of the printing presses. But how seriously should we take this final scene where villainy triumphs in a melodrama gone wrong? What complexities does the reassuringly simple truth versus lies scenario conceal? In this Machiavellian mode is Le Roux really saying anything terribly disturbing? He will more than likely either confirm the audience's preexisting distrust of newspapers or arouse their outrage at the flaunting of ethical standards in the press. Neither outcome does much to challenge the traditional frameworks within which the news is conceptualized.

In both the 'foundry of lies' statement and the longer one which preceded it there is in fact much to comfort an audience. Le Roux (a loose cipher for the Australian newspaper tycoon Rupert Murdoch, who acquired both *The Times* and the *Sun* in the early 1980s) may currently be the victor, and there may be no signs of his imminent defeat, but at least we know that a clear distinction between truth and lies can still be made because here we have the arch-liar brazenly confessing before us. If we examine more closely his rebuttal to Andrew on the moor, we find him claiming that truth and lies are *contents* independent of the means by which they are communicated. In the same breath, Le Roux compares the lies told in newspapers with those told by wives to husbands, by the healthy to the ill, and he wonders why any special exception should be made for the papers. He thus gives the impression that there is no difference between words whispered in an ear and those printed and read by hundreds of thousands of readers. If we learn anything from the play it is that we must not take this man at his word, and everything in the play suggests that he knows better than this – that there are in fact special rules for newspapers. The most important rule? Marshall McLuhan said it many years ago and Jean Baudrillard has been repeating it ever since: 'The medium IS the message.' It is not so much *what* a newspaper prints (although it can obviously get its facts wrong) but *how* it does so that matters most.

For Baudrillard, the advent of the mass media means that it is no longer always relevant to talk in terms of the 'truth' because this term assumes a 'real' that is more and more de-realized by the endless proliferation of images, messages and information which characterizes consumer society. Baudrillard would instead have us think in terms of *simulation*, perhaps the most notorious term in his lexicon. Simulation can be usefully contrasted with *representation*: whereas representation always implies a thing which is represented – that is, an object antecedent to the representation – simulation takes place without reference to any original. Representation, it follows, can be false or poor; simulation, in contrast, can never be 'unfaithful'. 'Simulation', writes Baudrillard, 'is no longer that of a territory, a referential being, or a substance. It is the generation by models of a real without origin or reality: a hyperreal.'[9] Baudrillard explains further by distinguishing between faking (or pretending) and simulating. If you fake an illness, you simply stay in bed and convince everyone you are ill; the simulator, on the other hand, actually generates some of the *symptoms* of illness.[10] In this way simulation spells at once the end of the real, since it is divorced entirely from any referent, and at the same time moves closer to the real – simulation is a simulation of the real. Simulation is troubling because, ever since Plato, Western philosophy has upheld a distinction between the real and its copy, with the real always given priority. Simulation, on the contrary, is a copy of a copy.

Baudrillard excels at terse summaries of his key concepts. There have been, he claims, four 'phases' of the image, of which simulation is the fourth:

   it is the reflection of a profound reality;
   it masks and denatures a profound reality;
   it masks the *absence* of a profound reality;
   it has no relation to any reality whatsoever: it is its own pure simulacrum.[11]

In terms of journalism the good investigative reporter, the noble and idealistic editor, would have an investment in the first phase of the image. Andrew May rather incoherently accuses Le Roux of subscribing to the second phase, though it is yet to be determined where exactly he does fall – presumably either in the third or

135

the fourth camp. When Baudrillard writes of phases it is not clear whether he means distinct historical periods or overlapping moments. It is also sometimes hard to tell if he thinks that we currently live exclusively in an era of simulacra.

To understand better what Baudrillard means, we can look at what he says about the way the media report on important global events. In the past Baudrillard has raised the ire of commentators by saying that wars have not taken place, or that for all intents and purposes they take place only on television. Is he willfully ignoring the death and mutilation of modern warfare? Yes and no. Contrary to much opinion, Baudrillard is unlikely to deny that people die in wars. His point is that our experience of warfare – and most national and international events – is entirely limited to television and press coverage. This creates a strange effect: we have the impression of intimate knowledge of worldwide conflagrations from the safety of our living-rooms. As he puts it in *The Transparency of Evil*: 'Already, in any case, the filter of screens, photographs, video images and news reporting allows us access only to that which has already been seen by others. We are indeed incapable of apprehending anything that has not already been seen.'[12] Since we rarely, if ever, have access to the real without mediation, it is a short step to the conclusion that in news reporting the images and stories are effectively detached from the real, following their own preprepared models and protocols. It is not that the media 'make up' stories, or fake the news (the occasional exposed 'hoax' story on television serves to reassure us that the rest of it must be 'true'), but that everything happens first on TV:

> What else do the media dream of besides creating the event simply by their presence? Everyone decries it, but everyone is secretly fascinated by this eventuality. Such is the logic of simulacra, it is no longer that of divine predestination, it is that of the precession of models, but it is just as inexorable. And it is because of this that events no longer have meaning: it is not that they are insignificant in themselves, it is that they were preceded by the model, with which their processes only coincided.[13]

Take, for example, the total eclipse of the sun over Britain in August 1999. If there were ever an example of an event of 'divine predestination' which the media cannot create, an eclipse must be it. And yet the media took up the challenge to their supremacy with extraordinary vigour. Not only did television, radio, newspapers and the internet prepare us for weeks in advance for those two minutes of 'totality' but they provided a better view of the spectacle than was available on the ground. Because it was cloudy, and because of the danger of looking directly at the eclipse (such is the power of the real!), the mass media stepped into the breach, generating for us a simulacrum of the event much more impressive than the real thing. Before, during and after the event we were bombarded with endless images – slow-motion, frozen, computer-generated – of the eclipse, such that we experienced a surfeit of the real, or what Baudrillard might call the *hyperreal*. The eclipse was eclipsed by its own blanket coverage: the media managed to blot out the 'once in a lifetime' natural event. Walking into a newsagent the next day one was greeted by the extraordinary sight of the papers then blotting themselves out, for every single one carried an identical photo on its front cover (a 'close-up' of the eclipse taken by a military jet above the clouds), making it impossible to distinguish between the different newspapers.

More real than Disney

Just after sacking Andrew from his editorship at the *Victory*, Lambert Le Roux gives his own version of 'the precession of models' as it applies to his newspapers:

> LE ROUX: I provided the formula. (*He picks up a copy of the Victory.*) It worked in South Africa. Page one, a nice picture of the Prime Minister. Page two, something about actors. Page three, gossip, the veld, what you call the countryside, a rail crash if you're lucky. Four, high technology. Five, sex, sex crimes, court cases. Then it's editorials, then letters. All pleasingly like-minded, all from Kent. Then six pages of sport. Back page, a lot of weather and something nasty about the opposition. There you are. (*He closes the paper.*)[14]

None of the elements in Le Roux's formula are what we would traditionally call lies, but then neither are they what we might call the truth. The elements of repetition and sameness ('all from Kent') put paid to usual notions of accuracy while remaining flexible enough to accommodate and even anticipate chance events – a rail crash, the weather. The newspapers make the news, and not the other way round. Brenton and Hare make this point theatrically as well with the 'Newsvendors', who pass across the stage at the start of scenes shouting out increasingly sensational headlines:

FIRST NEWSVENDOR: HEADLESS MURDER CASE: WHOSE HEAD IS IT?

SECOND: SEX TUTOR SAYS 'SHE LOVED ME'.

THIRD: TWELVE GO-GO DANCERS FOUND IN CRATE AT HEATHROW: TWELVE EXCLU-SIVES.[15]

In each case the headlines loudly proclaim an astonishing uniqueness – a detached head, a teacher's confession, *twelve* exclusives. And yet this is only the simulacrum of the exceptional because the stories are effectively all the *same*. We can easily distinguish the endlessly repeated categories they fall into – sex scandal, sex crimes, shocking violence. They all refer back to an internal code rather than pointing to any real external event, a fact that is reinforced by the tautological nature of the headlines themselves. One of the favourite such simulacra in the British press is of course reporting on the royal family, a phenomenon that is captured perfectly by the headline 'ROYAL HAIR-DO. CUT OUT AND KEEP'.[16] Each photo of a princess or duke does not so much refer to a real blue-blood as to an endless sequence of similar photos printed on a daily basis; the cut out and keep royal hair-do is a logical step whereby the simulacrum becomes an artefact in its own right. In possibly the best joke in the entire play, Le Roux rubbishes the lamentable former editor of the *Victory* with the line: 'He's a fool. A joke. Mickey Mouse has a Fruit-Norton watch.'[17] To wear a Mickey Mouse watch is to display a lack of seriousness, a capitulation to the world of simulation by transposing this creature of pure simulation, reproduced everywhere and endlessly, on to the real world of temporality, a watch. The joke, then, is a sort of *mise-en-abyme* of simulation, where Mickey Mouse can also wear a watch and a supposedly real person appears on its face, arms turning mechanically to keep Mickey on time. Disney is often invoked as the finest case of a self-sufficient world removed from the real, and Brenton and Hare exploit these associations again later. Andrew thinks he has uncovered a dark past for Le Roux and exposes him in the pages of the *Usurper*, his new rival newspaper,

138

only to discover that Le Roux has himself simulated the scandal. The 'legal deposition' attesting to Le Roux's crimes is signed by the South African, Donald Eende. 'Eende' is Afrikaans for duck.[18]

In the face of the dominance of models and simulacra, it is understandable if we feel a little anxiety, a touch of nostalgia for the real and for meaning. Two potential responses are articulated by Andrew May. Alone on the moor with Le Roux, he pitifully laments the loss of his metaphysical moorings: 'I just cling to this idea of the language. That a sentence means something. I hang on to the sentence.'[19] It is a plea for a depth in journalism to which he never had access in the first place. This is clear from the moment Le Roux cursorily examines the first paper Andrew edits for him, the *Leicester Bystander*. He does so without actually reading: '*He steps forward, feet apart, holding the paper at arm's length. He looks at the front page, turns it, looks at the back page, not reading and hands it back to* ANDREW.'[20] The mass media generate images and information that appear and disappear with equal rapidity and do not allow for the slower processes of reading and reflection. Le Roux treats the newspaper almost as if it were a television, where speed is everything. The second option is taken up by Andrew at the end of the play when he throws himself into his new position as editor of the *Daily Tide* by judging the 'big tits competition'. Like royal hair-dos, the breasts in newspapers are part of an endless sequence of such images, effectively detached from the real. It is at this very moment that criteria of 'authenticity' are ironically reintroduced. Displaying an extraordinary zeal for a real rendered frivolous, Andrew's predecessor, Hannon Spot, informs him: 'We're on the look-out for silicon fraud [...] At this job you get good at spotting a fraudulent tit.'[21] The journalist's traditional fact-checking is thereby reduced to policing implants.

It is hard to tell whether Brenton and Hare hold out any hope for the great British institution of Fleet Street so overrun by simulacra. There are indications that their concerns go beyond exposing the wild formulaic spectacle that newspapers have become. By staging the process of production of a single story about a peace camp, *Pravda* signals that there is still a profound reality that is being masked and denatured by its mis-representation (Baudrillard's second phase of the image, what we might also call the ideological). An idealistic young reporter, Larry Punt, submits a story about the brutal treatment of women in a peace camp by policemen. We are lead to believe that this is a case of a good image in the sense that it faithfully reflects a profound reality (first phase of the image). However, the story undergoes a transformation at the hands of the night editor, Doug Fantom, who judiciously edits the piece, making it look as if the women provoked the police, caused the violence themselves, were scum to begin with, and so on. Fantom does not suppress the story; he simply changes its inflection through deft rhetorical manipulation.[22] One of the dictionary definitions of 'simulacrum' is 'a phantom', and the 'night' editor's name signals that he is a sort of ghost-writer. Ghosts, phantoms and shadows have had a bad name in Western theories of representation ever since Plato. The Greek philosopher imagined humans trapped in a cave filled only with shadows, and he called on us to make our way out of the cave and into the sunlight to look at actual things, to grasp them directly rather than through the mediation of these shadows.[23] By making Fantom the villain here, *Pravda* appears to reassert an age-old prejudice against simulacra and, by association, all the mass media, which are only so many phantoms. But then theatre, which on and off through history has been attacked for its own artificiality, needs to defend itself, as a first-order simulacrum, against the incursions of simulacra of a higher order.

Theatre – for or against technology?

Baudrillard elaborates thus his schema of first-, second- and third-order simulacra:

> The *operatic* (the theatrical status of theatrical and fantastical machinery, the 'grand opera' of technique) ... corresponds to the first order, the *operative* (the industrial, productive status, productive of power and energy) ... corresponds to the second order, and the *operational* (the cybernetic, aleatory, uncertain status of 'metatechnique') ... corresponds to the third order ... only the last order can still truly interest us.[24]

The first order is the era of dramaturgy and the stage, the second of the factory and the printing press and the third of the screen and the electronic circuit. Baudrillard implies that the second and third make the first redundant, or at least anachronistic. At a purely material level it is true that modern theatre has a task on its hands in competing with the enormous productive capacity of commodity culture and the endless dissemination of images and sounds carried out by the mass media. In response, the strategy of *Pravda* is to distance itself from mass forms through satire, with little hope held out for a positive recuperation of Fleet Street. It was not always like this with theatre from the left. In fact, epic theatre, of which *Pravda* is a late example, originally embraced the new aesthetic forms that came with the advent of the age of mechanical production.

The German director Erwin Piscator is often credited with initiating the theatrical technique about which Brecht later theorized at length as the epic theatre. Piscator felt that in the early twentieth century theatre was stagnating because it lagged so far behind the industrial and technological developments of the time: 'With the exception of the revolving stage and electric light the stage at the beginning of the twentieth century was still in the same position that Shakespeare had left it in.'[25] He did not advocate technical innovations for their own sake, but he did argue that the theatre must catch up:

> It is not mere chance that in an age whose technical achievements tower above its achievements in every other field the stage should become highly technical ... Intellectual and social revolutions have always been closely bound up with technical upheavals. And a change in the function of the theatre was inconceivable without bringing the stage equipment technically up to date.[26]

In the 1920s, in Berlin, Piscator put this theory into practice by combining stage action with the projection of slides and filmstrips of historical material. Thus, second-order simulacra were brought into alliance with theatre in a montage style unlike anything seen before. The legacy of Piscator can be found in *Pravda* with its episodic structure and its juxtaposition of theatrical levels (from the newsvendors shouting headlines to the instant TV press conferences to the dog-track commentator and the mock advertisement for the *Daily Tide*). Like Piscator's theatre, *Pravda* was also almost prohibitively expensive to put on, largely due to the huge cast of characters. Nevertheless, some time between the 1920s and the 1980s, between the age of mechanical reproduction and the age of electronic transmission, optimism about technological advances was replaced by profound distrust.

Pravda has an even more specific theatrical antecedent than the epic theatre of Piscator. In the United States in the 1930s a unit of

141

the Federal Theatre Project, a state-funded organization, produced six 'Living Newspapers'. Using documentary sources and techniques of reportage, the didactic Living Newspapers brought to audiences information about social issues ranging from the war in Abyssinia to federal housing policy and farming conditions. Perhaps the best-known British equivalent is Theatre Union's *Last Edition*, a 'living newspaper' scripted by Joan Littlewood and Ewan MacColl. Using a narrator figure something like a modern-day newsreader, *Last Edition* dramatized events such as the Gresford pit disaster, the Anglo-German naval agreement, the Spanish Civil War and the Munich Pact.[27] A character called 'newsboy' fulfills the function of the newsvendors in *Pravda*, shouting out headlines. This character first appeared in *Newsboy*, an adaptation of a New York play by the Workers' Theatre Movement. Already in 1933 we can see the model for Brenton and Hare's newsvendors:

> As the play opens the Newsboy, who represents the establishment bourgeois newspapers, stands in the amber spot and shouts in staccato fashion.

> NEWSBOY: News Chronicle Empire (*repeat*). Plans for royal Jubilee. SIX KINGS AT ROYAL WEDDING. CUP FINAL LATEST.[28]

As the sketch progresses other voices intervene and contest the banalities of the newsboy's headlines, offering instead news about workers being laid off, exploitation of Indian labour and so on. In some ways, then, nothing has changed between the 'newsboy' of 1933, representative of the bourgeoisie, and the grotesque news-vendors of *Pravda* shouting tittle-tattle about a simulated royalty. But while *Pravda* is uniformly convinced of the poisonous nature of news reporting, these earlier documentary theatres maintained a more ambivalent stance, recognizing the ideological function of newspapers and yet at the same time holding out hope for the counterideological features of the news.

Just as Piscator believed that the theatre must accommodate modern technological advances or risk becoming anachronistic, the creators of documentary theatre felt it essential to incorporate the staccato, quick-fire information-delivery techniques of the mass press in order to capture the imagination of new audiences raised on such methods. Critical distance could still be maintained – as in this scene from *Newsboy*, which questions the deadening sameness of the popular press:

VOICE: Don't you get tired, Newsboy, shouting all the time about

CHAR. GENT: Hold ups

YOUNG LADY: And divorces

ALL: AND DUCHESSES IN GAMBLING DENS![29]

However, the popular press did not just have to be an organ of mystification, a means to stupefy the masses. It was also a wonderful weapon for distributing information about oppression to the very masses that were being exploited. In other words, at this stage newspapers were still seen to have a pedagogic value in disseminating images belonging to Baudrillard's first phase. The news could transparently convey a reality about world politics or working-class exploitation that simply needed to be revealed. *Last Edition* and *Newsboy* trod a fine line between suspicion of the products of mass culture and enthusiasm for these new tools. In the process they forged a new theatrical style, which is a synthesis of older methods and new media. *Pravda* carries on this tradition of mixed-media performance, but one cannot help thinking that it is with a certain reluctance and dismay.

A major change took place on the left between the inter-war period of documentary theatre and the late twentieth-century moment of *Pravda*. In the 1920s the masses were seen as a potentially revolutionary force, a great energy waiting to explode. Consequently, mass culture was also potentially a revolutionary tool. Here is Piscator again: 'It is no longer the private, personal fate of the individual, but the times and fate of the masses that are the heroic factors in the new drama.'[30] Where are these heroic masses in *Pravda*? The newspaper readership is silent and nowhere to be seen, and the single representative of this mute public is Moira Patterson, owner of a health-food shop. She has been wrongly identified in the *Bystander* as the mother of a cocaine dealer and her business is suffering. She asks for a retraction, but Andrew brushes her aside. Michael Quince, MP, at one time Le Roux's man in parliament, paints a sorry picture of the lot of the public after he is deposed from his position of influence: 'I'll never appear again on "Speak or Shut Up". I have to sit at home shouting at the television like ordinary people.'[31] As for the audiences of *Pravda* itself, they were hardly the surging masses of Piscator's imagination. The play enjoyed a long and successful run at the National Theatre, much to the dismay of some of Brenton and Hare's critics on the left. As Carol Homden remarks, the ideal audience was composed of media insiders: 'One reason for *Pravda*'s undoubted success on the media-oriented South Bank was precisely the fun audiences could take in matching up the real events to the stage caricatures.'[32] She goes on to roundly condemn the overall direction of the play: '*Pravda* may be about a political phenomenon but became a conceited comedy for the theatre-going elite.'[33]

Homden's disapproval of *Pravda* is based on the desire to make productive use of images. Baudrillard is dismissive of such desires:

> we all remain incredibly naïve: we always look for a good usage of the image, that is to say a moral, meaningful, pedagogic or informational usage, without seeing that the image in a sense revolts against this good usage, that it is the conductor neither of meaning nor good intentions, but on the contrary an implosion, a denegation of meaning.[34]

With an optimistic view of the masses, documentary theatre still believed in the pedagogic value of the representations they were producing, an optimism that has all but disappeared with Brenton and Hare. These two in fact come closer to Baudrillard's position on the masses. He claims that the masses are usually imagined as either passive and stupefied or as wildly energetic, when in fact they are silent, indifferent, imploded.[35] Through opinion polls, elections and statistical surveys the silent majorities are urged to speak and express themselves, but they remain sullenly unresponsive. Perversely, Baudrillard argues that the power of the masses lies in their very refusal to participate: 'the masses scandalously resist this imperative of rational communication. They are given meaning: they want spectacle. No effort has been able to convert them to the seriousness of the content, nor even to the seriousness of the code.'[36] If anything, *Pravda* subscribes to a notion of the brute stupidity of the masses, whose appetite for idiotic stories about sex, violence and royalty seems bottomless. But we can only hazard a guess that this may be the play's stance because Brenton and Hare give no direct clues on where they stand. *Pravda* focuses almost exclusively on media insiders, and the notable absence of the reading masses indicates an inability or unwillingness to account for this silent thing.

Heaven and hell

The media is the devil.

Bob Dylan

As Dominic Strinati has demonstrated, the advances of mass culture in the twentieth century have invariably been associated with 'Americanisation':

Because mass culture is thought to arise from the mass production and consumption of cultural commodities, it is relatively easy to identify America as the home of mass culture since it is the capitalist society most closely associated with these processes. So much mass culture comes from America that if it is perceived as a threat then Americanisation becomes a threat as well. For critics of mass culture this represents a threat not just to aesthetic standards and cultural values, but to national culture itself.[37]

Baudrillard goes along with this thesis for the most part: a large proportion of his examples of the culture of simulation are American and he has dedicated an entire book to the United States.[38] Of course, he does not see the advance of American mass culture as a threat so much as an inevitability. That American culture lurks somewhere behind the simulating world of Fleet Street is implied by the Disney motif in *Pravda*. More to the point, the play starts with Rebecca's return from America, where there were 'Too many dazzling salads'.[39] In what can be nothing but a pastiche, in the opening lines she soliloquizes about an English rural idyll holding out against globalization: 'The low green English countryside unchanged. In the village church always fresh flowers on the altar. On the village green late in the season, the wicket taking spin.'[40] She asks Andrew in the same scene whether he has been to America, and he confesses that he fears he would be seduced by it. Instead he is seduced by the advance of American culture as it manifests itself in the newsroom of major newspapers.

There are no American characters in *Pravda*, but if Americanization is intimately linked with the process known as 'globalization' – international capitalism extending everywhere and making borders more porous and national identities less secure – then America has left its mark on the play. The wicket taking spin and the old-school tie are shown to be defenseless against the international partnership of a ruthless South African entrepreneur and his plain-talking Australian henchman, Eaton Sylvester. As Howard Brenton made clear in an interview, the writers' intent was not to scapegoat former colonies for the decline of Britain: 'We loved the satirical offence of these two characters from the edge of our colonial past, turning up and taking over the country. The satire's not against Australia, it's against Britain.'[41] Indeed, the British characters are made to look incompetent and antiquated in comparison with the vigorous post-colonials. But as much as Le Roux is marked by his South African identity, he is above all a transnational phenomenon. The audience first encounters him alone on an empty stage waxing poetic about the unique South African landscape, but we quickly see that he can take or leave his national identity as his global financial interests are revealed: he now stands in '*a huge featureless exhibition hall*' and a large banner unfurls overhead to read '*SPORTSWEAR INTERNATIONAL – WELCOME TO FRANKFURT*'.[42] His ability to move as freely as international capital is further demonstrated when he purchases a British passport to expedite his acquisition of the up-market *Victory*.

The ease with which Le Roux and his money cross borders, and the facility with which he sweeps away any resistance he encounters, make him a sinister, almost demonic force. By all accounts, Anthony Hopkins' *tour de force* in rendering this part in the original National Theatre production only added to the effect. Just imagine Hopkins warming up for the role of Hannibal Lecter in *The Silence of the Lambs* (1991) and you may get a sense of Lambert Le Roux on stage. Indeed, like Lecter, that strange phenomenon of recent horror movies – the monster whom audiences adore – Le Roux is a villain who is easily the most charismatic character on stage. He certainly gets all the best lines, from the Mickey Mouse joke to his extraordinary performance in sacking half the staff of the *Victory* at the close of Act One. Other characters find him charming in spite of the terror he inspires, and even though, as Eaton Sylvester puts it, 'He's totally without morality'.[43] It is implied that he has blood on his hands from a past in South Africa, and fascist tendencies are intimated by his fondness for Leni Riefenstahl movies. Embodying the principle of evil, he remains the dynamic focal point of the play and the source of its manic energy. This is mildly surprising, it must be stated, in a play from two prominent left-wing playwrights.

Pravda, National Theatre 1986. Anthony Hopkins as Lambert Le Roux.

Commentators on the play have been quick to identify Le Roux as a uniquely malevolent force. Robert Wilcher claims that *Pravda* is a medieval morality play for the 1980s and that Le Roux is a vice or devil-figure tempting Everyman Andrew May into damnation.[44] Christopher Innes traces Le Roux's pedigree to a more recent dramatic tradition: '[he] belongs to nineteenth-century melodrama. Unredeemably evil, he is also omnipotent.'[45] Richard Boon, meanwhile, registers a distinct ambivalence towards the arch-villain, finding him 'by turns attractive, appalling, seductive, and terrifying'.[46] In by far the most complete analysis, Carol Homden claims that Le Roux is connected to both Hitler and Shakespeare's Richard III. She observes that by making Le Roux South African, Brenton and Hare ensure that his accent alone carries with it a whole set of negative associations: 'the charges of state violence, oppression of the majority, racism and self-seeking capitalism of the apartheid regime'.[47] The white South African accent may have been rehabilitated somewhat in a post-apartheid era, but at the peak of protest against the regime in the mid-1980s Brenton and Hare could be assured of an additional *frisson* of fear and loathing every time their hero-villain opened his mouth.

The consensus, then, is that *Pravda* gives a starring role to evil. In the same interview Brenton himself admitted as much:

> As we got into it, *Pravda* began not to be about Fleet Street, but about the nature of evil. 'Evil' is a difficult subject for a paid-up atheist. We wrote about the sheer power of a strong entrepreneur and what people call his 'charm' – 'the charm of Hitler'.[48]

Brenton puts his finger on the problem of Le Roux when he says that evil is 'a difficult subject for a paid-up atheist'. What is such an archaic dramatic device doing in a left-wing play? Should *Pravda* not be analysing the material basis of the power of newspapers rather than attributing their malign cultural influence to some transcendent force? Such has been the gist of the many criticisms levelled at the play. One early reviewer warns that 'An uneasy respect for the glamour of the rapist emerges' (but then paradoxically proceeds to praise to the skies Hopkins' 'virtuoso performance'.)[49] Homden is equally disapproving: 'by failing to show just how the rise is/was resistible, he ... inevitably becomes the hero ... not only do they give a major platform to what they would oppose, but they further naturalise that phenomenon ... Le Roux stopped being the embodiment of bare-toothed capitalism and became instead an eternal universal force against which there is no recourse.'[50] Homden's critique is at least as old as the beginnings of modern British political drama. George Bernard Shaw disdained the melodrama of the nineteenth century for summoning up categories of transcendent vice and virtue that masked the underlying economic and social basis of dramatic situations. Blaming capitalism and not individual capitalists for the world's inequities, he proposed a stage realism that did without heros and villains. His injunction has been followed fairly closely among political playwrights in the twentieth century, with the possible exception of the cartoon sketches of agit-prop. *Pravda* dispenses pretty much with virtue but boldly resurrects in Lambert Le Roux the wicked capitalist.

It is peculiar how easy critics find it to spot evil while at the same time declaring the category obsolete. Indeed, evil is so much a product of a religious world-view that it is difficult to discuss it in a secular society, as Brenton, the 'paid-up atheist', acknowledges. While most of us think of evil as the residue of an outdated mode of thinking, and therefore find it somewhat out of place in a modern play, Jean Baudrillard has consistently analysed evil as a very modern phenomenon. He does not advocate a return to pre-modern belief systems where good could once again be distinguished from bad in the return of normative value systems. He suggests, though, that in the West the loss of the category of evil has had its consequences: 'We have become very weak in terms of Satanic, ironic, polemical and antagonistic energy; our societies have become fanatically soft ... hunting down all of the accursed share in ourselves and allowing only positive values free rein.'[51] The implication is that secularism appeared to banish good–evil distinctions but really only got rid of evil while clinging to a positive notion of the good. Elsewhere, Baudrillard reflects on the dominance of the Good in Western thinking on representation:

> Metaphysics allows only the good radiations to filter through; it wants to make the world a mirror of the subject ... a world of forms distinct from its double, from its shadow, from its image: that is the principle of Good. Here the object is always the fetish, the false, the *feticho*, the factitious, the delusion – all that embodies the abominable integration of a thing and its magical and artificial double ... this is the principle of Evil.[52]

This definition of evil is useful for understanding how Lambert Le Roux functions in *Pravda*. He too is unconcerned with true images and merrily mimics the language of Good. For instance, at the end of the savage series of sackings at the *Victory* he says 'Let's make a good, a lovely paper, a family paper full of love.'[53] Again, at the end, he apes the rhetoric of virtue when Andrew comes to work for him again: 'There is more rejoicing in heaven over the one who returns to me than there is over the ten thousand lazy bastards who are loyal.'[54] This is not irony in the smug, knowing English sense, but in Baudrillard's sense of Evil mockingly dressing itself up as the Good.

There is no doubt that the false, that delusion, can be seductive. Equally, we can always count on the moralists to condemn seduction. But does seduction care if it is condemned? As Baudrillard points out, the good assumes a dialectic between good and evil, while evil refuses such fair play:

> Evil consists in the negation of this dialectic, in a radical dissociation of Good and Evil, and by extension in the autonomy of the principle of Evil ... Evil is founded on itself alone, in pure incompatibility. Evil is thus master of the game, and it is the principle of Evil, the reign of eternal antagonism, that must eventually carry off the victory.[55]

It is easy enough to condemn the likes of Lambert Le Roux, but the point that *Pravda* seems to make is that this is only so much water off a duck's back. It is all fine and well to take the moral high ground against the arch-simulator, but it will not get us very far. Simulacra are untroubled by the moral high ground, and simulation carries on regardless of the protestations of the Good. Instead of censuring Brenton and Hare for making Le Roux glamorous, perhaps they are to be congratulated for correctly characterizing the master of newspaper simulation as the embodiment of evil. Finally, it is also appropriate that Anthony Hopkins, who so ably acted the demonic South African, went on to win an Oscar for *The Silence of the Lambs*. The Academy, the guardian at the gate of Simulation Central, was right to see in Hopkins' depiction of a serial killer just the sort of evil it is after. The serial killer, just like Le Roux, makes no distinction or attribution of value and copies the same act over and over without concern for its origin.

Notes

1 Jean Baudrillard, *The Transparency of Evil: Essays on Extreme Phenomena*, trans. James Benedict (London and New York: Verso, 1993 [1990]), p. 54.
2 Baudrillard, *Transparency of Evil*, p. 57.
3 This designation comes from Zygmunt Bauman in his chapter on Baudrillard in *Intimations of Postmodernity* (London: Routledge, 1992).
4 Jean Baudrillard, *Simulacra and Simulation*, trans. Sheila Faria Glaser (Ann Arbor: Michigan University Press, 1994 [1981]), p. 149.
5 Jean Baudrillard, *The Evil Demon of Images*, trans. Paul Patton and Paul Foss (Annadale: Power Institute, 1987). There is no direct French equivalent for this text, but it serves to demonstrate how easily Baudrillard's writings can be combined and recombined and still be intelligible – undoubtedly a function of their aphoristic quality.
6 To be more precise, it is normal to divide Baudrillard's output into two periods. In the first, which includes *The System of Objects* (1968), *The Consumer Society* (1970) and *The Mirror of Production* (1973), Baudrillard carries out a systematic analysis of consumer society and a thoroughgoing critique of traditional Marxism. The second phase, which I am drawing on here, starts around 1976 with *Symbolic Exchange and Death*. This periodization is made by Douglas Kellner in *Jean Baudrillard: From Marxism to Post-Modernism and Beyond* (Cambridge: Polity, 1989).
7 Howard Brenton and David Hare, *Pravda: A Fleet Street Comedy* (London: Methuen, 1986), pp. 103–4. I am using the readily available revised version of the play from the second production in 1986 rather than the edition of 1985, which reflects the original production.
8 Brenton and Hare, *Pravda*, p. 113.
9 Baudrillard, *Simulacra and Simulation*, p. 1.
10 Baudrillard, *Simulacra and Simulation*, p. 3.
11 Baudrillard, *Simulacra and Simulation*, p. 6.
12 Baudrillard, *Transparency of Evil*, p. 167.
13 Baudrillard, *Simulacra and Simulation*, pp. 55–6.
14 Brenton and Hare, *Pravda*, p. 76.
15 Brenton and Hare, *Pravda*, p. 10.
16 Brenton and Hare, *Pravda*, p. 11.
17 Brenton and Hare, *Pravda*, p. 102. Appropriately, Brenton and Hare got this joke from the political editor of the *Daily Mirror*. Howard Brenton, 'Writing for democratic laughter', *Drama* 157 (1985), p. 11.
18 Brenton and Hare, *Pravda*, p. 105. Baudrillard on Disney: 'Disneyland exists in order to hide that it is the "real" country, all of "real" America that *is* Disneyland', *Simulacra and Simulation*, p. 12.
19 Brenton and Hare, *Pravda*, p. 108.
20 Brenton and Hare, *Pravda*, p. 40.
21 Brenton and Hare, *Pravda*, p. 112.
22 Brenton and Hare, *Pravda*, pp. 60–2.
23 In Book 7 of *The Republic*, trans. G. M. A. Grube (Indianapolis: Hackett Publishing Co., 1974), pp. 183–4.

24 Baudrillard, *Simulacra and Simulation*, p. 127.

25 Erwin Piscator, 'Basic principles of a theory of sociological drama' (1929) in Richard Drain, ed., *Twentieth-Century Theatre: A Sourcebook* (London: Routledge, 1995), p. 103.

26 Piscator, 'Theory of sociological drama', p. 103.

27 Joan Littlewood and Ewan MacColl, *Last Edition*, in Howard Goorney and Ewan MacColl, eds, *Agit-Prop to Theatre Workshop: Political Playscripts 1930–50* (Manchester: Manchester University Press, 1986), pp. 21–33.

28 *Newsboy* in *Agit-Prop to Theatre Workshop*, p. 14.

29 *Newsboy*, p. 15.

30 Piscator, 'Theory of sociological drama', p. 102.

31 Brenton and Hare, *Pravda*, p. 97.

32 Carol Homden, *The Plays of David Hare* (Cambridge: Cambridge University Press, 1995), p. 88.

33 Homden, *Plays of David Hare*, p. 99.

34 Baudrillard, *The Evil Demon of Images*, p. 23.

35 Jean Baudrillard, *In the Shadow of the Silent Majorities* (New York: Semiotext(e), 1983), pp. 2–4.

36 Baudrillard, *Silent Majorities*, p. 10.

37 Dominic Strinati, *An Introduction to Theories of Popular Culture* (London: Routledge, 1995), p. 22.

38 Jean Baudrillard, *America*, trans. Chris Turner (London: Verso, 1988 [1986])

39 Brenton and Hare, *Pravda*, p. 10.

40 Brenton and Hare, *Pravda*, p. 9.

41 Howard Brenton (interview), 'The red theatre under the bed', *New Theatre Quarterly* 11 (1987), p. 196. He also says in this interview, 'I like stories about world citizenry … I want to crack open English insularity.' p. 195.

42 Brenton and Hare, *Pravda*, p. 27.

43 Brenton and Hare, *Pravda*, p. 97.

44 Robert Wilcher, '*Pravda*: a morality play for the 1980s', *Modern Drama* 33 (1990), pp. 42–56.

45 Christopher Innes, *Modern British Drama 1890–1990* (Cambridge: Cambridge University Press, 1992), p. 211.

46 Richard Boon, *Brenton: The Playwright* (London: Methuen, 1991), p. 253.

47 Homden, *Plays of David Hare*, p. 89.

48 Brenton, 'Red theatre under the bed', p. 196.

49 Michael Ratcliffe, 'London: press gang', *Drama* 157 (1985), pp. 32 and 33.

50 Homden, *Plays of David Hare*, pp. 96–7.

51 Baudrillard, *Transparency of Evil*, p. 82.

52 Jean Baudrillard, 'Fatal strategies', in *Jean Baudrillard: Selected Writings*, ed. Mark Poster (Cambridge: Polity, 1988), p. 200.

53 Brenton and Hare, *Pravda*, p. 59.

54 Brenton and Hare, *Pravda*, p. 111.

55 Baudrillard, *Transparency of Evil*, p. 139.

8

Culture and colonies – Wertenbaker with Said

Culture in Botany Bay

In the late nineteenth century, when the British, French, Belgian and German empires were at their height, 'imperialism' was by and large considered a positive global force, at least by those who controlled the empires. Aside from the obvious material gain derived from empires and their strategic value in world politics, it was generally considered by the imperialists that the work of empire was carried out for the good of the subject peoples, the natives of lands far from the metropolitan centre. The French called this their *mission civilisatrice*. Imperialism was not thought of as an unjust exploitation of people and territory but as a bold and brave project. In the early twenty-first century, some forty to fifty years after the final dismantling of the last European empires, in what is known as the post-colonial period, it is rare indeed to find anyone extolling the virtues of imperialism. With the exception of the most conservative of commentators, Europe's imperial past is now viewed as an indication not of its civilization but of its barbarism. In retrospect, the brutalities carried out in the name of imperialism in the eighteenth and nineteenth centuries are seen to prefigure the massive violence wrought by the Western world in the bloody twentieth century. This does not mean, however, that imperialism has somehow come to an end. On the contrary, it continues on a regular basis – most notably in the various interventions of Western powers in the nations of the 'Third World', as well as the Middle East. In the name of democracy and liberty, the United States in particular has, since World War II, protected its economic interests in countless regions far from its shores. The difference lies in nomenclature. Call these interventions by their dirty name – imperialism – and great protestations rise up on all sides, denying that modern economic imperialism bears any resemblance to the colonial imperialism of the past.

Whether or not imperialism carries on by another name is a much debated issue. Certainly, the old name and the practices it implies have been thoroughly discredited. As a result, there has been for some time now a reassessment of all aspects of Europe's imperial past, with the emphasis not on the glories of empire but on its devastating effects. Timberlake Wertenbaker's *Our Country's Good* is one instance of this general trend. It takes as its subject the foundation of modern Australia. Until relatively recently the exact facts about this foundation have often been obscured both by the British, who established the convict colony in New South Wales, and by latter-day Australians, the ultimate beneficiaries of the initial settlement. The British, understandably, would prefer to forget that they treated a whole group of largely petty criminals as a form of human waste to be shipped under appalling conditions to the far side of the earth; Australians, meanwhile, have spent a large part of their modern history trying to erase the 'convict stain' of their past which forever shadows their modern, law-abiding lives. Robert Hughes, historian of the system of convict transportation, describes a sort of collective amnesia, even in the 1970s:

> An unstated bias rooted deep in Australian life seemed to wish that 'real' Australian history had begun with Australian respectability – with the flood of money from gold and wool, the opening of the continent, the creation of an Australian middle class. Behind the bright diorama of Australia Felix lurked the convicts, some 160,000 of them, clanking their fetters in the penumbral darkness.[1]

The task of a post-colonial history, then, is to excavate the aspects of empire which, repressed by subsequent respectability, have been plunged into 'penumbral darkness'.

The First Fleet of convicts and their jailers landed at Botany Bay in 1788 after a harrowing journey of eight months. In 1988 Australia celebrated its bicentennial, but since it is difficult to celebrate the 'dumping' of thousands of criminals or the devastation of an indigenous population, the history of transportation and the treatment of Australian Aborigines were mentioned as little as possible. Naturally, Aborigine groups protested against the celebrations; and, in the lead up to the anniversary, several critics, historians and artists set out to memorialize the less than savoury aspects of Australia's convict past in the spirit of remembering rather than occluding colonial history. Robert Hughes' *The Fatal Shore* and Paul Carter's *The Road to*

Botany Bay, published in 1986 and 1988, respectively, were central to the rethinking of imperial history at a moment when attempts were being made to celebrate Australia's founding in an uncritical fashion.[2] Thomas Keneally's novel *The Playmaker* (1987) also contributed, on a fictional level, to the critical re-examination of Australia's past.[3] Keneally builds his story around the fact that the first play produced in colonial Australia, George Farquhar's *The Recruiting Officer*, was performed by an all-convict cast in 1789. Drawing on cultural history and populating the play with real figures from early Sydney, Keneally scrutinizes the social and sexual politics of the colony in a work of what Linda Hutcheon might call historiographical metafiction.[4] Wertenbaker's play, *Our Country's Good*, was commissioned by the Royal Court Theatre as an adaptation of Keneally's novel. It therefore shares with that novel a desire to shed light on the 'penumbral darkness' of early Australian history. And since it was first performed in 1988, it coincided neatly with the bicentennial celebrations.

Like the histories which inform them, the novel and the play pull no punches when it comes to detailing the manner in which the British treated their own in the late eighteenth century. What distinguishes *The Playmaker* and *Our Country's Good* from historical works like *The Fatal Shore* is, of course, the freedom of fiction. From within that freedom these two works of imagination exhibit an intense concern with the status of culture – in the shape of Farquhar's play – in a place presumably far removed from civilization. They are not just historical accounts of a moment of imperialism, but they ask, what is the relationship between the *culture* of the metropolitan European power and its imperial activities on a distant shore? While it is hardly controversial any more to be critical of imperialism, it is another matter when it comes to the link between culture and imperialism. Can a novel or a play actually *participate* in the processes of imperialism? What is the nature of that participation? Or do the unpalatable day-to-day workings of empire have nothing at all to do with the productions of high culture? Should we divorce the one entirely from the other? These are precisely the sort of questions Edward Said asks in *Culture and Imperialism*. His answer is unequivocal: the process of dissociating culture and imperialism has gone on too long and the intimate connections between the two must finally be acknowledged.

155

Said and Wertenbaker, then, share an interest in culture *and* imperialism; indeed, their understandings of both terms are quite close to each other. However, there the similarity ends, for *Our Country's Good* and *Culture and Imperialism* hold almost diametrically opposed views on the nature of the link between the two. Said asserts, again and again, that the 'great' (a qualifier he employs unashamedly) works of Western culture are implicated in complex ways with the imperial activities of Western powers. He does not go so far as to claim that Jane Austen's novels are propaganda for overseas expansion, but he refuses to exculpate them from involvement in the ongoing workings of empire. Wertenbaker, on the other hand, sees culture at odds with imperialism. For the convicts in *Our Country's Good*, participation in the production of *The Recruiting Officer* is clearly an escape from the harsh rigours of colonial life. In some cases culture, in the shape of the play, provides nothing less than redemption for convict and jailer alike. *Our Country's Good* places culture and imperialism side by side, only to claim that the former transcends the latter. It is a claim that Edward Said would take issue with.

The imperial uses of culture

Said's thesis in *Culture and Imperialism* could not be clearer, particularly since he repeats it so often. There has been, he effectively says, a cover-up on a massive scale by the guardians of the Western cultural heritage. In what he calls a 'radical falsification', 'Culture is exonerated of any entanglements with power.'[5] Imperialism is, and was, about the brute exercise of power over others, and in the nineteenth century it was the common currency almost the entire globe over. But critics who study, for instance, the nineteenth-century novel quarantine their object of inquiry, refusing to take into account the ongoing impact of imperialism at the moment the novels were being written. This is a form of aesthetic blindness that ignores a major factor in the formation of those novels. Said believes that there is almost something intrinsic in the link between culture and imperialism which encourages this blindness:

> Few full-scale critical studies have focused on the relationship between modern Western imperialism and its culture, the occlusion of that deeply symbiotic relationship being a result of the relationship itself.[6]

His objective, then, is twofold: to explain 'how culture partici-
pates in imperialism yet is somehow excused for its role' and to
prove that 'the great cultural archive … is where the intellectual and
aesthetic investments in overseas domains are made'.[7] What is at
stake, therefore, is the supposed innocence of culture in imperial
matters. At the outset of *Culture and Imperialism* Said makes it very
clear who is responsible for the exoneration of culture, and what it is
exonerated of:

> Most professional humanists … are unable to make the connection
> between the prolonged and sordid cruelty of such practices as
> slavery, colonialist and racial oppression, and imperial subjection on
> the one hand, and the poetry, fiction, and philosophy of the society
> that engages in these practices on the other.[8]

Right near the end of his book Said puts this in another way by
invoking Walter Benjamin's 'Theses on the Philosophy of History',
the essay considered in Chapter Six of this book. 'There is no document of civilization which is not at the same time a document of
barbarism', Benjamin says in Thesis VII.[9] These words could easily
stand as shorthand for Said's entire book. He does not want to
reduce the works of civilization (culture) to barbarism, but neither
does he want to divorce the two entirely. Instead, he constantly
emphasizes their simultaneity, or co-existence. The phrase Benjamin
uses captures Said's intent perfectly: 'at the same time'.

One of the reasons 'professional humanists' are blind to culture's
participation in imperialism is the very definition of culture they
work with. Said offers two definitions of culture, the second of which
he attributes to the humanists. The first definition is the broadest,
taking in a wide range of human products:

> those practices, like the arts of description, communication, and rep-
> resentation, that have relative autonomy from the economic, social,
> and political realms and that often exist in aesthetic forms …
> Included … are both the popular stock of lore about distant parts
> of the world and specialized knowledge available in such learned
> disciplines as ethnography, historiography, philology, sociology, and
> literary history.[10]

This definition takes in almost anything that is written about
'the distant parts of the world'. The second definition of culture he
gives derives from the mid-nineteenth century, the period of rapid

imperial expansion, but he claims that it is still very much in force today:

> culture is a concept that includes a refining element, each society's reservoir of the best that has been known and thought, as Matthew Arnold put it in the 1860s. Arnold believed that culture palliates, if it does not altogether neutralize, the ravages of modern, aggressive, mercantile, and brutalizing urban existence.[11]

This version of culture is remarkably close to that promoted by the first governor of New South Wales, Captain Arthur Phillip, in *Our Country's Good*. Phillip, unlike many of his officers, supports the idea of a play performed by convicts on the grounds that it can only improve them: 'Theatre is the expression of civilisation ... The convicts will be speaking a refined, literate language and expressing sentiments of a delicacy they are not used to. It will remind them that there is more to life than crime, punishment.'[12] Phillip, like Arnold, sees culture as a form of compensation for the more unpleasant aspects of life (in this case, flogging, leg-irons, exile). There is a hint of anachronism in attributing to a late eighteenth-century naval officer the views of a late nineteenth-century poet and critic, but as the earlier chapter on Caryl Churchill argues, anachronism is the privilege, even the prerogative, of history plays.

Although Said himself regularly, and approvingly, invokes an idea of the 'best that has been known and thought', he is extremely suspicious of the Arnoldian view of culture.[13] He worries that Arnold's perspective involves a narrow view of culture as national culture, which inevitably leads to a valuing of one's own culture over and above that of other nations. Certainly, Captain Phillip, for one, draws direct links between high culture and national identity: 'We belong to a great country which has spawned great playwrights: Shakespeare, Marlowe, Jonson.'[14] The 'trouble with this idea of culture', thinks Said, 'is that it entails not only venerating one's own culture but also thinking of it as somehow divorced from, because transcending, the everyday world.'[15] The 'everyday world' in this case is the daily business of empire. Said also offers a concise definition of imperialism: '"imperialism" means the practice, the theory, and the attitudes of a dominating metropolitan centre ruling a distant territory; "colonialism", which is almost always a consequence of imperialism, is the implanting of settlements on distant territory.'[16] This account captures perfectly the colonial experience enacted in

Our Country's Good. It is the status of culture in that colony which is at odds with Said's account.

Said gives countless examples of how culture and imperialism are not divorced one from the other but intimately inter-implicated. Rather fortuitously, the first example he gives concerns colonial Australia and its penal history. He calls attention to the character of Magwitch in Charles Dickens' *Great Expectations*. Early in the narrative the hero of the novel, Pip, helps Magwitch elude arrest in England, and although Magwitch is subsequently caught and sent to Australia as a convict, he does not forget Pip's act of kindness. In fact Magwitch, with the money he makes in Australia, is responsible for Pip's transformation into a gentleman. Pip does not know the identity of his anonymous benefactor, and he is dismayed to discover it is a former convict. Far from being a minor point in plot development, the dependence of Pip's development on the spoils of empire is crucial, claims Said. Pip goes on to be a successful colonial businessman in the denouement of the novel. In Said's reading, then, even while Australia is kept on the fringes of the plot, Dickens tacitly acknowledges a growing colonial empire as the condition of possibility of social relations at home in the metropolitan centre. Said presents a similar reading of Jane Austen's *Mansfield Park*, pointing out that the polite society occupied by Austen's English characters in the novel is in many ways contingent on the plantations in Antigua owned by Sir Thomas Bertram. The lessons in the novel about moral conduct, about property and money, are in fact intimately tied up with the imperial enterprise. 'According to Austen we are to conclude that no matter how isolated and insulated the English place (e.g. Mansfield Park), it requires overseas sustenance.'[17] As with Dickens, the sustenance of England by the overseas holdings is not explored in depth; in fact it is almost taken for granted. Nevertheless, these canonical novels cannot help but concede the interdependence of culture and imperialism while at the same time effacing that relationship.

Coercion or redemption?

Although *Our Country's Good* is in the main concerned with culture in the sense of Said's second, Arnoldian definition, it also touches on the broader understanding of culture in Said's first definition. Said writes about the production of 'specialized knowledge' about

159

imperial holdings, and he implies that this is one way of gaining control over newly colonized territories. It is a view that Wertenbaker would appear to endorse in a scene of deep black humour when the audience is introduced to the officers of the First Fleet as they discuss the punishment of convicts:

> COLLINS: This land is under English law. The court found them guilty and sentenced them accordingly. There: a bald-eyed corella.
> PHILLIP: But hanging?
> COLLINS: Only the three who were found guilty of stealing from the colony's stores. And that, over there on the Eucalyptus, is a flock of 'cacatua galerita' – the sulphur-crested cockatoo. You have been made Governor-in-Chief of a paradise of birds, Arthur.[18]

The naming of flora and fauna is a way of taking possession of a new continent, a colonization in and through language, wittily reinforced in this scene by the fact that the men are also shooting the birds. Therefore, *Our Country's Good* does not consider scientific enquiry a neutral activity but a cultural practice (in Said's sense) that is directly linked with the violence of imperialism. Shortly afterwards, when Lieutenant Ralph Clark bemoans his failure to gain promotion, Harry Brewer hints that he should participate in such *cultural* activities:

> RALPH: His excellency never seems to notice me [...] He finds time for Davey Collins, Lieutenant Dawes.
> HARRY: That's because Captain Collins is going to write about the customs of the Indians here – and Lieutenant Dawes is writing about the stars.[19]

Dawes and Collins are taking part in the mapping of the new colony, a necessary prelude to its further exploitation. It is at this point that Ralph hatches his plan to stage a play to impress the Governor. In other words, his initial investment in an idea of culture appears to be motivated purely by a desire for personal advancement.

The audience is asked, then, to treat with a certain amount of skepticism one kind of cultural work carried out during the establishment of colonial New South Wales. Does this skepticism extend to the rather rosy redemptive picture of high culture painted by Governor Phillip and already cited? After all, *Our Country's Good* sets out for the most part to give the point of view of the convicts, to allow them to tell their otherwise untold stories. Arthur Phillip was a lenient and reforming Governor who insisted that rations for convicts and marines should be equal, but he was, nevertheless, in a position of power, and his views inevitably reflected that position. Does the play as a whole support his Arnoldian perspective and therefore the perspective of the rulers? It is a difficult question to answer because one of the strengths of the play is the way in which it presents many different voices without privileging any single one. Max Stafford-Clark, director of *Our Country's Good* and other Wertenbaker plays, identifies this multi-vocality as a regular feature of her theatre:

> there is usually a reluctance to see events through the eyes of one person, and that challenge seems to be refreshing and structurally and stylistically new. Timberlake Wertenbaker's plays are also sometimes criticised for lacking a narrative line, for lacking a principal character. And sometimes those criticisms are also a critic's limitations to come to grips with a new form which is a strength as well as a weakness.[20]

It is true that *Our Country's Good* lacks a principal character who expresses the play's philosophy, and it is for this reason that we need to be cautious in attributing Phillip's view to the play as a whole. However, as will be seen, much in the play does push us in that direction.

In *Our Country's Good* there are almost as many opinions about the performance of *The Recruiting Officer* as there are characters. Among the officers this ranges from the indifference and disdain of Dawes and Faddy to the distrust and outright opposition of Major Robbie Ross. Ross is, in Matthew Arnold's terminology, a philistine, who considers the play subversive, a potential threat to the hierarchics of the colony. 'The theatre leads to threatening theory' he blusters, and he blames the rehearsals for thefts of food: 'I said it from the beginning. The play will bring down calamity on this colony.'[21] For Ross, culture is just one step on the road to anarchy, a neat reversal of Arnold's formula in *Culture and Anarchy*. Ross is also the most violent and repressive of the officers in New South Wales, sadistically doling out punishment to convicts at every opportunity and disrupting rehearsals by confining the convict players. The play is therefore arguing that the harshest expression of

161

imperialist practices will be found among those who reject culture most vociferously. If Ross read a little more poetry, perhaps he would not be so quick with the lash. He may explicitly contradict Phillip's theories about the value of culture, but, through his actions, Ross implicitly confirms them, while at the same time violently dissociating the activities of empire from the culture produced by that empire.

Among the convicts, John Arscott and Dabby Bryant present apparently contrasting views on the uses of theatre. Arscott testifies to the capacity of theatre to raise him above his current circumstances: 'I don't want to play myself. When I say Kite's lines I forget everything else. I forget the judge said I'm going to have to spend the rest of my natural life in this place getting beaten and working like a slave [...] I don't have to remember the things I've done, when I speak Kite's lines I don't hate any more.'[22] In many ways Arscott is the ideal recruit to Phillip's vision, forgetting temporarily that his life is dominated by punishment when he enters into the part of Kite. This power of theatre to elevate is borne out by nearly every participant in the play. The director, Ralph Clark, claims that convict women, who are 'no better than animals', 'seemed to acquire a dignity' when they read Farquhar's lines. Ketch Freeman, the hangman, tainted by his part in the death of so many fellow convicts, seeks redemption through acting in the play. And theatre even has the magical effect of making leg-irons vanish: 'WISEHAMMER: How can I play Captain Brazen in chains? MARY: This is the theatre. We will believe you.'[23] Dabby Bryant is an exception to this general acquiescence to the Governor's benevolent ideal. She recognizes that the transcendence offered by theatre is only temporary: 'ARSCOTT: When I say my lines, I think of nothing else. Why can't you do the same? DABBY: Because it's only for one night.'[24] Dabby also articulates most eloquently the discrepancy between the material conditions of the convicts and the parts of the wealthy London-dwellers they are asked to play in The Recruiting Officer. And yet even Dabby finds a character to identify with in Kite, the male soldier.

The play does allow for dissenting and dissonant opinions about the relative value of culture, but the collective weight of these voices, even in the shape of Ross's philistinism, serves to confirm Phillip's thesis that culture is distinct from imperialism and may even help to alleviate the worst aspects of colonial life. And it is not just the opinions of the characters that build up this consensus but the action of the play itself. The first scene of *Our Country's Good*, 'The Voyage Out', takes place in the hold of one of the convict ships bound for Botany Bay. In this scene Ralph Clark oversees the flogging of Robert Sideway. The hierarchies of colonial Australia could not be more strictly drawn, with the distant officer administering rough justice to an abject convict. When Clark calls auditions for *The Recruiting Officer*, however, Sideway comes forward, and as the play progresses he emerges as one of the main comic actors in the convict company. As a result, what was once a strict hierarchical relation begins to blur. During rehearsals Ralph must negotiate with Sideway, giving way to an acting style he does not altogether approve. The same goes for the other convicts, who find that in the world of the rehearsal they are able to challenge the authority of Clark:

RALPH: It's completely wrong.
WISEHAMMER: It's right for the character of Brazen.
RALPH: No it isn't. I'm the director Wisehammer.
WISEHAMMER: Yes, but I have to play the part. They're equal in this
            scene. They're both Captains and in the end fight for
            her.[25]

Were Wisehammer to contradict Ralph thus in the world of the colony, he could expect 50 lashes for his impudence. Furthermore, in the play he is able to take on the persona of one of his oppressors, an army officer. In fact, both rehearsal scenes show the convicts and Ralph cocooned in a miniature democracy where they can debate freely, test ideas, disagree and compromise – options foreclosed to them in the daily life of the colony.

It is hard for an audience to miss the message of *Our Country's Good* about the potentially transformational and transcendent capacities of theatre. But if we have any doubts, the published version of the play attempts to set us straight. Wertenbaker includes a preface as well as a series of letters written to her by long-term prisoners and an epigraph from *Pygmalion in the Classroom* by Rosenthal and Jacobsen. In the preface Wertenbaker tells of a performance she attended of Howard Barker's *The Love of a Good Man* in HM Prison Wormwood Scrubs, and of a subsequent performance of *Our Country's Good* in Blundeston prison. The experience validated culture as transformational: 'it confirmed all our feelings about the power and the value of theatre.'[26] The letters from prisoners, which sound remarkably like some lines spoken by convicts in *Our Country's Good*, echo Wertenbaker's claim: 'Drama, and self-expression in general, is a refuge and one of the only real weapons against the hopelessness of these places' writes Joe White.[27] Finally, the epigraph from *Pygmalion in the Classroom* recalls a pedagogical experiment in which a set of teachers were given lists of supposedly bright children in their classes. The lists were in fact generated at random, but the teachers treated these children as if they were brighter, and they in turn showed 'significantly greater gains in IQ' than other children.[28] Matthew Arnold would be very pleased because the lesson here is clear: if only we expose the underprivileged to higher culture, they will become better people.

I do not want to diminish the achievements of theatre in prisons or question the power of rehearsal as a space of exploration, of working through new ways of thinking and seeing. However, if we recall Edward Said's warning about the dangers of totally separating culture and imperialism, we need to pause over some of *Our Country's Good*'s more optimistic formulations. Take, for instance, the special Prologue to *The Recruiting Officer* which Wisehammer pens with the aid of Mary Brenham. It contains the title of Wertenbaker's play, and even though Ralph forbids Wisehammer to speak it lest the officers be offended, it is taken as an example of the 'self-expression' the convicts have finally been allowed through participation in the play. It is at once a lament for a nation lost and an ironic complaint against that nation:

> From distant climes o'er wide-spread seas we come,
> Though not with much éclat or beat of drum,
> True patriots all; for be it understood,
> We left our country for our country's good;
> No private views disgraced our generous zeal,
> What urg'd our travels was our country's weal,
> And none will doubt but that our emigration
> Has prov'd most useful to the British nation.[29]

With this piece of poetry the downtrodden convicts seem to have come full circle, voicing their dilemma in heartfelt lyrics – all made possible by their access to high culture.

The historical circumstances of this prologue differ somewhat from the use to which *Our Country's Good* puts it, though. It was, indeed, written during the eighteenth century, but not for the origi-

nal production of *The Recruiting Officer* in Sydney in 1789, as Robert
Hughes explains:

> Its prologue, supposedly written by some nameless felon bard, was to
> become famous in and beyond Botany Bay ... Alas, later research has
> shown that this was not penned by a convict in Port Jackson, but by
> Henry Carter, a hack journalist in London, well after he heard the
> play had been performed ... even without its imperishable second
> couplet, [it] deserves to be remembered as the first of a long series of
> gibes directed by the supercilious Pommy at cultural efforts in
> Australia.[30]

The prologue was written in the first instance for a metropolitan
audience as a way of understanding its colonial fringes. And in the
view of the post-colonial historian, Hughes, it is in fact the first in a
long line of satirical broadsides aimed at the inferior denizens of
the far-off colony. By recycling Carter's doggerel as sentimental
'self-expression', *Our Country's Good* may be reappropriating the
language of the colonizers on behalf of the colonized, but it is probably more accurate to say that it obscures the link between culture
and imperialism for the sake of a feel-good ending.

The play has in fact already drawn criticism on grounds similar to
those just laid out. Ann Wilson, for instance, has expressed doubts
about the optimistic conclusion of the play, suggesting that what we
witness at the end of *Our Country's Good* is the successful pacifi-
cation of an underclass by the ruling class of New South Wales.[31]
Esther Beth Sullivan is even more explicit in her suspicions. Where
Our Country's Good attempts to sever the ties between culture and
imperialism, Sullivan insists on uniting them:

> *The Recruiting Officer* indeed recruits the convicts to England's impe-
> rialist project, making them willing rather than resistant participants
> ... Through the material of great English drama, a group of social
> outcasts learns to act in a 'mannered' way, in a way that can be toler-
> ated and put to more 'productive' uses.[32]

Sullivan goes even further than Said, finding a one-to-one correspon-
dence between the project of culture and the project of imperialism.
Said does acknowledge that culture was perceived as a potential
pacifier: 'what Arnold had to say about culture was specifically
believed to be a deterrent to rampant disorder – colonial, Irish,
domestic.'[33] He is, however, reluctant to interpret culture as simply

coercive, as it is in Sullivan's reading. 'Texts are protean things', he insists, and while they should not be separated out from questions of power, they are never simply at the service of power.

Our Country's Good may endorse a slightly conservative vision of culture and, in doing so, occlude the implications of culture *in* empire. But such is the protean nature of this play – its openness to different interpretations – that it has been successfully performed against itself, as Susan Carlson's survey of reviews of the play shows. By analysing the press responses to *Our Country's Good* on three different continents, Carlson demonstrates that the lessons it offers about culture and imperialism are not, in fact, clear cut. The contrast between the British and Australian receptions of the play is particularly instructive. In London, the reviewers almost uniformly embraced the first production as a celebration of the power and value of theatre. Not only this, but the play was taken as proof of the vitality of a national culture: 'anchoring such theatre-based reviews is also the assumption that British theatre is not just the barometer of British culture: it *is* British culture.'[34] In London, then, issues of colonization were pushed into the background. Not so in Australia where, in 1989, Max Stafford-Clark's Royal Court production played in Sydney at the same time as an Australian production in Melbourne. Not only did the Australian reviews focus much more on colonial history, but the Melbourne production brought to the foreground the submerged 'issue of native displacement'.[35] In Melbourne the message about the transformative power of theatre was also very much downplayed. If we follow Edward Said's thesis in *Culture and Imperialism*, it should come as no surprise that in London, the heart of the former empire, a celebration of culture should take precedence over memories of colonialism, while in the former colony, where empire is not so easily forgotten, such celebrations of culture are less palatable.

For happy endings go to Australia

It seems a little churlish to criticize a play for having a (relatively) happy ending. It is, after all, rather unusual to find optimism or uplifting messages at the conclusion of modern British plays, and *Our Country's Good* should come as something of a relief to audiences trained in despair. It is worth comparing the ending of *Our Country's Good* with those of the other plays addressed in this book because it is so strikingly different in its resolution. It ends with a beginning – the convicts' production of *The Recruiting Officer*, which is greeted by '*the triumphant music of Beethoven's* Fifth Symphony *and the sound of applause and laughter from the First Fleet audience*'. (p. 91) There is no 'triumph' in any of the eight other plays, which together make up a fair cross-section of post-war British drama. At best there is irony, at worst deep cynicism. *Look Back in Anger* concludes with Alison's miscarriage and her unconvincing and surely temporary reconciliation with Jimmy. This bleak vision of the domestic sphere continues in *The Homecoming*, where Ruth acquiesces in her role as mother and whore. *Rosencrantz and Guildenstern are Dead* finishes with the death and/or disappearance of its title characters, while its fellow comedy, *What the Butler Saw*, unleashes a series of revelations about incest before the sardonic *deus ex machina* lifts the characters from the stage. In *Comedians*, the comics who sell out to commercialism succeed and Waters tells Price an inconclusive anecdote about Nazi concentration camps. Angie's dire words, 'Frightening, frightening', punctuate *Top Girls*, and *Pravda*'s final scene shows the total victory of Lambert Le Roux as Andrew May's feeble resistance is extinguished. Finally, Sarah Kane's *Blasted*, the subject of the next chapter, leaves nothing but shattered, mutilated characters on stage. This is not to say that not a single happy ending was to be found on British stages between 1950 and the present, but they were more likely to be encountered in West End musicals than at the Royal Court Theatre, where *Our Country's Good* was premiered.

The paucity of happy endings on the modern British stage may be a result of playwrights' reluctance to send their audiences away contented, preferring them to leave the theatre thinking; and as post-war audiences for theatre have shrunk, theatre has generally taken up a critical role in relation to society, a role not conducive to providing happy endings. Furthermore, if we examine *The Grace of Mary Traverse* (1985) and *Three Birds Alighting on a Field* (1991), two Wertenbaker plays staged at the Royal Court before and after *Our Country's Good*, we find, perhaps not bleak final scenes, but certainly scenes that tend towards *diminuendo*. And although Wertenbaker insists that *Three Birds*, like *Our Country's Good*, asserts 'the theme of the redemptive value of art', that play, set in the London art world, contains some crushing satire against the pretensions of the cultural elite of the metropolis.[36] What is it that makes *Our Country's Good* exceptional? Could it be the play's locale?

In *Culture and Imperialism* Edward Said notices a similar discrepancy in the outlook of novels of the late nineteenth and early twentieth centuries. He compares the work of Rudyard Kipling (and *Kim* specifically) with that of his contemporaries Thomas Hardy, Henry James, George Eliot, Gustave Flaubert and Marcel Proust. According to Said, Kipling is the equal of these writers in artistic achievement and yet radically different from them in philosophy:

> the works of these writers are essentially novels of disillusion and disenchantment, whereas *Kim* is not. Almost without exception the protagonist of the late nineteenth-century novel is someone who has realized that his or her life's project – the wish to be great, rich, or distinguished – is mere fancy, illusion, dream ... This awakening is not to be found in *Kim*.[37]

Why does Kipling's hero, the Irish outcast boy who has gone native in India, escape the dismal fate of his fellow protagonists? He escapes because his environment, the colonial world, is infinitely receptive to the desires and needs of the colonizer. He succeeds in Kipling's narrative because the culture of the West imagines the colonial space as pliant, available, expansive:

> what one cannot accomplish in one's own Western environment – where trying to live out the grand dream of a successful quest means coming up against one's own mediocrity and the world's corruption and degradation – one can do abroad. Isn't it possible in India to do everything?[38]

Said's critique is clear: the Westerner, unable to control his surroundings, may feel world-weary in Europe; but in the outlying empire, there at least he is in command, the dominant, superior force among so many subordinate peoples. It is a fantasy, but it is a powerful one, which, through cultural means, serves to solidify and confirm colonial relations.

The relevance of Said's analysis is apparent when we see that *Our Country's Good* reproduces much the same idealized model of the colonial sphere almost a century after *Kim*. The nature of this post-colonial projection can be seen in the forward-looking plans the convicts make as they wait backstage for *The Recruiting Officer* to begin.

WISEHAMMER: I don't want to go back to England now [...] Here, no one has more of a right than anyone else to call you a foreigner. I want to become the first famous writer.

[...]

SIDEWAY: I'm going to start a theatre company. Who wants to be in it?

[...]

LIZ: I'll be in your company, Mr Sideway.

KETCH: And so will I [...]

SIDEWAY: I'll hold auditions tomorrow.

DABBY: Tomorrow.

DUCKLING: Tomorrow.

MARY: Tomorrow.

LIZ: Tomorrow.[39]

Individual ambition, so cruelly suppressed in England, begins to blossom in the new colony. Even in the late twentieth century former colonies continue to be misrecognized as lands of opportunity, and the more brutal aspects of colonization can be forgotten amidst the celebration of theatre. That is not to say that negation is the only viable mode of closure. It is always worth recalling the Epilogue of Brecht's *Good Person of Szechwan*:

There's only one solution that we know:
That you should now consider as you go
What sort of measures you would recommend
To help good people to a happy end.
Ladies and Gentlemen, in you we trust:
There must be happy endings, must, must, must![40]

Yes, there must, but not just in Australia.

Notes

1 Robert Hughes, *The Fatal Shore: The Epic of Australia's Founding* (New York: Vintage, 1988 [1986]), p. xii.

2 Paul Carter, *The Road to Botany Bay: An Exploration of Landscape and History* (New York: Knopf, 1988).

3 Thomas Keneally, *The Playmaker* (London: Hodder and Stoughton, 1987).

4 See Linda Hutcheon, *A Poetics of Postmodernism: History, Theory, Fiction* (London and New York: Routledge, 1988).

5 Edward W. Said, *Culture and Imperialism* (London: Vintage, 1994 [1993]), p. 67.

6 Said, *Culture and Imperialism*, p. 40.
7 Said, *Culture and Imperialism*, pp. 128, xxiii.
8 Said, *Culture and Imperialism*, p. xiv.
9 Said, *Culture and Imperialism*, p. 373.
10 Said, *Culture and Imperialism*, p. xii.
11 Said, *Culture and Imperialism*, p. xiii.
12 Timberlake Wertenbaker, *Our Country's Good* (London: Methuen, 1991), p. 21.
13 This phrase of Arnold's can be found in 'The function of criticism at the present time' (1865), where he says that the 'business' of criticism is 'simply to know the best that is known and thought in the world, and by in its turn making this known, to create a current of true and fresh ideas'. Raman Selden, ed., *The Theory of Criticism: From Plato to the Present* (London and New York: Longman, 1988), p. 495. Said's adherence to this perspective can be seen in his impassioned defense of high culture: 'Yet I do believe that some literature is actually good, and that some is bad, and I remain as conservative as anyone when it comes to, if not the redemptive value of reading a classic rather than staring at a television screen, then the potential enhancement of one's sensibility and consciousness by doing so, by the exercise of one's mind.' *Culture and Imperialism*, p. 386.
14 Wertenbaker, *Our Country's Good*, p. 21.
15 Said, *Culture and Imperialism*, p. xiv.
16 Said, *Culture and Imperialism*, p. 8.
17 Said, *Culture and Imperialism*, p. 107.
18 Wertenbaker, *Our Country's Good*, p. 2.
19 Wertenbaker, *Our Country's Good*, p. 8.
20 Interview with Max Stafford-Clark. *The European English Messenger* 7:2 (1998), p. 38.
21 Wertenbaker, *Our Country's Good*, pp. 25, 51.
22 Wertenbaker, *Our Country's Good*, pp. 73–4.
23 Wertenbaker, *Our Country's Good*, p. 56.
24 Wertenbaker, *Our Country's Good*, p. 85.
25 Wertenbaker, *Our Country's Good*, p. 72.
26 Wertenbaker, *Our Country's Good*, p. v.
27 Wertenbaker, *Our Country's Good*, p. vii.
28 Wertenbaker, *Our Country's Good*, p. xvi.
29 Wertenbaker, *Our Country's Good*, p. 89.
30 Hughes, *The Fatal Shore*, p. 340.
31 Ann Wilson, 'Our Country's Good: theatre, colony and nation in Wertenbaker's adaptation of *The Playmaker*', *Modern Drama* 34:1 (1991), p. 33.
32 Esther Beth Sullivan, 'Hailing ideology, acting in the horizon, and reading between plays by Timberlake Wertenbaker', *Theatre Journal* 45:2 (1993), p. 143.
33 Wertenbaker, *Our Country's Good*, pp. 157–8.
34 Susan Carlson, 'Issues of identity, nationality and performance: the reception

of two plays by Timberlake Wertenbaker', *New Theatre Quarterly* 35 (1993), p. 276.

35 Carlson, 'Issues of identity', p. 280.
36 Timberlake Wertenbaker, 'Introduction', *Timberlake Wertenbaker: Plays 1* (London: Faber and Faber, 1996), p. ix.
37 Said, *Culture and Imperialism*, pp. 188–9.
38 Said, *Culture and Imperialism*, p. 192.
39 Wertenbaker, *Our Country's Good*, pp. 85–6.
40 Bertolt Brecht, *The Good Person of Szechwan*, in *Brecht: Plays Two* (London: Methuen, 1987), p. 291.

9

Trauma and testimony in *Blasted* – Kane with Felman

The scenes of trauma

In reading Sarah Kane's *Blasted* (1995) alongside what has become known as 'trauma theory', this final chapter takes up a play of the 1990s and a theory of the same decade. Since they are both so recent, it is to be expected that in many ways the jury is still out on them. Sarah Kane, who committed suicide in February 1999 at the age of 28, has just had her complete plays published by Methuen (December 2000), a sure sign of canonization; but opinion on her dramatic output – five full-length plays – is divided to say the least. Excoriated by many leading theatre reviewers for her first play (*Blasted*) and all the others that followed, she also found powerful allies in Harold Pinter, Caryl Churchill and Edward Bond, who hailed her as an important new dramatic voice.[1] Her death by her own hand not only punctuates her *œuvre* with a depressing finality but inevitably brings retroactive, and possibly distracting, meanings to her plays. It is not, however, for such biographical meanings that this chapter turns to 'trauma theory'. By invoking a genre of theory first, rather than a specific theoretical text, I am breaking for the first time with the pattern of this book. I am doing this because of the very early stages in which 'trauma theory' still finds itself – as an incomplete and still generally untested theory – and because no one specific text or writer yet defines the field. Shoshana Felman's *Testimony: Crises of Witnessing in Literature, Psychoanalysis, and History* (1992) has been chosen, not as a final statement on trauma and testimony, but as one of the theory's earliest texts, which set some of the terms of the debate. It is very much in response to this book – co-authored with Dori Laub, a practicing psychoanalyst – that other important theorists in this area, such as Cathy Caruth and Dominick LaCapra, have set out their arguments. Caruth has generally followed the route taken by Felman, while LaCapra has been more critical; both will be important reference points.

The link between trauma theory and *Blasted* (or any of Kane's plays for that matter) is hardly contentious. Trauma is a kind of brutalizing shock, and it is for submitting her audiences to exactly this, in heavy doses, that Kane has been both applauded and dismissed. *Blasted* is set in an expensive hotel room in Leeds during what appears to be a civil war or *coup d'état*, a fact which only becomes apparent in the second scene. The first scene introduces us to Ian, a journalist whose smoking and drinking have propelled him to within days of death, and Cate, his former girlfriend, much younger than him, whom he has invited to stay the night in the hotel. He fails to convince her to have sex with him, but she does eventually help him to masturbate before they go to bed. Between scenes he rapes her, and when she faints early in the next scene he appears to do so again (the stage directions are ambiguous; they read: '*He puts the gun to her head, lies between her legs, and simulates sex. As he comes,* CATE *sits bolt upright with a shout.*'[2]) Slightly later, Cate bites hard on Ian's penis while performing oral sex. When she is in the shower a soldier bursts into the room and holds Ian at gunpoint; Cate meanwhile has fled through the bathroom window. As the soldier threatens Ian a massive explosion blasts a hole in one of the room's walls. In the following scene the soldier relates to Ian some of the atrocities he has committed; he then rapes Ian, after which he sucks out his eyes and eats them. In between this scene and the next the soldier shoots himself, leaving Ian alone until Cate returns with an injured baby, who dies. In the final scene Cate leaves to search for food, and Ian, in what may be a hallucinatory episode, attempts to strangle himself, defecates on stage and eats the dead baby. This synopsis does not in any sense summarize the play, leaving out, as it does, most of the dialogic developments, but it does give a pretty clear picture of the sequence of traumatizing events undergone by the three characters and imposed on the audience. It should be added that the play was performed in the Royal Court Theatre Upstairs, which seats only 65 people, so no member of the audience would have been very far from the stage.

Repetition and displacement

Trauma theory, as it is manifested in the work of Felman, Caruth and LaCapra, is primarily an American development. There are good reasons why the United States, and more specifically humanities departments in American universities, have provided fertile ground for this theory. However, its historical and intellectual roots lie very much in Europe. Perhaps the founding text of trauma theory is Sigmund Freud's long essay *Beyond the Pleasure Principle* (1920), where the founder of psychoanalysis tries to explain a seemingly perverse psychic phenomenon: *repetition compulsion*. In repetition compulsion a subject unconsciously relives, or even acts out, a traumatic, unassimilated experience from the past, not just once, but repeatedly. Why, Freud asks, when humans generally try at all costs to avoid psychic pain do they in this case appear to deliberately seek it out? He by no means satisfies himself with an answer, but he suggests that through repetition a trauma from the past may eventually be recognized and mastered.[3] The debt owed by 'trauma theory' to Freud can be seen in Cathy Caruth's economical definition of trauma in *Unclaimed Experience*:

> In its most general definition, trauma describes an overwhelming experience of sudden or catastrophic events in which the response to the event occurs in the often delayed, uncontrolled repetitive appearance of hallucinations and other intrusive phenomena. The experience of the soldier faced with sudden and massive death around him, for example, who suffers only in a numbed state, only to relive it later on in repeated nightmares, is a central and recurring image of trauma in our century.[4]

The second part of Caruth's definition gives us a clue to the historical provenance of the theory. It was no accident that Freud 'discovered' repetition compulsion shortly after World War I, which generated so many shell-shocked soldiers who, in retrospect, can be described as suffering from trauma. Unable to come to terms with what they saw and experienced on the front, soldiers found its horrors returning to them later, after they had left the actual fighting.

The atrocities acted out and narrated in *Blasted* may be shocking, even horrifying, but they are not totally unfamiliar since the traumas of the twentieth century did not end, but began, with World War I. As the century proceeded modern technology and politics combined to bring about the Nazi genocide of European Jews in the Holocaust and the nuclear destruction of two Japanese cities. In the aftermath of these seismic events memory itself undergoes a crisis: the events are too awful to contemplate, and yet they must be memorialized. The vexed, and often impossible, difficulties associated with remembering and understanding such events is the task which trauma theory sets itself. There is at this stage a useful distinction to be made. Felman and Caruth are first and foremost literary critics and LaCapra is an intellectual historian, but *trauma* has a complicated existence as a medical and psychiatric phenomenon. Post-traumatic stress disorder (PTSD) is an accepted, if somewhat controversial, medical condition which has come to have more and more applications since its initial use in the United States in 1980 in the wake of the Vietnam War.[5] Its use has extended beyond the experiences of war, most notably in relation to forms of sexual trauma – rape and child abuse – which are also often coped with in a delayed and belated fashion. Felman, Caruth and Lacapra are clearly not qualified to comment in any expert fashion on medical conditions or on sexual abuse, although Felman strengthens her credentials with the presence of her co-author, whose name appears on the cover of *Testimony* as 'Dori Laub, M.D.'[6] No doubt these writers of the 1990s took their cue from medical developments of the 1980s, but apart from the occasional detour into pseudo-psychiatry they are careful to stick to what they know. As a result, 'trauma theory' is mainly linguistic in orientation, interested for the most part in trauma as it relates to literary and historical issues such as representation, narrative and truth.[7]

If the legacy of the Vietnam war provided the impetus for the study of trauma in the United States, it is now above all the Holocaust, or *Shoah*,[8] which animates the work of trauma theory. In fact, trauma theory can be seen as one aspect of the much larger field of Holocaust studies, which has expanded of late, but which has, of course, been undertaken ever since Auschwitz. Dominick LaCapra, in his analysis of the work of Shoshana Felman, traces – very perceptively if somewhat mischievously – the genealogy of the literary strand of Holocaust studies that arose in American Departments of English and Comparative Literature in the 1990s. He reads this development as a displacement activity: the recent interest of Felman and others, such as Jacques Derrida, in the Holocaust and the philosophical legacy of the Nazis (Heidegger's affiliation with Nazism, to be precise) is a way of dealing indirectly with the trauma of the revelations in 1988 about Paul de Man, long-time professor at Yale University, where Felman also teaches. With his special brand of uncompromising attentiveness to textuality, de Man exerted a powerful intellectual influence on a generation of

American literary scholars, and he was mourned widely on his death in 1983. Five years later it was revealed that in his early twenties in Belgium, during the first years of World War II, he wrote many articles for the collaborationist newspaper *Le Soir*, including one particularly negative piece about Jewish literature in 1941. The fallout from the revelations rippled right through an American academy populated by de Man's former students and generated a great many accusations and exonerations of varying degrees of sophistication, including a chapter in *Testimony*.[9] In that chapter Felman goes to great lengths to explain and justify de Man's post-war silence in the United States over his wartime activities. In fact, she uses de Man's silence as an exemplary instance of the necessary silence of the witness in the face of the horror of the Holocaust.

This long digression about Paul de Man is not immediately relevant for the discussion of *Blasted*, but it is important background to the whole subject of trauma theory. We need to approach Felman and others cautiously because of the number of potentially submerged issues at work in their writing. On the other hand, it could also be argued that the heavy presence of such unarticulated anxieties is part and parcel of trauma theory, which is concerned above all with the complex and often painful and distorted ways in which the past continues to haunt and affect the present. Furthermore, the ways in which the intellectual and emotional processing of the de Man controversy worked themselves out in a displaced fashion may be instructive for understanding *Blasted*'s peculiar relation to the atrocities in the former Yugoslavia, which for many reviewers and commentators it evidently evoked, if in a 'blurred' or 'shrouded' manner.[10]

Three versions of trauma

It should already be clear that all three characters in *Blasted* seem to have undergone some form of potentially traumatizing experience. However, neither their traumas, nor their manner of dealing with them, are undifferentiated. In fact, the play presents us with three distinct possibilities for the (re)manifestations of traumatic experience. The soldier has both suffered and inflicted horrific violence during the course of whatever war is taking place, and he continues to reenact these crimes in their full brutality. Ian, it appears, has also been involved as a perpetrator in some sort of atrocities, but he revisits his possible war crimes as phantasms, or, rather, they revisit

176

him. In his abuse of Cate, though, he seems simply to repeat what has gone before. Finally, Cate, as a victim, is thrust into a compulsive repetition of her previous scenes of abuse and yet, at the same time, resists the pattern of repetition and attempts to halt it.

What the soldier wants when he breaks into the hotel room is never exactly spelt out. He is ravenous and devours the two breakfasts Ian has ordered; he inquires after Cate, and implies that he wants to have sex. His main concern, though, seems to be to tell Ian of his crimes. His first confession is as brutal as anything the play stages:

SOLDIER: Went to a house just outside town. All gone. Apart from a small boy hiding in the corner. One of the others took him outside. Lay him on the ground and shot him through the legs. Heard crying in the basement. Went down. Three men and four women. Called the others. They held the men while I fucked the women. Youngest was twelve. Didn't cry, just lay there. Turned her over and –
Then she cried. Made her lick me clean. Closed my eyes and thought of –
Shot her father in the mouth. Brothers shouted. Hung them from the ceiling by their testicles.
IAN: Charming
SOLDIER: Never done that?
IAN: No.
SOLDIER: Sure?
IAN: I wouldn't forget.
SOLDIER: You would.[11]

Leaving aside for the moment the actual acts carried out by the soldier, it is worth examining his extraordinary claim that such brutal things are necessarily *forgotten*. How is it possible to forget the anal rape of a twelve year-old, or hanging men by their testicles? Surely they would be imprinted forever on the memory? According to Cathy Caruth, though, there is a constitutive forgetting at the heart of all trauma: 'The historical power of the trauma is not just that the experience is repeated after its forgetting, but that it is only in and through its inherent forgetting that it is experienced at all.'[12] Why is the forgetting 'inherent'? It is inherent because the experience is too extreme to be assimilated by consciousness, to enter into the regular routes of memory, and it is therefore repressed, pushed out of consciousness. Only in its circuitous returns, then, is it experienced at all.

Caruth is writing in this instance about *victims*, and it is entirely justified to protest that the soldier is a *perpetrator* and should not be treated with the same sympathy or interest as his victims. That way lies the dangerous road to claiming, for instance, that the Nazis were as traumatized by their actions as those they victimized. Clearly, though, the forgetting (repression) of the Holocaust by Nazis is of an entirely different order, and motivated by absolutely different aims, than its forgetting by Jews. *Blasted*, nevertheless, chooses to blur the distinction between perpetrator and victim by giving the soldier an originary trauma. He reveals, in a much shorter piece of narration, that his girlfriend is also a casualty of the fighting, having been killed in a fashion already familiar to us from his first story: 'Col, they buggered her. Cut her throat. Hacked her ears and nose off, nailed them to the front door.'[13] We do not know which event took place first, the mutilation and anal rape of his girlfriend or his anal rape of the twelve year-old and mutilation of her brothers, but at the end of the scene he rapes Ian and bites out his eyes.[14] Perhaps what made reviewers (unconsciously for the most part) so uneasy about *Blasted* is that the soldier's compulsive repeating of the same brutalities appears to be partly mitigated by his own trauma, which he is acting out again and again. And perhaps they were right.

The soldier is not the only character who leaves the audience feeling morally and ethically ambivalent. Charles Spencer of the *Daily Telegraph* rather peevishly chastized the play for not telling him whether he should loathe or pity Ian, the dying, racist journalist.[15] It is much harder to pass judgment on Ian because he is not as forthcoming about what he has done in the past. However, his own fragmented and incomplete confession immediately precedes the arrival of the soldier; it may, indeed, prompt the arrival. Ian, like the soldier, is a perpetrator; but unlike the soldier his status as a victim is not clear, although his physical suffering in the present is graphically and repeatedly shown. At the beginning of the second scene, for instance, he collapses on the floor: '*His heart, lung, liver and kidneys are all under attack, and he is making involuntary crying sounds.*'[16] It is no doubt this continuing spectacle of pain that elicits the sympathies of the uncertain spectator.

Ian is guilty on two counts as a perpetrator: he apparently sexually abused Cate when she was a child, and he engaged in shadowy activities with an unnamed government organization. The abuse of Cate is never articulated outright, but there are some heavy hints.

At one point Cate, who is 21, says 'We always used to go to yours' (his place), to which Ian replies, 'That was years ago. You've grown up.'[17] The verbal implications are confirmed by visual clues: Cate sucks her thumb throughout the play, even when, as Paul Taylor reports, she is helping Ian to masturbate.[18] Ian's confession of his 'war' efforts emerges in fragments as Cate fellates him: 'Signed the official secrets act [...] Done the jobs they asked. Because I love this land [...] Driving jobs. Picking people up, disposing of bodies, the lot [...] Now/ I do/ The real job/ I/ Am/ A/ Killer' (pp. 28–9). So Ian has supplemented his journalistic work with some secret government detail – possibly counter-terrorism, certainly assassination. He carries on the abuse of Cate, but he appears to have retired from killing. What, if any, trauma is involved here, and what mitigation does the play offer for it?

On the face of it, *Blasted* neither shows Ian working through unspeakable repressed events from his past, nor does it offer any mitigation for what he has done. However, there are good reasons to assume that not everything that occurs on stage happens at the level of a single 'reality' but that at least some aspects of the civil war raging outside the hotel, and the arrival of the soldier, are in fact phantasms of Ian's memory, externalizations of the previously unspoken. The reviewer for the *Sunday Telegraph* complained of the legion of 'implausibilities' in the play, and Michael Billington claimed that 'the play falls apart' because 'there is no sense of external reality – who is exactly meant to be fighting whom out on the streets?'[19] Billington also correctly pointed out the peculiar normality of Leeds in the middle of a civil conflagration (room service continues, football matches are played at Elland Road).[20] Are these inconsistencies simply poor plotting? There are hints in the text of the play that another reading is in order. For instance, Cate is never in the room at the same time as the soldier, and there is therefore no confirmation of his existence outside Ian's imagination. The uncertain materiality of the soldier is hardly resolved by the short shrift Cate gives him when she returns to the room: '*She steps over the* SOLDIER *with a glance.*' (p. 48) Furthermore, the actuality of the range of distressing acts Ian carries out in Cate's absence in scene five (masturbating, strangling himself, defecating on stage, eating the baby) is called into doubt by the staging – the lights come up and then go down for each 'vignette' – but most of all by the final miniature scene: '*He dies with relief.*' This death must be a wish fulfilment, realized in Ian's imagination, because he clearly does not die in the world of the play: it ends with his survival with Cate.

Given the doubt that hangs over many of the 'events' the audience witnesses in *Blasted*, it is legitimate to speculate that at least some of them act as manifestations *for the first time* of trauma Ian has inflicted in the past. For the first time because, as trauma theorists repeatedly assert, it is only in the remembering of a traumatic occurrence that it takes on reality:

> Massive trauma precludes its registration; the observing and recording mechanisms of the human mind are temporarily knocked out, malfunction. The victim's narrative – the very process of bearing witness to massive trauma – does indeed begin with someone who testifies to an absence, to an *event that has not yet come into existence*, in spite of the overwhelming and compelling nature of the reality of its occurrence.[21] (Emphasis added)

It cannot be emphasized enough that *Blasted* gives the perpetrator's narrative, not the victim's, and this is what makes it so troubling from the point of view of trauma theory, which is usually concerned with the repressed memories of victims. In any case, there are at least two good reasons for suspecting that the soldier's appearance is a catalyst for Ian's memories, or that the soldier is even the embodiment of them. The first has already been hinted at in the soldier's counterclaim to Ian's 'I wouldn't forget': 'You would' inevitably suggests 'You have already'. Furthermore, the crimes the soldier compulsively repeats bear a remarkable resemblance to those we suspect Ian has committed. In particular, the raping of the young girl resonates with the abuse of Cate as a child. This is not to say that the play makes a *direct* correlation between Ian's past and the soldier's actions: it is careful to keep any possible connections very much in the realm of possibility rather than certainty, and it would be dangerous to start making simple equations – to claim, for instance, that the soldier's crimes are in fact Ian's. However, *Blasted* does play with the vagaries of memory, and the soldier is part and parcel of this cloudy vista of memory. The danger, then, is that Kane has produced a sort of melodrama (or even *grand guignol*) of traumatic memories – one that, if not glamorizing the violence of the perpetrator, at least privileges it because so fascinated by it.

The presence of Cate, a victim and not a perpetrator, presumably offsets this danger since she seems the most reluctant to participate in the violent acting out of the past. On the one hand, she *has* returned to spend the night with the man who victimized her, which implies she is repeating past patterns. On the other hand, her main mode of engagement with Ian is negation: she constantly contradicts what he says and consistently rejects his advances point blank. There is a hint (it is always hints in *Blasted*) that she has been abused by an older man before Ian. She suffers from fainting fits, brought about by moments of crisis and marked by the disjunction in subjectivity associated with trauma: 'The world don't exist. Not like this. Looks the same but –/ Time slows down./ A dream I get stuck in'.[22] The fits started, she tells Ian, 'Since dad came back', and we can guess from this that her father sexually abused her, if his reappearance brings on a crisis that is not fully addressed in consciousness.[23] The 'numbingly traumatic event', as LaCapra tells us, 'does not register at the time of its occurrence but only after a temporal gap or period of latency, at which time it is immediately repressed, split off, or disavowed.'[24] At the risk of over-psychologizing, fainting (a sudden loss of consciousness) could well be interpreted as a mechanism for immediately repressing or disavowing a thought or memory that is too distressing to contemplate. Tellingly, though, Cate faints for the last time early in the second scene, after which she seems able to pass judgment on Ian – 'You're cruel' she tells him more than once.[25] And in her desire to bury the dead baby, she alone among the three shows a willingness to mourn the past rather than simply dig it up again, or reenact it in all its violence. In this sense she is closer to 'working through' trauma than 'acting it out'.[26]

The crisis in witnessing

This three-part analysis of trauma in *Blasted* is a piece of speculative excavation, a narrative constructed from bits and pieces of information which the play lets fall without ever assembling them in a coherent fashion. It cannot be otherwise with trauma, Shoshana Felman would argue. It is in the very nature of trauma to resist being accounted for in a completely coherent or easily comprehensible way. If *Blasted* is disorientating as a spectacle, if much of what it shows its audience is 'shrouded in mystery',[27] it is because atrocities of this sort cannot be simply digested. Felman writes of 'a memory that has been overwhelmed by occurrences that have not settled into understanding or remembrance, acts that cannot be constructed as knowledge nor assimilated into full cognition, events in excess of our frames of reference.'[28] Certainly, in *Blasted* there could not be a more literal exceeding of the frames of reference than the blast which opens a hole in the wall at the end of scene two. Trauma is not just a crisis in the memory of the traumatized subject but a crisis in representation and narration. It is this crisis in representation precipitated by trauma that particularly interests Felman. She uses the associated terms, *witnessing* and *testimony*, to describe the tortuous way in which trauma comes to be represented and/or narrated.

In what may be an extravagant claim, Felman says that literature since World War II is the 'literature of testimony' in that it cannot but reflect on that war and on the Holocaust in particular. But literature, and by association theatre and cinema,[29] does not, indeed cannot, approach the Holocaust directly – as if that were the literary equivalent of staring at the sun – and instead treats it allegorically, or even thematizes its own inability to bear adequate witness to the Holocaust. One of her key examples is the writing of Albert Camus, who in two novels, *The Plague* and *The Fall*, writes indirectly about the *Shoah*. In neither case does Camus mention the Holocaust explicitly, and it is almost this refusal to name it straightforwardly that Felman finds exemplary. It is her very special understanding of 'testimony' that leads her to this conclusion. A standard dictionary definition of the word is 'evidence; declaration to prove some fact; proof'.[30] But Felman wants to free testimony from such a strict legalistic meaning: 'testimony cannot be subsumed by its familiar notion ... texts that testify do not simply *report facts* but, in different ways, encounter – and make us encounter – *strangeness*.'[31] Later she makes a special case for the witness: 'what constitutes the specificity of the innovative figure of the witness is ... not the mere telling, not the mere fact of *reporting* of the accident, but the witness's readiness to become himself a *medium of testimony* – and a *medium of the accident*.'[32] The dictionary, in contrast, gives the mundane 'a person who gives evidence', which seems pretty undemanding compared to what Felman expects.

In Felman's view the events of the Holocaust (and other traumatic events, although the Holocaust is given a special status and is in some ways incomparable to any other) are too problematic to be 'merely reported', and therefore traditional historical writing inevitably fails to capture the trauma adequately. Only literature, which proceeds indirectly, by narrative, metaphor and other figures of speech, can approach the Holocaust with enough subtlety. Only literature and art are capable of being sufficiently self-conscious about their own impossible status as witnesses to do justice to extreme trauma. In *Representing the Holocaust* LaCapra usefully points out the shortcomings of 'conventional history' when it comes to the Holocaust. He criticizes the historian Arno Mayer for trying to write about the *Shoah* as if it were any other historical event, 'in a case where certain basic procedures of conventional history may well be necessary but not sufficient'. Mayer's book is 'an example of what may occur when one does not heed sufficiently the special demands – at times the impossible choices or aporias and in any event the pressures on the use of language – that confront the historian ... when he or she attempts to account for certain events'.[33] In other words, the cool objective stance of the professional historian, armed with commonsense and notions of causality and accuracy, is too cool for the emotional freight of the Holocaust.

It is interesting that LaCapra claims that conventional history is not 'sufficient' but does not want to do away with it entirely. Felman, on the other hand, wants to go much further. In their introduction to *Testimony*, Felman and Laub summarize this non-conventional, non-historiographical approach:

we underscore the question of the witness, and of witnessing, as non-habitual, estranged *conceptual prisms* through which we attempt to apprehend – and to make tangible to the imagination – the ways in which our cultural frames of reference and our preexisting categories which delimit and determine our perception of reality have failed, essentially, both to contain, and to account for, the scale of what has happened in contemporary history.[34]

They do not acknowledge it, but this position is effectively an adaptation of the theory of art and literature proposed by Russian Formalist critics such as Victor Shklovsky, who said that the task of literary language (unlike 'ordinary' language) was to 'defamiliarise' an object or experience for the reader. He says that 'as perception becomes habitual, it becomes automatic' and that 'The technique of art is to make objects "unfamiliar," to make forms difficult ... Art removes objects from the automatism of perception'.[35] 'Nonhabitual' and 'estranged' are the terms used by Felman and Laub, and the point they seem to be making is that certain events should never undergo an 'automatism of perception'; they should *always* seem extraordinary and unfamiliar lest they ever become 'normal' or 'ordinary'.

In trying to understand what Felman and Laub are asking for, it is appropriate to turn to *Blasted*, which shares at least some of their convictions. Whether or not *Blasted* fulfills the stringent criteria *Testimony* lays down for authentic witnessing (it is hard to know *what* exactly *Blasted* is witnessing, to start off with) is open to debate, but it does echo Felman's doubts about the capacity for mere reporting to account adequately for the ethical weight and emotional charge of trauma. It is no coincidence that Ian is a journalist and, as such, putatively responsible for witnessing on a daily basis. There are plenty of representations of heroic journalists witnessing the violence of the twentieth century (for instance, the films *Salvador* and *The Killing Fields*[36]). *Blasted* is not one of these. The traditional role of the journalist as the bearer of historical testimony is reduced here to a hack churning out lurid clichés down a telephone. Here is how the play depicts him delivering copy to his (unidentified) newspaper:

> A serial killer slaughtered British tourist Samantha Scrace in a sick murder ritual comma, police revealed yesterday point new par. The bubbly nineteen-year-old from Leeds was among seven victims buried in identical triangular tombs in an isolated New Zealand forest point new par. Each had been stabbed more than twenty times and placed face down, comma, hands bound behind their backs point new par. Caps up, ashes at the site showed the maniac had stayed to cook a meal, caps down point new par. Samantha comma, a beautiful redhead with dreams of becoming a model comma [etc][37]

The lesson here is almost too clear: the journalist writes of a horrific event from which he is removed by thousands of miles in hackneyed language repeated in different variations in countless stories in countless newspapers. There is clearly a formula, *Blasted* is telling us, for rendering atrocities in a familiar, easily digestible fashion. The language for doing so is habitual and determined in advance: there is nothing strange or defamiliarizing about the murder of seven people. This is presumably the sort of thing Felman is referring to when she says 'our preexisting categories which delimit and determine our perception of reality have failed'. Journalistic haste – to meet a deadline, to capture a readership – only represses further the meaning of a traumatic event.

Ian is obviously a bad witness: not only does he make the events he reports seem routine and commonplace but he is detached, both literally and symbolically, from those events. The play, of course, is the story of the revenge of events on the bad witness, culminating, somewhat predictably, in the removal of his eyes. Only then, in what is a fairly laboured paradox, can he see the necessity of witnessing. When Cate returns to him he is insistent that she should take on the burden of the witness, that she should relate something (he does not specify) to his son Matthew:

IAN: You seen Matthew?
CATE: No.
IAN: Will you tell him for me?
CATE: He isn't here.
IAN: Tell him –
          Tell him –
CATE: No.
IAN: Tell him –
CATE: No.
IAN: Don't know what to tell him.[38]

The crisis in witnessing here is startling. Whereas the tale of Samantha Scrace rolled off the tongue, language now fails entirely: the attempt ends in silence. There is no simple way to assimilate what has happened into knowledge.

This crisis has been prefigured by the encounter between the soldier and Ian in the previous scene. The soldier has just told the story of his girlfriend's rape and murder:

IAN: Enough.
SOLDIER: Ever seen anything like that?
IAN: Stop.
SOLDIER: Not in photos?
IAN: Never.
SOLDIER: Some journalist, that's your job.
IAN: What?
SOLDIER: Proving it happened. I'm here, got no choice. But you. You
             should be telling people.[39]

The soldier has a fairly conventional view of the journalist's responsibility to bear witness, but Ian's sudden involvement in events demonstrates that the good witness, the one who is not detached, cool and objective, is often overwhelmed and therefore paradoxi-

185

cally unable to bear witness. This is perhaps what Felman means when she writes of 'the witness's readiness to become himself a *medium of the testimony* – and a *medium of the accident*'.[40] The ravages Ian's body undergoes are the testimony, written on the body, of the events he has participated in. He is no longer neutral but fully implicated in the trauma he has seen and inflicted.

We are entitled to ask, I think, what *Blasted* is bearing witness to. I will offer two tentative, and related, answers. The first picks up on the Russian Formalist-style argument put forward by Felman and Laub in their introduction. *Blasted* implies that modern Britain is a society where potentially traumatizing events, such as rape and murder, are rendered inconsequential by the constant diet of them provided by the press. In a language at once sensational and habitual the reporting of 'limit events' is evacuated of any significance and real trauma is buried without a trace. It could also be argued that television and cinema participate in this process, but the play does not invoke them directly. *Blasted*, on the other hand, makes those events strange by presenting them so graphically and in such an intimate environment. This is where theatre has a capacity to defamiliarize the kinds of images television and film bombards us with, breaking up the 'automatism of perception' of horrific events.

The second answer takes up the notion put forward by many trauma theorists that a traumatic episode cannot, or should not (there is often an element of prescription about this theory), be represented or narrated directly. As has already been pointed out, there is a good deal of displacement at work in *Blasted*, and inevitably, given their closeness to the time of the play's first production, it is assumed that the play is in some way or other a reworking of the atrocities committed in Bosnia in the immediate post-Yugoslav era. To depict those atrocities directly on stage in order to elicit pathos from a British audience would no doubt be trite, or even offensive: an appropriation of the sufferings of another and distant group of people. To depict them in a displaced fashion – by imagining a similar civil war and its consequences in West Yorkshire – might merit the same opprobrium. Alternatively, the final four scenes of the play (the scenes which incorporate the 'implausible' civil war) could be read as a displacement of the very local sexual and racial abuse of scene one, in which there is no indication that a war rages outside apart from Ian's possession of a revolver. In that scene Ian verbally attacks Cate and lets forth a string of racist statements, some of it generalized, some of it directed at the offstage black hotel worker. Keeping in mind that Ian rapes Cate between scene one and scene two, the remainder of the play could be seen as a tortured re-articulation of the traumas of sexual and racial politics in contemporary Britain. In other words, the play deliberately establishes parallels between the sexual and racial politics of the first scene and the civil strife of the rest of the play.[41] But even these tentative interpretations may rush to reclaim *Blasted* for knowledge.

Pity the witness

Finally, it is worth sparing a thought for those innocents who bore the first burden of witnessing *Blasted* – the London theatre reviewers. It is far too easy to reel off a string of quotations from the dailies and Sundays to show the sort of hysteria that broke out in 1995 in the wake of Kane's debut. Although many of those first reviewers stuck to their guns and continued to lambaste Kane's subsequent plays, others recanted and came around to Harold Pinter's view that Kane's 'was a very startling and tender voice ... appalled by the world in which she lived and the world within herself'.[42] Unlike Pinter, those first reviewers were not able to ponder and process slowly some of the shocking scenes they had been subjected to. Instead, as with any production, they are expected to be immediately eloquent, not only describing it but passing judgment on behalf of others (a readership whose expectations put even more limitations and pressures on the witness[43]). Like Ian, they possess only a habitual, hasty language which is inadequate under the circumstances.[44] The speed of the mass media forecloses the possibility of trauma's gradual, belated emergence, long after the fact, and in difficult, attenuated forms. It is perhaps no coincidence, then, that 'trauma theory' has arisen in the wake of the global triumph of the mass media, as a tentative attempt to slow them down.

Notes

1 For an account of the media storm *Blasted* generated and the heated exchange of letters in the *Guardian* that followed, see Tom Sellar, 'Truth and dare: Sarah Kane's *Blasted*', *Theater* 27:1 (1997), 29–34.
2 Sarah Kane, *Blasted*, in *Blasted and Phaedra's Love* (London: Methuen Drama, 1996), p. 25.
3 Sigmund Freud, *Beyond the pleasure principle*, in *On Metapsychology*,

Penguin Freud Library vol. 11, trans. James Strachey, ed. Angela Richards (Harmondsworth: Penguin, 1984), pp. 269–338.

4 Cathy Caruth, *Unclaimed Experience: Trauma, Narrative, and History* (Baltimore and London: Johns Hopkins University Press, 1996), p. 11.

5 Caruth, *Unclaimed Experience*, pp. 130–1.

6 There are seven chapters in *Testimony*, five signed by Felman and two by Laub. In a foreword the authors state that they wrote their chapters independently but that they are each 'the product of this intellectual and conceptual interaction and of this continuous dialogue of insights'. Shoshana Felman and Dori Laub, *Testimony: Crises of Witnessing in Literature, Psychoanalysis, and History* (London and New York: Routledge, 1992), p. xiv. I will be concentrating on the chapters by Felman, which bear all the hallmarks of her earlier work.

7 The way in which 'trauma theory' straddles disciplines is evident from the fact that the work of Laub, Felman and Caruth was first collected together in a special issue of a journal exploring psychoanalysis and culture: Cathy Caruth, ed., 'Psychoanalysis, culture and trauma', *American Imago* 48:1 (1991).

8 Dominick LaCapra is illuminating on the problems of naming the Holocaust. See LaCapra, *Representing the Holocaust: History, Theory, Trauma* (Ithaca: Cornell University Press, 1994), p. 45; and *History and Memory After Auschwitz* (Ithaca: Cornell University Press, 1998), pp. 53–4.

9 Chapter 5, 'After the apocalypse: Paul de Man and the fall to silence', in Felman and Laub, *Testimony*. Many of the responses to the revelations are collected in Werner Hamacher, Neil Hertz and Thomas Keenan, *Responses: On Paul de Man's Wartime Journalism* (Lincoln, NE: University of Nebraska Press, 1989). LaCapra's chapter on the de Man controversy in *Representing the Holocaust*, 'Paul de Man as object of transference', is an excellent summary of the issues.

10 'Blurred' is the term used by Paul Taylor in his review in the *Independent*, 20 January, 1995, p. 27; 'shrouded' the one used by Charles Spencer in his in *The Daily Telegraph*, 20 January, 1995, p. 19.

11 Kane, *Blasted*, pp. 40–1.

12 Caruth, *Unclaimed Experience*, p. 17.

13 Kane, *Blasted*, p. 45.

14 The predilection of 1990s playwrights for representing anal sex as brutalizing (see, for instance, Mark Ravenhill's *Shopping and Fucking*) might be read as unconscious homophobia. Anal sex is made literally 'unspeakable' in the soldier's account, implying that it is the *worst* thing he did: 'Then I turned her over and – / Then she cried'. Why is anal sex always introduced as a sort of limit act, and a necessarily violent one, if there is not some paranoia about it?

15 Spencer, *The Daily Telegraph*, 20 January, 1995, p. 19.

16 Kane, *Blasted*, p. 23.

17 Kane, *Blasted*, p. 13.

18 Taylor, *Independent*, 20 January, 1995, p. 27.

19 John Gross, 'Review' section, *Sunday Telegraph*, 22 January, 1995, p. 6; Michael Billington, *Guardian*, 20 January, 1995, p. 22. Billington subsequently changed heart about *Blasted* and apologized to Kane for dismissing it out of hand. See Simon Hattenstone, 'A sad hurrah', 'The Guardian Weekend', *Guardian*, 1 July, 2000, p. 31.

20 Although, as Melissa Jacques pointed out to me, it is quite common in a situation of civil strife to see many aspects of quotidian life carry on regardless.

21 Felman and Laub, *Testimony*, p. 57

22 Kane, *Blasted*, p. 21.

23 Kane, *Blasted*, p. 9.

24 LaCapra, *Representing the Holocaust*, p. 174.

25 Kane, *Blasted*, p. 30.

26 This is a distinction that LaCapra makes frequently in his two books. He claims that Caruth and Felman place too much emphasis on 'acting out' trauma, which does not allow for any 'beyond' of the painful memory. He offers the Freudian notion of 'working through', which is closer to mourning, as an alternative that eventually sees trauma dealt with and interpreted, however provisionally.

27 Spencer, *The Daily Telegraph*, 20 January, 1995, p. 19.

28 Felman and Laub, *Testimony*, p. 5

29 Felman's main case study, and the one the whole book leads up to, is Claude Lanzmann's film *Shoah* (1985), which contains nine and a half hours of interview footage with survivors of the Holocaust, as well as perpetrators and Polish bystanders.

30 *Chambers Paperback Dictionary* (Edinburgh: W & R Chambers, 1992).

31 Felman and Laub, *Testimony*, p. 7.

32 Felman and Laub, *Testimony*, p. 24.

33 LaCapra, *Representing the Holocaust*, p. 80.

34 Felman and Laub, *Testimony*, p. xv.

35 Victor Shklovsky, 'Art as technique' (1917), *Debating Texts: Readings in 20th Century Literary Theory and Method*, ed. Rick Rylance (Toronto: University of Toronto Press, 1987), pp. 48–9.

36 It should be said that both these films, while driving home the importance of witnessing, present the central American journalist as compromised by ambition or ethical failings, and they therefore bring across the complexities of the witness as 'survivor' rather than victim.

37 Kane, *Blasted*, p. 12.

38 Kane, *Blasted*, pp. 48–9.

39 Kane, *Blasted*, p. 45.

40 Felman and Laub, *Testimony*, p. 24.

41 I am indebted to Sarah E. Evans for this idea and its phrasing.

42 Quoted in Hattenstone, 'A sad hurrah', p. 31.

43 I am thinking of poor Jack Tinker of the *Daily Mail*. Writing for that paper on 20 January, 1995, what choice did he have but to entitle his notorious

review 'The disgusting feast of filth'? (Quoted in Sellar, 'Truth and dare', p. 31.)

44 Núria Triana-Toribio pointed out to me that much of the overreaction to the play may be attributed to the playwright being a woman; that the same play written by a man would not have sparked such outrage because it would not have offended the taboo on women writing about violence or writing violently.

Bibliography

Althusser, Louis, 'Ideology and ideological state apparatuses', in *Lenin and Philosophy*, trans. Ben Brewster (London: New Left Books, 1971), pp. 121–73.

Arnold, Matthew, 'The function of criticism at the present time' (1865), in Raman Selden, ed., *The Theory of Criticism: From Plato to the Present* (London and New York: Longman, 1988), pp. 494–5.

Aston, Elaine, *An Introduction to Feminism and Theatre* (London and New York: Routledge, 1995).

Babula, William, 'The play–life metaphor in Shakespeare and Stoppard', *Modern Drama* 15:3 (1973), 279–81.

Barrett, Michele, *Women's Oppression Today*, rev. edn (London: Verso, 1988).

Baudrillard, Jean, *America*, trans. Chris Turner (London: Verso, 1988 [1986]).

——, *The Evil Demon of Images*, trans. Paul Patton and Paul Foss (Annadale: Power Institute, 1987).

——, *In the Shadow of the Silent Majorities* (New York: Semiotext(e), 1983).

——, *Simulacra and Simulation*, trans. Sheila Faria Glaser (Ann Arbor: Michigan University Press, 1994 [1981]).

——, *The Transparency of Evil: Essays on Extreme Phenomena*, trans. James Benedict (London and New York: Verso, 1993 [1990]).

——, 'Fatal strategies', in *Jean Baudrillard: Selected Writings*, ed. Mark Poster (Cambridge: Polity, 1988), pp. 185–206.

Bauman, Zygmunt, *Intimations of Postmodernity* (London: Routledge, 1992).

Beckett, Samuel, *Waiting for Godot* (London: Faber and Faber, 1956).

Belsey, Catherine, *Critical Practice* (London: Methuen, 1980).

——, *Desire: Love Stories in Western Culture* (Oxford: Blackwell, 1994).

Benjamin, Walter, *The Arcades Project*, trans. Howard Eiland and Kevin McLaughlin (Cambridge, MA, and London: Harvard University Press, 1999).

——, *The Origin of German Tragic Drama*, trans. John Osborne (London: New Left Books, 1977).

——, *Understanding Brecht*, trans. Anna Bostock (London: New Left Books, 1973).

——, 'Theses on the philosophy of history' [1940], in *Illuminations*, ed. Hannah Arendt, trans. Harry Zohn (New York: Shocken Books, 1969), pp. 253–64.

Bigsby, Christopher, *Joe Orton* (London and New York: Methuen, 1982).

Billington, Michael, Review of *Blasted*, *Guardian*, 20 January, 1995, p. 22.

Bond, Edward, *Lear*, in *Plays: Two* (London: Methuen Drama, 1978).

Boon, Richard, *Brenton: The Playwright* (London: Methuen, 1991).

Boxall, Peter, *Samuel Beckett: Waiting for Godot/Endgame: A Reader's Guide to Essential Criticism* (Cambridge: Icon Books, 2000).

Bowie, Malcolm, *Lacan* (London: Fontana, 1991).

Brecht, Bertolt, *Brecht on Theatre*, trans. & ed. John Willett, 2nd edn (London: Methuen, 1974).

——, *The Good Person of Szechwan*, in *Brecht: Plays Two* (London: Methuen, 1987).

Brenton, Howard, 'Writing for democratic laughter', *Drama* 157 (1985), 9–11.

Brenton, Howard (interview), 'The red theatre under the bed', *New Theatre Quarterly* 11 (1987), 195–201.

Brenton, Howard, and David Hare, *Pravda: A Fleet Street Comedy* (London: Methuen, 1986).

Brown, Janet, 'Caryl Churchill's *Top Girls* catches the next wave', in Phyllis Randall, ed., *Caryl Churchill: A Casebook* (New York and London: Garland, 1988).

Cairns, David, and Shaun Richards, 'No good brave causes? The alienated intellectual and the end of empire', *Literature and History* 14 (1988), 194–206.

Callinicos, Alex, *Against Postmodernism: A Marxist Critique* (Cambridge: Polity, 1989).

Carlson, Susan, 'Issues of identity, nationality and performance: the reception of two plays by Timberlake Wertenbaker', *New Theatre Quarterly* 35 (1993), 267–89.

Carter, Angela, *Wise Children* (London: Chatto & Windus, 1991).

Carter, Paul, *The Road to Botany Bay: An Exploration of Landscape and History* (New York: Knopf, 1988).

Caruth, Cathy, *Unclaimed Experience: Trauma, Narrative, and History* (Baltimore and London: Johns Hopkins University Press, 1996).

——, ed., 'Psychoanalysis, culture and trauma', *American Imago* 48:1 (1991).

Case, Sue-Ellen, *Feminism and Theatre* (London and New York: Routledge, 1988).

Charney, Maurice, *Joe Orton* (Basingstoke: Macmillan, 1984).

Chedzgoy, Kate, *Shakespeare's Queer Children* (Manchester: Manchester University Press, 1996).

Churchill, Caryl, *Plays: One* (London: Methuen, 1985).

——, *Top Girls*, in *Plays: Two* (London: Methuen, 1990), pp. 51–141.

Cixous, Hélène, 'Fiction and its phantoms: a reading of Freud's Das Unheimliche (the "uncanny")' [1972], *New Literary History* 7 (1976), 525–48.

Cousin, Geraldine, *Churchill: The Playwright* (London: Methuen, 1989).

Dawson, Helen, 'Oh! Calcutta! at the Roundhouse' (Sept 1970), in Peter Roberts, ed., *The Best of Plays and Players: Volume 2: 1969–1983* (London: Methuen Drama, 1989), pp. 36–7.

de Jongh, Nicholas, *Not in Front of the Audience: Homosexuality on Stage* (London and New York: Routledge, 1992).

——, *Politics, Prudery and Perversion* (London: Methuen, 2000).

Derrida, Jacques, *Dissemination* [1972], trans. Barbara Johnson (London: Athlone Press, 1981).

——, *Writing and Difference* [1967], trans. Alan Bass (London: Routledge, 1978).

Diamond, Elin, *Unmaking Mimesis: Essays on Feminism and Theatre* (London and New York: Routledge, 1997).

——, 'Parody play in Pinter', *Modern Drama* 25:4 (1982), 477–88.

Dolan, Jill, *The Feminist Spectator as Critic* (Ann Arbor: UMI Research Press, 1988).

Dollimore, Jonathan, 'The challenge of sexuality', in Alan Sinfield, ed., *Society and Literature 1945–1970* (London: Methuen, 1983), pp. 51–85.

Eagleton, Terry, *The Illusions of Postmodernism* (Oxford: Blackwell, 1996).

——, 'Ideology and its vicissitudes in Western Marxism', in Slavoj Žižek, ed., *Mapping Ideology* (London: Verso, 1994), pp. 179–226.

Elam, Keir, *The Semiotics of Theatre and Drama* (London and New York: Methuen, 1980).

Esslin, Martin, *The Field of Drama: How the Signs of Drama Create Meaning on Stage and Screen* (London: Methuen Drama, 1987).

——, *Pinter: the Playwright* (London: Methuen, 1982 [1970]).

Felman, Shoshana, and Dori Laub, *Testimony: Crises of Witnessing in Literature, Psychoanalysis, and History* (London and New York: Routledge, 1992).

Fitzsimmons, Linda, ed., *File on Churchill* (London: Methuen, 1989).

Fortier, Mark, *Theory/Theatre: An Introduction* (London and New York: Routledge, 1997).

Foucault, Michel, *The History of Sexuality: Volume 1, An Introduction*, trans. Robert Hurley (London: Penguin, 1981 [1976]).

Freud, Sigmund, *Jokes and Their Relation to the Unconscious* [1905], trans. & ed. James Strachey (Harmondsworth: Penguin, 1976).

——, *Beyond the pleasure principle*, in *On Metapsychology, Penguin Freud Library* vol. 11, trans. James Strachey, ed. Angela Richards (Harmondsworth: Penguin, 1984), pp. 269–338.

——, 'Mourning and melancholia', in *On Metapsychology, Penguin Freud Library* vol. 11, trans. James Strachey, ed. Angela Richards (Harmondsworth: Penguin, 1984), pp. 245–68.

——, 'The "uncanny"' [1919], in *Art and literature, Penguin Freud Library* vol. 14, trans. James Strachey, ed. Albert Dickson (Harmondsworth: Penguin, 1985), pp. 335–76.

Gabbard, Lucina P., *The Dream Structure of Pinter's Plays: A Psychoanalytic Approach* (Rutherford, NJ, and London: 1976).

Gallop, Jane, *Reading Lacan* (Ithaca and London: Cornell University Press, 1985).

Ganz, Arthur, ed., *Pinter: A Collection of Critical Essays* (Englewood Cliffs, NJ: Prentice-Hall, 1972).

Goodman, Lizbeth, 'Overlapping dialogue in overlapping media: behind the scenes of *Top Girls*', in Sheila Rabillard, ed., *Essays on Caryl Churchill: Contemporary Representations* (Winnipeg and Buffalo: Blizzard Publishing, 1998), pp. 69–101.

Goorney, Howard, and Ewan MacColl, eds, *Agit-Prop to Theatre Workshop: Political Playscripts 1930–50* (Manchester: Manchester University Press, 1986).

Griffiths, Trevor, *Comedians* (London: Faber and Faber, 1976).

Gross, John, Review of *Blasted*, 'Review' section, *Sunday Telegraph*, 22 January, 1995, p. 6.

Hall, Peter, 'Directing Pinter: an interview with Catherine Itzin and Simon Trussler' [1974], in Michael Scott, ed., *Harold Pinter: The Birthday Party, The Caretaker and The Homecoming: A Casebook* (Basingstoke: Macmillan, 1986), pp. 44–71.

Hamacher, Werner, Neil Hertz and Thomas Keenan, *Responses: On Paul de Man's Wartime Journalism* (Lincoln, NE: University of Nebraska Press, 1989).

Hamilton, Paul, *Historicism* (London and New York: Routledge, 1996).

Hattenstone, Simon, 'A sad hurrah', 'The Guardian Weekend', *Guardian*, 1 July, 2000, pp. 26–34.

Heath, Stephen, 'Lessons from Brecht', *Screen* 15:2 (1974), 103–28.

——, 'Narrative space', *Screen* 17:3 (1976), 68–112.

Hertz, Neil, 'Freud and *The Sandman*', in Josué V. Harari, ed., *Textual Strategies: Perspectives in Post-structuralist Criticism* (Ithaca: Cornell University Press, 1979), pp. 296–321.

Homden, Carol, *The Plays of David Hare* (Cambridge: Cambridge University Press, 1995).

Hope-Wallace, Philip, 'Feeling Cheated' [1965], in Michael Scott, ed., *Harold Pinter: The Birthday Party, The Caretaker and The Homecoming: A Casebook* (Basingstoke: Macmillan, 1986), pp. 196–7.

Hughes, Robert, *The Fatal Shore: The Epic of Australia's Founding* (New York: Vintage, 1988 [1986]).

Hutcheon, Linda, *A Poetics of Postmodernism: History, Theory, Fiction* (London and New York: Routledge, 1988).

Innes, Christopher, *Modern British Drama 1890–1990* (Cambridge: Cambridge University Press, 1992).

Kane, Sarah, *Blasted*, in *Blasted and Phaedra's Love* (London: Methuen Drama, 1996).

Kellner, Douglas, *Jean Baudrillard: From Marxism to Post-modernism and Beyond* (Cambridge: Polity, 1989).

Keneally, Thomas, *The Playmaker* (London: Hodder and Stoughton, 1987).

Kofman, Sarah, 'The double is/and the devil: the uncanniness of *The Sandman* (*Der Sandmann*)', in *Freud and Fiction* [1974], trans. Sarah Wykes (Cambridge: Polity, 1991), pp. 119–62.

Kristeva, Julia, *Strangers to Ourselves*, trans. Leon S. Roudiez (New York and London: Harvester Wheatsheaf, 1991).

Lacan, Jacques, 'The mirror stage as formative of the function of the I as revealed in psychoanalytic experience', in *Écrits: A Selection*, trans. Alan Sheridan (New York and London: W. W. Norton and Co., 1977 [1966]), pp. 1–7.

——, 'The signification of the phallus', in *Écrits: A Selection*, trans. Alan Sheridan (New York and London: Norton, 1977).

LaCapra, Dominick, *Representing the Holocaust: History, Theory, Trauma* (Ithaca: Cornell University Press, 1994).

LaCapra, Dominick, *History and Memory after Auschwitz* (Ithaca: Cornell University Press, 1998).

Lacey, Stephen, *British Realist Theatre: The New Wave in its Context* (London and New York: Routledge 1995).

Laclau, Ernesto, *Emancipation(s)* (London: Verso, 1996).

Lahr, John, *Prick Up Your Ears: The Biography of Joe Orton* (London: Penguin, 1978).

——, ed., *The Orton Diaries* (London: Methuen, 1986).

Laing, R. D., *The Divided Self* (Harmondsworth: Penguin, 1965).

Lane, Harry, 'Secrets as strategies for protection and oppression in *Top Girls*', in Sheila Rabillard, ed., *Essays on Caryl Churchill: Contemporary Representations* (Winnipeg and Buffalo: Blizzard Publishing, 1998), pp. 60–8.

Lilly, Mark, 'The plays of Joe Orton', *Gay Men's Literature in the Twentieth Century* (Basingstoke: Macmillan, 1993).

Littlewood, Joan, and Ewan MacColl, *Last Edition*, in Howard Goorney and Ewan MacColl, eds, *Agit-Prop to Theatre Workshop: Political Playscripts 1930–50* (Manchester: Manchester University Press, 1986), pp. 21–33.

Lyotard, Jean-François, *The Postmodern Condition: A Report on Knowledge*, trans. Geoff Bennington and Brian Massumi (Manchester: Manchester University Press, 1984 [1979]).

MacCabe, Colin, 'Realism and the cinema: notes on some Brechtian theses', *Screen* 15:2 (1975), 7–27.

——, 'Theory and film: principles of realism and pleasure', *Screen* 17:3 (1976), 7–27.

Marcuse, Herbert, *Eros and Civilization: A Philosophical Inquiry into Freud* (London: Allen Lane, 1969 [1955]).

Marwick, Arthur, *British Society since 1945* (Harmondsworth: Penguin, 1982).

Marx, Karl, *The German Ideology*, in Eugene Kamenka, ed., *The Portable Karl Marx* (Harmondsworth: Viking Penguin, 1983), pp. 162–95.

Masters, William H., and Virginia E. Johnson, *Human Sexual Response* (New York: Bantam, 1980 [1966]).

Melrose, Susan, *A Semiotics of the Dramatic Text* (Basingstoke: Macmillan, 1994).

Merrill, Lisa, 'Monsters and heroines: Caryl Churchill's women', in Phyllis Randall, ed., *Caryl Churchill: A Casebook* (New York and London: Garland, 1988), pp. 71–90.

Mitchell, Juliet, and Jacqueline Rose, eds, *Feminine Sexuality: Jacques Lacan and the École freudienne* (New York: Norton, 1982).

Newsboy (anon.), in Howard Goorney and Ewan MacColl, eds, *Agit-Prop to Theatre Workshop: Political Playscripts 1930–50* (Manchester: Manchester University Press, 1986), pp. 13–20.

Norris, Christopher, *What's Wrong with Postmodernism?: Critical Theory and the Ends of Philosophy* (London: Harvester Wheatsheaf, 1990).

O'Higgins, Paul, *Censorship in Britain* (London: Thomas Nelson, 1972).

Orton, Joe, *What the Butler Saw*, in *Orton: The Complete Plays* (London: Eyre Methuen, 1976), pp. 361–448.

Osborne, John, *Look Back in Anger* (London: Faber and Faber, 1960 [1957]).

Page, Adrian, ed., *The Death of the Playwright?: Modern British Drama and Literary Theory* (Basingstoke: Macmillan, 1992).

Pavis, Patrice, *Languages of the Stage*, trans. Susan Melrose (New York: Performing Arts Journal Publications, 1982).

Pinter, Harold, *The Homecoming* [1965], in *Plays: Three* (London: Methuen, 1978).

——, 'Writing for the Theatre', in *Plays: One* (London: Methuen, 1976), pp. 9–16.

Piscator, Erwin, 'Basic principles of a theory of sociological drama' (1929), in Richard Drain, ed., *Twentieth-Century Theatre: A Sourcebook* (London: Routledge, 1995), pp. 102–4.

Plato, *The Republic*, trans. G. M. A. Grube (Indianapolis: Hackett Publishing Co., 1974).

Quigley, Austin E., 'Creativity and commitment in Trevor Griffiths's *Comedians*', *Modern Drama* 24 (1981), 404–23.

Rabillard, Sheila, ed., *Essays on Caryl Churchill: Contemporary Representations* (Winnipeg and Buffalo: Blizzard Publishing, 1998).

Randall, Phyllis, ed., *Caryl Churchill: A Casebook* (New York and London: Garland, 1988).

Ratcliffe, Michael, 'London: press gang', *Drama* 157 (1985), 32–4.

Ravenhill, Mark, *Shopping and Fucking* (London: Methuen, 1996).

Rebellato, Dan, *1956 and All That: The Making of Modern British Drama* (London and New York: Routledge, 1999).

Reinelt, Janelle, *After Brecht: British Epic Theatre* (Ann Arbor: Michigan University Press, 1994).

Roberts, Philip, 'Tom Stoppard: serious artist or siren?', *Critical Quarterly* 20 (1978), 84–92.

Rowe, M. W., 'Pinter's Freudian homecoming', *Essays in Criticism* 41:3 (1991), 189–207.

Said, Edward W., *Culture and Imperialism* (London: Vintage, 1994 [1993]).

Scott, Michael, ed., *Harold Pinter: The Birthday Party, The Caretaker and The Homecoming: A Casebook* (Basingstoke: Macmillan, 1986).

Selden, Raman, ed., *The Theory of Criticism: From Plato to the Present* (London and New York: Longman, 1988).

Sellar, Tom, 'Truth and dare: Sarah Kane's *Blasted*', *Theater* 27:1 (1997), 29–34.

Shepherd, Simon, *Because We're Queers* (London: Gay Men's Press, 1989).

Shklovsky, Victor, 'Art as technique' [1917], in *Debating Texts: Readings in 20th-Century Literary Theory and Method*, ed. Rick Rylance (Toronto: University of Toronto Press, 1987), pp. 48–56.

Silverstein, Marc, *Harold Pinter and the Language of Cultural Power* (Lewisburg, PA: Bucknell University Press, 1993).

Sinfield, Alan, *Out on Stage: Lesbian and Gay Theatre in the Twentieth Century* (New Haven and London: Yale University Press, 1999).

——, 'The theatre and its audiences', in Alan Sinfield, ed., *Society and Literature 1945–1970* (London: Methuen, 1983), pp. 173–97.

——, 'Who was afraid of Joe Orton?', *Textual Practice* 4 (1990), 259–77.

Spencer, Charles, Review of *Blasted*, *The Daily Telegraph*, 20 January, 1995, p. 19.

Stafford-Clark, Max (interview), *The European English Messenger* 7:2 (1998), 38.

States, Bert O., 'Pinter's *Homecoming*: the shock of nonrecognition' [1968], in Arthur Ganz, ed., *Pinter: A Collection of Critical Essays* (Englewood Cliffs, NJ: Prentice-Hall, 1972), pp. 147–60.

Stoppard, Tom, *Rosencrantz and Guildenstern are Dead* (London: Faber and Faber, 1967).

Stoppard, Tom (interview), 'Ambushes for the audience: towards a high comedy of ideas', *Theatre Quarterly* 4.14 (1974), 3–17.

Storch, R. F., 'Harold Pinter's happy families' [1967], in Arthur Ganz, ed., *Pinter: A Collection of Critical Essays* (Englewood Cliffs NJ: Prentice-Hall, 1972), pp. 136–46.

Strinati, Dominic, *An Introduction to Theories of Popular Culture* (London: Routledge, 1995).

Sullivan, Esther Beth, 'Hailing ideology, acting in the horizon, and reading between plays by Timberlake Wertenbaker', *Theatre Journal* 45:2 (1993), 139–53.

Taylor, Paul, Review of *Blasted*, *The Independent*, 20 January, 1995, p. 27.

Thomas, Jane, 'The plays of Caryl Churchill: essays in refusal', in Adrian Page, ed., *The Death of the Playwright* (Basingstoke: Macmillan, 1992), pp. 160–85.

Todd, Jane Marie, 'The veiled woman in Freud's *Das "Unheimliche"'*, *Signs* 11:3 (1986), 519–28.

Trussler, Simon, 'A case against *The Homecoming*' [1973], in Michael Scott, ed., *Harold Pinter: The Birthday Party, The Caretaker and The Homecoming: A Casebook* (Basingstoke: Macmillan, 1986), 178–85.

Ubersfeld, Anne, *Lire le théâtre* (Paris: Éditions Sociales, 1977).

Wandor, Michelene, *Carry On, Understudies: Theatre and Sexual Politics*, 2nd edn (London: Routledge and Kegan Paul, 1986).

——, *Orlando's Children: Sexuality and the Family in Post-War British Plays* (London: Methuen, 1986).

Wardle, Irving, 'The territorial struggle' (1971), in Michael Scott, ed., *Harold Pinter: The Birthday Party, The Caretaker and The Homecoming: A Casebook* (Basingstoke: Macmillan, 1986), pp. 169–71.

Weber, Samuel, 'The sideshow, or: remarks on a canny moment', *Modern Language Notes* 88 (1973), 1102–33.

Weeks, Jeffrey, *Coming Out: Homosexual Politics in Britain from the Nineteenth Century to the Present*, rev. edn (London: Quartet Books, 1990).

Weigel, Sigrid, *Body- and Image-Space: Rereading Walter Benjamin*, trans. G. Paul (London and New York, Routledge, 1996).

Wertenbaker, Timberlake, *Our Country's Good* (London: Methuen, 1991).

——, 'Introduction', in *Timberlake Wertenbaker: Plays 1* (London: Faber and Faber, 1996).

197

Wilcher, Robert, 'Pravda: a morality play for the 1980s', Modern Drama 33 (1990), 42–56.

Wilson, Ann, 'Our Country's Good: theatre, colony and nation in Wertenbaker's adaptation of The Playmaker', Modern Drama 34:1 (1991), 23–34.

Wohlfarth, Irving, 'On the messianic structure of Walter Benjamin's last reflections', Glyph 3 (1978), 148–212.

Worth, Katherine, 'Pinter and the realist tradition' [1972], in Michael Scott, ed., Harold Pinter: The Birthday Party, The Caretaker and The Homecoming: a casebook (Basingstoke: Macmillan, 1986), pp. 23–39.

Wright, Elizabeth, 'The uncanny and surrealism', in Peter Collier and Judy Davies, eds, Modernism and the European Unconscious (Cambridge: Polity Press, 1990), pp. 265–82.

Žižek, Slavoj, Enjoy your Symptom: Jacques Lacan In Hollywood and Out (London and New York: Routledge, 1992).

——, Looking Awry: An Introduction to Jacques Lacan through Popular Culture (London and Cambridge, MA: MIT Press, 1991).

——, The Sublime Object of Ideology (London: Verso, 1989).

Index